A DOLL'S LEG

YAACOV HAELYON

A DOLL'S LEG

The Story of a War Injury

John Malherbe Pty Ltd
P.O. BOX 1207 · CAPE TOWN
1974

ISBN 0 86966 080 2

Translated from the Hebrew by Louis Williams

©

Hebrew copyright: Am Oved Publishers Ltd Tel Aviv 1973
English copyright: John Malherbe Pty Ltd 1974
Printed by Citadel Press Lansdowne Cape

CONTENTS

FOREWORD

Dear Yaacov,

When I turned the last page of your book A DOLL'S LEG, my faith in man's indomitable spirit was reinforced.

You and your book are both testimony to man's ability to succeed, by sheer willpower, in overcoming every obstacle, even if this requires hard struggle and unfailing human fortitude.

You have attained what but the very few attain: to serve as a guide and a source of hope to others who may have to undergo a similar fate.

Twice I read your book – before the Yom Kippur War and after. Many things were changed by the war. Only your book, unfortunately, gains in tragic actuality, an actuality which you as its author would no doubt be the first to forgo if it were up to you.

I read with bated breath. From my talks with the wounded and injured as well as with their families I learned that the volume is of great help to them. It aids them to overcome the fears and apprehensions they have to face, and teaches that bodily tribulations cannot daunt the spirit.

With friendly greetings,

YIGAL ALLON

Israeli Deputy Prime Minister
and Minister of Education and Culture.

April 1974

7

PREFACE

I was twenty-nine plus, a journalist, married eight years, father of a two and a half year old girl, three months in a new flat – and the war came.

And with the war, shells. Two, addressed to me. One, fired by an artillery piece, its red-hot splinters found a haven in my head. The second left the mouth of a mortar to complete the job in the lower half of my body.

I don't know what hour it was when the artillery-shell hit me. War was raging; I had no time to glance at watches. I also don't know when the mortar-shell hit. I was in a crazed and sometimes pleasant daze, apparently characteristic of a man on the brink of losing consciousness.

Days would pass before I would recover and know that I was wounded – and I would be proud without cause; months would pass, many trips in and out of the world of bodily and spiritual torment – before a new reality materialized – and I would know that I was a cripple; and then I was not so proud.

Years would pass before I could gauge myself and decide that it would be a lie if I told myself or others that I had accepted what had happened to me. But I would also know that not making peace, coupled with compulsion to pay a debt, the promissory notes of which I must meet to the end of my days – does not mean non-adaptation.

I will always carry a card that says 72% disability, which is in fact 115%. Why both? The explanation is too complicated. I will have a special tax-free car, I will enjoy special rights, I will meet doctors more often than the average man. I will be cripple forever. But I will also know that if I so wish, I can be a man among men.

But the road is long, beset by obstacles, bereft of high courage and paved with travail, but occasionally illuminated by a smile. This is the story of my book. Most of its events are the whole truth, and only a few are slightly inaccurate, both because time has blurred unimportant details and because I felt the need not to offend people living among us.

BOOK 1

THE NINTH OF JUNE

1

A steel fist slammed my head. One sharp, short blow. A thousand bells began to ring in insane cacophony. My head fell downwards as though my neck was folding in on itself. The upper half of my body began to move backwards and forwards, backwards and forwards as though in time with a wild rhythm. I couldn't stop it.

Hot streams spurted off my temples and soaked my neck. I lifted a heavy hand to feel what I had thought was my head, but was in fact an anvil beaten by hundreds of small hammers. My hand stuck to my temple. A hot fluid poured between my fingers and over my palm.

My torso was still oscillating. I dropped on hard metal. For a second I realised the coolness of steel.

Come back to your senses, concentrate, grab hold of your fleeting thoughts. Be clear-headed. Something has happened. Something isn't clear. Where am I? What happened? Think! Think! Think! If I don't think – I will drown!

God! Don't panic. Don't lose control. Strange – the blow didn't hurt. Only in the first instant. Then why am I so heavy? What's happening to me? Did I take drugs? Am I drunk? From what? Perhaps from drugs? Yes. But no, never . . .

Thank God, I begin – at least begin – to regain awareness. Stunned, but still able to think. It's night. Darkness. Where was I when it happened? Perhaps it isn't night now. Perhaps it's not dark and it only seems so? Maybe the eyes have simply closed. Hand, go and check. Yes, they're stuck closed. That fluid, it's like carpenter's glue. If only I could open them, perhaps I would understand what has happened. But I can't. Somebody must tell me what happened. There's nobody here. Not a living soul. There's nothing. Drugs. I'm drunk. My body doesn't obey me. Why is it so difficult to think? Why are my thoughts moving with such maddening slowness?

But then, why should I care what's happening? Perhaps it's better this way. Yes, really, I begin to feel comfortable. Comfortable with my eyes closed. Perhaps I'll fall asleep. Sleep. That will be good. Mother! I'm dying to sleep . . .

Who's that screaming? Whose voices are those? Wake up! Wake up! You know these voices. They belong to people you know. But to whom? They're screaming. You must get up, wake up. I must wake up. I must lift my head, move it. Perhaps my eyes will open and I will see what's going on around me. What is it? Am I blind? Somebody's screaming *all the time*. If I concentrate, perhaps I'll know who it is.

God! My crew. The crew I command. Then perhaps I'm in the tank. Of course. This cool steel – it's the turret. I'm lying on it. Albert, my radio operator-loader, is screaming. Clearer, Albert. I don't understand. You – what? Wounded? Then why are you screaming, for pete's sake? Somebody else is screaming. A chorus of shrieks of pain. Who is it? Amram? Shimon? Abrusha? The noise is killing me. Somebody over there is screaming that he's wounded. Why suddenly wounded?

Think! Think! Think! We went to war. We were moving up the Syrian Heights. Suddenly, the blow came. A blow that doesn't hurt . . . Idiot! What are you waiting for? They're screaming that they're injured. Do something. Perhaps the tank has stopped moving. Perhaps we're standing facing Syrian anti-tank guns and bazookas. Maybe the tank is on fire. Something is scalding my hands and back. Another moment and the tank will blow up; all the shells carefully laid in its bowels will explode. In all, we didn't fire many. The tank is still full. A lousy state of affairs – a tank full of exploding ammunition. I must call for help, report that my tank has been hit. If only I could see something. I must dive into the turret and try to operate the radio. How do you find the radio? I can't see anything. Don't scream down there below, I'm going to call for help. I'm a fool! I speak, but the words don't come out of my mouth. Fact: I don't hear them. Something strange has happened to me. I'm in a daze. The radio. God, I must find the right switch. "Ziva, this is 3C. My crew is wounded. My crew, they're wounded. Do you hear? Over."

Now I spoke. I heard my voice through the ringing in my ears. Why don't they answer? Why doesn't anybody answer? I can't hear anything in the earphones. They're dead. The screams have stopped inside the turret. Maybe they're dead? The tank can blow up at any minute. I saw things like that in the last war, in 1956. It's gruesome. Turrets flew through the air like tennis-balls. There was a smell of roasting flesh. My boys down below will burn alive.

Again I feel the cold steel on my cheeks. I don't remember getting out of the turret. Strange. I'm sinking again. I'm lost again. I'm in a tank – that much is certain. I've been around tanks for twelve years, but never in a situation like this. My crew is injured, and here I lie in apathy. No energy to do anything. Just want silence and to drift. A moment! I've got it! I too am wounded. Must be blind. So it's happened. It doesn't scare me. Now that too is strange. If I'm wounded, then that dampness on my face is perhaps – blood? It's already flowing down my back like streams of sweat. It's also spurting from my head onto my cheeks. And inside, in the skull, as though my internal pipe system has disintegrated. It's rushing into my throat. How could I have gotten hit in the head? It was protected by two thicknesses. A tank crew helmet and a heavy steel helmet. What can get through that? Mamma mia! How this helmet has disintegrated! It's terrifying to touch. All in shreds. Lucky I wore it. Before we set off for battle I wanted to throw it on the turret floor. It felt too heavy on my burning head. What luck! If the helmet disintegrated like this – my head would have come apart! I never thought you feel like this when you're wounded. They didn't teach this in training.

Somebody's approaching. He's talking. Can't follow a word. His voice is pleasant, familiar, soothing. He touches me. Let me be! I've got no strength for you now. Who are you? Why are you dragging me out? How much time has gone by? A minute? An hour? Where do you find the strength to pull like that? I will try to help. It must be difficult for you. Stop! The blood in my head is flowing into my throat again. Maybe I shouldn't be moved! Who's tugging at me? Why go to all that trouble? My body's sliding over the tank. Now my legs are being pulled down on the ground. The blood is flowing. It terrifies me. The stranger lays me down and starts doing something to my head.

"There's no point in bandaging the head. Lost case!"

Who did he say that to? Why did he say it in such a sad voice? He puts the steel helmet on me. Why is there nothing to bandage? Look again! No, leave me alone. I want to rest. It's so good to lie on the ground. So very, very comfortable.

Here I lie on foreign soil. In Syria. It was marvellous and terrifying to climb those slopes, to snake up those serpentine paths, to drink

15

in the view of the valleys and boulders, with their tattered mantles of low, sickly and neglected grain. To keep on up, to look by chance to the left and discover the Huleh Valley on the other side! Not where we usually see it.

A sudden rush of warm excitement. We did it! We smashed them! We're right in the middle. Those hated slopes, exuding a smell of death and malevolence, are so beautiful as they are mauled and crushed under the tracks of my tank.

I was sorry for my crew. I thought: poor devils. Buried in the tank, hardly seeing the path through a periscope. Our beautiful green valley, the green-blue checkered fields and fish-ponds – they can't see them! War or no war, this mustn't be missed. Perhaps they'll come back this way alive. Even if they come here again, it won't have the same taste. To the devil with war and discipline! To hell with having to travel with closed flaps. I ordered the driver to slow down, urged the men to stick their heads out. I told them: "Boys, this is an historic moment!" But the words rang in my ears like some empty phrase from a Zionist orator . . .

I felt the warm, pleasant heat of the sun on my face. What time is it? My body is spreadeagled on sharp stones, but they don't bother me. In the dark vacuum where I find myself, there is no noise, no pretty views and no voices. Emptiness. Nobody bothers me. Sleep. I'm exhausted. I drop down, down, down . . .

2

What was that?!

What was that terrible thunder-clap that burst so close and ripped at my ear-drums? It fell . . . it fell right next to me, right on me. It's so . . . Oh ah ah! Mother! It hurts! It hurts so much. My leg. My leg's bursting. It's coming apart. The bones are breaking. God, they're broken! One bone, a second, a third . . . The splinters are tearing into the flesh. Ssss, a sound like a cigarette being put out in water.

Who is screaming next to me? He's wounded. I won't scream. Nothing will make me . . . Nevertheless, I screamed like a madman. Like an animal. I really didn't want to. But the voice screaming next to me tore a shriek out of my throat as well.

16

I've been wounded again. A second time. That's not fair.

I knew that something would happen to me. Well before the war a voice whispered inside me. I wrote something like a last will and testament. But why twice? Once would have been enough. The first time, at least, it didn't hurt. Now it's hurting like nothing has ever hurt before. It's uncalled for, this business with the leg. It's no big deal to wound a blind man who can't move. In any case, the Syrians have already put me out of action.

I've heard that when it hurts very much, you lose consciousness. Why isn't it happening to me? Why aren't I losing it? I want to faint . . .

Voices shout. It's Meir Tzuk, the platoon commander. He's bawling out his crew: why did they get out of the tank without their Uzzis? Has anything happened to them? Perhaps they were also wounded. Perhaps not. Perhaps the Syrians are charging them? If them, then me as well. They are near me. God, anything but not a prisoner; not blind in Syrian captivity!

They're approaching. They stop by me and say something about me in hysterical voices, as though panic-stricken. Tzuk, I can't answer you. But I can hear you. It's O.K. I'm alright. Don't get worked up. There's no need to calm me down. You can see I'm not panicking – just lying quietly. Who's wetting my face with water? David Elimelech. What? What are you telling them? My brain's spilling out? That's bad. It's very bad if your brain spills out. I thought that only the blood was flowing.

They lift me up. Where do they want to take me? Poor Tzuk. You're strong, but I'm heavy. It's no mean task to carry me, even with your kibbutznik's strong hands.

Noooo! No! No! No! Don't touch my leg. You're murdering me! No! Don't touch. My leg's smashed. Leave it alone. Leave that leg alone, you fools! You're killing me!

I screamed at the top of my lungs. They pay no attention to me. This is terrible. Please, hold me by the thigh and not the lower leg, because there, down there, it's hell. They don't understand. Why don't they teach them at school the difference between the thigh and the shin? The thigh, my comrades – is the upper part of the leg. That's the place to clip it – high up.

At last they left me alone. They meant well, but only hurt me. I sobbed like a child. I could hear a half-track coming near. They'll crush me. The track rumbled by. Again they're lifting me. Putting me inside. A lot of voices inside. Pandemonium. Somebody is probing me. Perhaps a doctor. Yes. They're calling him "doctor". I must explain to him what happened: "My name's Yaacov. My blood type – A. I was hit once when in the tank, and once on the ground." He wraps cool bandages, pleasant to the touch, around my head and face. He's tying my leg. He's doing the proper thing. A leg that's broken must be splinted. He says: "He must be given blood." That means – me. Somebody jabs me in the arm. Perhaps that's the blood transfusion.

It's crowded here. I can hear heavy breathing next to me. The half-track's moving. Leg, leg, what are you doing to me? Every jolt tears me to shreds. Why don't I faint? Why aren't I dead? Rivers of blood flow over and through me. Yet I'm completely awake. How wonderful it was to be in a daze. What do you do to make yourself faint? So I won't hear the groans here in the half-track. Who is that screaming all the time: "My leg! My leg!" Why does he shout so much? I'm also hurt, and I'm so quiet. I'm ashamed to scream. Why isn't he? His shrieks pound my head like hammers. If he keeps this up – I'll break down too. No. I'll stay silent. So they won't say afterwards that I whined like a dog that's been run over.

Who's that? Somebody's talking to me; it's a voice I know. A soft, pleasant voice. I know him from somewhere. I love his voice. I feel warm. A good warmth suffuses me. What? Yes, my name's Yaacov – Yaacov Haelyon. Why has he suddenly fallen silent? Hey, I want to hear you. Before, when you talked to me, it was pleasant. What?! It's you, Dan? Dan Shilon? What are you doing here? How did you get into this half-track? Dan, I'm happy! I haven't the strength to tell you, but I'm happy that you're here. It was bad, Dan. I was alone, and there were only strangers. No soul that I knew. Now you're here. I'm ashamed to admit it, but I need you. You must help me. Talk to me . . . I think I'm blind. I won't be writing for the paper any more. A blind man can't be a journalist. My leg! My leg! Help me. I saw you earlier. I saw the half-track you were in. I saw you fly from it like a shell. I wanted to run to you, to see what happened. Your half-track went up in flames. But I didn't stop. My tank moved on. Into the war.

Why is that fellow next to me screaming "My leg" all the time? Ask him to be quiet. I was scared that if I ran over to you, they'd

18

hit my tank meanwhile. The crew would go. A crew without a commander is like a blind horse or a mole. I acted without thinking. Everything seemed to be moving of its own volition. The tank also moved on past your burning half-track.

Answer me, Dan, answer me! I don't know whether I'm talking, or whether it only seems that I am. I can't hear myself. It's difficult to think of the words. I'm terribly worried about Yael. She'll be going mad from worry. I don't want her to know. On no account. Ring my friends. Tell them. Their daughter works in Israel Broadcasting. Perhaps you know her. Osnat. But on no account are they to tell my wife. She won't be able to bear it. She mustn't suffer. Tami, my little girl! Your father will be blind, and won't be able to see you any more . . . How's Sara, your wife, Dan? How's the baby and the dog? Yes, ring my friends. Their number is 31357. Did you get that right? But they musn't tell Yael.

I'm thirsty, Dan. Very thirsty. Yes, thanks. That's good. More. Thanks. More water. I've never been so thirsty. It's like water from the Garden of Eden. But this lousy half-track's jolting. Every jolt is killing me. I'm thirsty, but I can't drink. The water's choking me. My throat's so dry. Dan, do me a favour. Ask the driver to slow down. Slower, not so fast, each jolt is purgatory. Thanks. Are you sure he heard you? Then why is he still driving so fast? Where are we going that it's taking so long? Water, Dan, water. I must drink.

. . . If I'm blind, I won't be able to write any more. Blood's pouring into my throat. My mouth's full of it, it's spilling out of my mouth. Like you see in the movies. What's the driver shouting there? His brakes have gone? Fantastic. That's all that was missing. Yes, yes, O.K., I'll spit out the blood, Dan. I know it can get into the windpipe and lungs – and choke me. Yes, I'm spitting. Can't you see? You've got a soothing voice, doctor. You keep saying: "Yaacov, spit. Yaacov, spit out the blood." It's nice of you. You've got other wounded. Take care of them. Each time I spit, doctor, more blood pours into my throat.

Why make the effort? Perhaps it would be better if I finished myself off? Swallow the blood, choke on it and die. Put an end to the agony in my leg, and Yael won't have a blind husband dependent on her for his whole life. What am I fit to be? A telephone operator, employed out of pity? What sort of a father can I be for little Tami? A father who can't see her, who can't look into her mischievous little eyes . . . Enough! I've got no strength to spit any more. Let it be. Who's shoving fingers down my throat?! Who's yanking the blood out? Dan, stop it!

It's O.K. I was only resting for a moment. Now, I'll make the effort and do it myself. Perhaps they've got something against pain? I can't bear it any more. Please, Dan, ask them. Maybe they've got something. They say that when it hurts, they give morphine and it helps. Talk to me, Dan, talk! I'm sinking into some place. It's hurting less. What are you tying on me? Ah, yes. A tag on my arm. That's what they do after a morphine shot. That must mean they've given me one. I didn't even feel it. It hurts less, Dan. Everything's getting dimmer. My leg's disappearing. The half-track's disappearing. I can't hear the screams. I can't hear the doctor's voice. Even you, Dan – you're not there. And me! I've vanished. Gone. Thanks, God!

3

Voices. Voices in the fog. Talking all around me. I can't catch a single word. They're talking quietly. The words flit around like small birds. Why can't I see anything? Where am I? They're dragging me somewhere. They're laying me down. On a stretcher? Is this a dream. What? – Yes. I'm wounded. Now I remember: I was wounded. Perhaps I'm in a field hospital? Don't mumble, speak loudly. My leg's killing me again. Somebody took pincers and is mauling my leg, especially on the heel. Somebody, why are you doing that to me? They're undressing me. They're tearing my clothes off. Don't lose Tami's doll's leg. It's my lucky charm. It's in my breast pocket. I hear! I'm alive! Is this a hospital? They've torn all my clothes off. I don't mind being naked. Wonderful! How did you succeed in cutting my boot leather? It eases me. When I'm discharged from the reserves, I have to fill in a form on lost equipment. Ask, ask, I can answer you. My name, Yaacov . . . Tank commander . . . Blood type . . . I took one on the head when I was on the tank. The second, when I was lying on the ground. Why are you laughing? I'm not a corpse yet. I'm talking. The body's been knocked about – but the head's working. No, don't take me. I don't want to travel on that miserable half-track again. I'm scared of it. I'll die – and not go.

Why do the words stick in my mouth? Why can't they be heard?
. . . Hey, Dan, where have you vanished to? I need you: they want
to cart me off in a half-track again.

Not a half-track. A helicopter. Somebody said: "Helicopter."
Very noisy. It rises. How much time has gone by since . . .? It's
coming, sleep. Is . . . is this what's meant by – unconsciousness? Is
this what they call – death . . .?

They're standing above me. I didn't notice that we stopped
moving. There's a woman among the bunch mumbling over me.
They're removing the bandages. I'm naked – and next to a
woman! Unpleasant. They're talking among themselves – alien
words – Latin? I can't understand anything. Doctors' language.
They're asking again. Every time the same questions. I already told
them: Name; blood type. The first time on the tank. The second
time on the ground. I think they were mortar-shells. Laughing
again? What's funny? The woman's amused that I can't talk?
Hands pawing over my body. Somebody says: "Work for the Plastics." Oho! Don't tell me I'm torn or burnt? A scarecrow. I must
look horrible. I'll scare Tami. I don't want her to pierce me with
big frightened eyes and say: "Mummy, I'm scared of Daddy." Like
she used to say: "Daddy, I'm afraid of the pigeon. It will bite me."

"Yes," the woman who laughed before said, "I'll have to deal
with him."

Who are you? What are you going to do to me? Are you from
Plastics? Are you one of those who fashion new noses for women?
It's good they don't mention the leg. Perhaps they don't know that
it's injured? If they dare touch it – I'll jump clear up to the sky. It
seems as though they're moving me. Somebody's probing a vein.
Like an injection. If only I could see what they're doing. Somebody
says: "Good night." What? It's already night? I thought only a few
moments had passed. I thought . . . only . . . only . . . only a few
moments . . . it's difficult . . . it's diff . . . to think . . . good . . . good
ni . . . ght . . .

4

Quiet! Quiet! Quiet! Have you gone mad? What are these fires?
Something's constantly exploding . . . fire. Fireworks. Camp fires.

A truck speeding along with crimson casualties. A half-track bursting into flames like a jerry-can of gasoline. Shells sputtering all around. Not so fast, Eli! What's going on here? Can't understand.
. . . Dan. Dan Shilon. I saw him Friday morning in Tal Grove. We were then so certain there wouldn't be a war. Dan suddenly appeared in a jeep with an infantry officer. "Hey, shalom, Dan. What are you doing here? Will there be a war or won't there?" He had a "military correspondent" tab on his shoulders. I thought: he must be well-informed about what's going on. Don't run away. Don't vanish. Don't back off. Wonderful: we've taken Jerusalem. I almost burst into tears. Many fell in Jerusalem, what? We'll go home shamefaced, because we didn't get the chance to lick the Syrians. It has its good side though – at least we'll come out of it in one piece. War is no joke. He's leaving. So long, Dan.

Yet, the war did break out. Coward. Yellow! The Sinai Campaign was a child's game to me. I was nineteen. But now there's a weight in my belly. Fear rumbles in my bowels. Now I've got a wife and a two and a half year old daughter, and debts on the new flat . . . The coming battle frightens me. I know that we've been placed in the vanguard to break into the Syrian fortifications. They want to finish – once and for all – every miserable Syrian in Tel Aziziyat who thinks that he's entitled to toss a shell at Kibbutz Dan, whenever the mood takes him.

We're going off to war. Good-natured Yuval, my best friend in the company. You're driving me. Look after yourself, Mr. Yuval Gold. You've also got a wife and little kid. Don't let anything happen to you, do you hear? Why does this place stink of cordite? Why is everybody shouting? Why are you screaming: My leg? You're not an only child here. Be a man! The shells are thundering all the time. We're bypassing Kfar Szold. What a disgrace! The only thing I know about Kfar Szold is that they are often a target for the Syrians.

Nahum Shuki's platoon went first and vanished from sight. Ezra was in the first tank. I was attached to his company. Namir, the company commander, was behind me. It's beautiful here, to hell with it. What a marvellous sight when you peek through the telescope. But why are we so exposed to Syrian eyes? They're so close to us . . . At least, we're not the first. There are tanks in front of us.

Tanks and half-tracks are ascending Givat Ha'em in a long, long line. The hill is right on the border. They also call it the Monk's Mound. Now masses of our tanks are rolling over it. Perhaps they're not ours. Perhaps theirs. If only my crew knew how to work the gun properly. They're new. I don't know them well enough. Albert was a machine-gunner. I turned him into a loader-wireless operator. If the loader doesn't know how to work the machine-gun, load it and especially take care of blockages – then a tank becomes a lump of steel that's only waiting for somebody to come and hit it. Afterwards they'll scrape us out with trowels.

No. The tanks on Givat Ha'em are ours. The Syrian positions are raining down a murderous fire on them. They're bursting into flames one after the other. God! There must already be dead and wounded! Why are we so exposed to the Syrians? They'll make mincemeat of us. Why is Namir, the company commander, silent? He's playing around with his earphones all the time. I've spotted some wild shrubs. "Driver! Hey Abrasha, wake up! Back up. Slowly, O.K., enough." Now the tank isn't so exposed. The shrubs hide us. Only the turret, and me, are sticking out. But what is important – we're no longer such a clear target for the Syrian guns. They're shelling us. The shells are getting closer. They're bursting in the ground and raising small clouds of dust. There are already fires in a few places. The thistles are burning. I'm no longer afraid. In Sinai, during the attack on Abu Ageila, shells burst all around me for a whole day. Nobody got hurt. Just noise. There's no need to get excited.

This lousy steel helmet is pressing down on my head like a steam-roller. The tanks are moving over there and beginning to get a foot-hold on the Syrian slopes. Bravo! Forward, comrades!

Now it's beginning to get monotonous. There's a long line of half-tracks drawn up alongside us on the road. The first one is sprouting a forest of radio aerials. I'm hungry. "Amram, as you know, a machine-gunner is also the crew chef, so for God's sake spread some of that stinking jam on biscuits and pass them up." Who's sitting on the half-track with the radio aerials? Even when you look at it through a telescope, all you can see are steel helmets. The faces aren't clear. Hey, would you believe it! Dan is sitting there. He looks funny under a steel helmet. It's a small world. To meet him here of all places. Our correspondent, Dan Shilon, reports: "At 11.30 a.m., our forces went up the Syrian Heights. But I was

23

getting bored down below at that hour." I'm also getting bored, pal. I'd love to go over and chat to pass the time. But what can you do? – we're at war now. He raises his head. He's got no binoculars, and so he can't spot me. "Hey, Dan! Dan Shilon! Hey! Look this way!" He turns around. Yes, he saw me. I stick up a thumb: "Good luck, comrade!" He waves his hand enthusiastically, and replies with his thumb. Such chance encounters warm the soul. He's a good guy and a clever bastard.

The helmet's like a vice. Rivers of sweat are pouring down beneath it. I've not yet found the most comfortable position in which to stand in. The guys who made this tank didn't give much thought to the comfort of its crew. Shimon, the gunner, squirms under me every time my heavy boots hit his back.

The radio comes alive after a long silence. Somebody's calling "Ziva". Ziva is our company call sign. A girl's name for hundreds of tons of steel. Whenever one of the other companies of the battalion would get the better of us during excercises, the men would say: "We've screwed Ziva . . ."

Who's calling Ziva? – Mussa Klein, Barak Battalion commander, to whom we're attached. Mussa asks where Nahum Shuki's platoon is. It should have been his point platoon, to lead the attack infantry. Shuki has moved off quite a way, and radio contact with him is broken. Mussa asks "Ziva" – our company – to send "another platoon of top-notch bastards" to take the lead. Namir offers my company. My stomach flips. So we'll be the vanguard. It means that our chances of returning are very slim. We are to be the cannon fodder, the soft belly that is first exposed. Where did I put the leg from Tami's doll? I search thoroughly through my breast pocket, open it, pull it out, kiss it, take a good look at the photos in my wallet, make my farewells and put them back. And we begin to move forward into hell.

A last look at Dan. He's talking to the men sitting next to him in the half-track. I can't see him. The road is narrow. I'm the fourth in the column. A river cuts across the road. The bridge thrown over it won't take the tanks' weight. We move over to the left to cut through the water. The tracks screech and throw up spurts of mud, the engines roar and struggle. The gun has to be turned backwards so that it won't stick in the river-bed. Our tank has not been lucky in recent days. Too many breakdowns.

5

. . . When we travelled from Sahnin to Ein Zeitim near Safed, during the tense days before the war, its clutch broke. The tank stopped and refused to move. Thirty-six hours passed till we got it back in shape. We were tense right through that one. Battle may be joined at any moment, and we sit unarmed. Everybody will rush onto the battlefield, and we'll remain in the shade of the green trees.

A few days later, when the battles in Sinai and Jordan were at their peak – the Syrians also tried to flex their muscles. They sent forces to attack Kibbutz Dan. We were summoned to the aid of the kibbutz from our tank park in Tel Hai Forest. We made a mad rush across the fields. Namir, the company commander, sat on my tank. I relieved him, and took over the command half-track. At the beginning of the road, following an unsuccessful turn, the tank got stuck on the ridge of a deep embankment and couldn't be extricated. Namir moved over to the half-track, and I went to try and move the tank which was blocking the road for the whole company. After a few manoeuvres we succeeded.

We continued on to the Hatzbani River. Here we also had to cross through water and treacherous mud. I warned Abrasha, the driver, that there is only one narrow lane through the water where we can pass without sinking. And then – the third breakdown: the tank slipped and began to slither about. We lost control and almost overturned. We barely made it across the river, while bashing into an ancient tree that stood on the banks.

Again we switched. Namir on the tank and me on the half-track. When we reached the fields of Kibbutz Dan, the Syrians were already close to the kibbutz fence. On the radio we could hear the desperate cries of the kibbutzniks for help. We rolled over the clover fields, spellbound by the sight of our planes incessantly working over the Syrian positions of Ramat Baniass.

Suddenly I heard somebody call me. I dropped my eyes from the heights of the half-track, and saw Namir. He ordered me to return to the tank. He climbed up into the half-track. I asked him where my tank was. Namir only pointed silently. I finally saw something flashing. I went towards it. My tank was, no more and no less, upside down in an anti-tank ditch. Namir in his mad rush forward hadn't noticed it, and it had swallowed the tank whole.

But this wasn't the end of it. When we returned that evening from the battlefield of Dan, weary and red-eyed, we were ordered to park in Tal Grove. Namir directed us from the ground. Suddenly the tank dipped, and most of its bulk vanished into a huge hole that was covered by dense foliage. I burst out laughing. That evening my tank was nicknamed – "The Tumbler".

Now, as we were about to cross the river, I was worried. But the crossing was easy and quick. We lurched out of the water wet and sparkling. We moved up onto Givat Ha'em. By now the hill was a focal point for incessant murderous fire. Before we began the climb up we were stopped by an officer on the roadside. He directed us into a wood by the road, or at least what was once a wood. Now it was lifeless. Blackened. Charcoal stumps were all that was left of its once proud trees. The heavy smell of fire was in our nostrils.

Suddenly a tremendous peal of thunder next to us. We dived into the tanks and crouched in terror. Tank crews don't have fox-holes and bunkers in which to take cover. Their only shelter is the tank's armour.

The Syrians had found us. Heavy mortar-shells landed next to us one after the other. Our ears were ringing. I quickly found myself wordlessly working out the course of events: a shrill whistle, a muffled drop, an immense explosion of the shell, and the hum of flying shrapnel. Then it was possible to breathe quietly for a moment.

It is in the nature of a soldier that he adapts to any situation. For how long can he remain frightened and crouching? As the shelling eased slightly, I cautiously lifted my head out of the turret. The heads of my comrades appeared from the tanks all around. My mouth was parched. I jumped from the turret onto the deck, to pull out the water container that was strapped to the tank's side. The crew began to call my name. I knew they were suffocating inside, and their bodies drowned in sweat.

"I'm dying to piss," Amram the machine-gunner shouted over the intercom. Everybody else joined in. I agreed, on condition that they come out one at a time. A long line of soldiers quickly drew up by the tank. I grinned at the sight, and was sorry that I hadn't brought a camera. I peeled an orange and no longer took the explosions seriously. I remembered the doll's leg and put my faith in it.

On the evening that I was called up, I felt in my bones that there

26

would be a war. I went into my little daughter's room, just as she had begun to fall asleep. I lifted her up and hugged her tight, breathing in her fresh baby smell. She giggled happily. She toyed with the hope that perhaps today we would break the rules and let her out of bed. She laughed – and I wanted to cry. Inadvertently my eye fell on her toy shelf. I noticed the doll's leg and put it in my pocket.

The doll's leg instilled in me greater security than the Uzzi which never left my shoulder. I knew that I was immune to all the shells exploding in this ghostly forest.

The tension of battle began to wane. The crews threw orange peels at each other, and began to exchange friendly insults. One of the half-track commanders peered at us through amused eyes: he said he had lived twelve years with tank crews, and he knew they were lazy, slow-moving animals. Twelve years – but he had never seen such a display of alacrity as we had exhibited a few moments ago when the shells exploded next to us . . .

Military police urged us along with sharp hand signals. Funny – I thought – they're directing traffic just like policemen in Dizengoff Square. Here, in the heart of battle, nobody mocked them – "Spit and polishers". They, like us, were risking their lives.

I was sorry that we were called to move on. We had just begun to enjoy the party, and the terror had been forgotten.

We screeched and clattered up the steep slope of Givat Ha'em. Fires were burning all around – dumb witness to the shells that had fallen. On both sides of the road soldiers were busy with various tasks. We paid no attention to what they were doing. Two of them came near, and tossed oranges up to us: "Eat, boys, to your health." We could read the anxiety in their eyes. Perhaps we wouldn't be coming back. We waved our hands at them. I fooled around with an orange and clutched it in my palm. Suddenly I was trembling all over. A tender rushed towards us, its siren wailing incessantly – from the top of the hill at a terrific speed. The driver signalled us to move off the road. He passed by. I followed him with my eyes. I could see that he was loaded with stretchers. These were the first wounded that I had seen since the battle started. The more we advanced, the more common this sight became. They lay at the roadside on stretchers or on the ground. Large bloodstains on their uniforms – their faces ashen. I felt sick. For a moment my fingers closed around the orange, and then I threw it on the ground. How low can you get! Here men are lying drained of blood, perhaps dying, and I – the sweet taste of orange juice in my mouth.

We reached the top of the hill, which was totally exposed to the Syrian positions. The path that was now being cleared by bull-dozers was very narrow. Half of it was taken up by a half-track that was burning like a huge red pyre. Large masses were flying out of the flames – shells exploding from the heat. A corpse seemed to be outlined in the blaze. I approached. I had almost to pass through the flames. I got down into the turret so that the flames and shrapnel wouldn't reach me. After we passed, I took a deep breath. One last look. I was saddened at the sight of a dying half-track.

At that very moment something happened inside me: the fear of war dropped away. The fear that had haunted me for so many days. The feeling was physical more than spiritual. Something was re-leased inside me. Steam that had accumulated had found a way out. I was overcome by the drunkenness of battle. The fear that had gnawed at me on the long nights of waiting, lying alongside the tank, dissolved into stars; the anxieties of the long briefing sessions when we were told that here we were going into battle; the knotted tension when we heard the ominous news bulletins pouring out of the transistor – all was at an end and discarded, as though purged by the burning half-track. I was now ready for anything. Battle drunkenness: the gift of a divine providence.

The tension was still there, but it was no longer rooted in fear. It was the heritage of willingness to do things right. Not make mis-takes. Not make a mess of it. To charge forward, while forgetting yourself. To finish the job quickly and well.

Givat Ha'em was wrapped in a heavy cloud of fog and dust. The first tanks had already begun to slide down the slope towards the Syrians. Why had the half-track in front of me stopped? It was blocking the way. Move! Move out, idiot! Can't you see that I can't advance? Move, the devil with you! Namir, behind me, was making wild hand-signals: "Advance!" What could I do? The road was blocked in front of me. The commander of the half-track in front finally decided to move. He got off the road. We had joined, it seemed, the Syrian patrol road. We were on their soil! We crossed the border. Syria, I'm inside you! The tanks were pulling well. The Sherman may be obsolete – but it's a work-horse. On reserve train-ing I hated it because it dragged me away from home, to a military regime where you can't be lord over your own destiny. Now it was flesh of my flesh. No, I was one of its limbs.

A group of houses. Perhaps a Syrian position. None of those lurching up in front of me were shooting at it. Pity. I wanted to try the machine-guns. I hadn't had a chance to try them so far – and I didn't know whether they were working.

The Hule! The Hule Valley spread out in front of us. Marvellous. Wonderful. Magnificent. What a view! You could reach out and hug and kiss the brown-green-blue jigsaw. "Boys, it's an historic moment! You can lift your heads out! . . ." The view was exhilarating. I felt at peace and forgot for a moment that we were fighting and not touring. Strange.

Yossi Cohen's tank, racing in front of me, stopped by the roadside. What happened? One tank already gone? Yossi announced over the radio that he had broken down. He shrugged his shoulders towards me as though to say: "What can be done?"

Great pity. Yossi's tank has the choice crew of the company. All of them, apart from the commander, are veteran tank men. Each of the four could fill any job in the tank with the same efficiency that he does his own. Yitzhakele Rivkin is a priceless gunner with record results on the ranges. Robert Cohen is a loader-wireless operator who has never had a blockage or malfunction that he couldn't clear quickly. Moshe Halfon, the driver, moves that tank not only with his hands, but also with his ears and heart. Amnon Yisraeli, the machine-gunner, an irreplaceable field cook with no competitors.

Yitzhakele, Amnon and Halfon were privates together with me in Moshe Brill's A Company that won a unit citation for taking Abu Ageila in Sinai, 1956. When we graduated to reserve service, I was separated from them. The three forged themselves into an elite tank crew. Nobody could split them. It was clear to everybody that they would make life a misery for anybody who tried. Over the years the three became known as the best of soldiers. I more than once regretted that I hadn't been given command of that crew, and I envied Yossi Cohen. Now they were stuck, and the company had lost their select talents.

I was now the third in the column. We were leaving the track down which we had come into the valley. Sparse corn grew here and there, and closely spaced terraces traversed its width. The terraces

29

were high, and I wondered how we would cross them. The landscape was nothing like the Negev wastes where we were used to operating. That was an ideal area for armour. Here it seemed that tanks couldn't function effectively. But the valley had its advantage. At last we were advancing as tanks are meant to: in a wide formation. Before we had travelled clumped together along the path, like a convoy of private cars on the Netanya-Tel Aviv highway.

Movement was now difficult and complicated. The terraces and rocks strewn across the valley were continually jolting us up and down. "Abrasha, pay attention! There are thousands of obstacles on the road. Think of your good and charming commander, and take pity on him." An incautious driver can literally "eliminate" his commander if he isn't careful about obstacles. Inside the tank the rocking and jolting isn't so obvious. The chief victim is the commander, stuck in the turret, taking heavy punishment from the armour and its projections. This is the time for a driver who doesn't care for his commander to settle his accounts . . .

A path facing us. The deviation alignment that the Syrians had prepared to stop our use of Jordan waters. We must move up onto this path. It's not easy. A steep escarpment blocks our advance. I look everywhere for an easy place to ascend. Namir, away om my right, does the same. Which of us will be the first? I am. Now I'm second after Ezra, who has already vanished beyond the twists in the road. To the right we can see ruins; but perhaps they're not ruins but mud houses, or even a Syrian-manned emplacement. Must be checked. I'll let my gunner have a go at it. "Gun, explosive, 700 yards, buildings opposite, fire!" – the order was carried out almost before I had finished giving it. Very nice. Now we'll sweep them up with some machine-gun fire. The machine-gun fires single rounds, and stops. "What's up, Albert? How the hell are you operating the gun? Bursts, for pete's sake. Come on, clear the blockage."

The machine-gun's dead. It would happen just now. After four lousy bullets. At the beginning of the battle. I peer down the turret and see Albert struggling with machine-gun parts, sweating and panting. "Do your best, Albert, do your best. That machine-gun's got to work! We'll be up against the Syrians any minute, and it's them or us." Albert shrugs helplessly in my direction. "O.K.," I instruct him, "switch to the other machine-gun. Amram will try meanwhile to clear the blockage."

30

The heights have by now turned into a boiling cauldron, with not a single square yard untouched by shells. It's difficult to see if these are our support shells, or whether the enemy is plastering his own soil, over which he is slowly losing control. The flat spaces in front of us are blazing up, and the shells are falling amid the flames. "Shimon, stick your head out. Can you see what's happening in front? Good. Aim there. No. I can't tell you whether you've hit. How can I find our shell among the hundreds that are exploding over there?"

On! On! "Abrasha, faster! Put your foot on it! Quicker. Give it everything it's got! No! No! No! Slow down!" In the Lord's name, how did that donkey get there ahead of us on the road? Out of it, donkey! You'll be run over. Move off the road, idiot. You'll die. You're not in this war. You're just a donkey. It canters ahead, frequently turning its head to gaze at us. I wonder: move fast and kill the animal, or be lax in my duty – slow down in the middle of a battle and let it live? "Faster, Abrasha, to the devil with the donkey. No! No! Stop! We're going to run it over."

God! Men are getting killed here and I take pity on a donkey?! I've never killed a man in cold blood. By virtue of being in a tank, I've been able to avoid face to face war. If I do kill – I needn't see my victim's face.

The donkey runs off the path. Ha! I'll have a tale to tell when I get home: "We were in the midst of battle. It was very hot. Suddenly a donkey thrust itself in the way, in front of the tank. I didn't have the guts to kill it . . ."

Again, buildings huddled in a cleft in the hills. Below, on the path, an officer is ordering me to fire on the buildings. Soldiers are climbing towards them with their guns at the ready. I must give them cover. "Shimon, put a few shells into them, and some wide long bursts. Enough! Stop! The tank behind will continue the job."

The trip, in a tight convoy on the narrow path, is against all the tank warfare rules that we learnt in training. We're ignoring them all now, in the heat of assault. I turn the tank towards the hill, to take up a convenient firing position.

The slope is very steep, almost vertical. In training I wouldn't have dared to scale rocks like these. Now, no trace of fear. The tank climbs with agonising slowness, and suddenly begins to roll backwards quickly. I panic: "Abrasha! Abrasha! Stop! You almost

31

killed us. You're forgetting yourself." My rage isn't justified. Through his periscope he can only see a narrow strip of road which doesn't give him any perspective of the steepness. He apologises. I'm the one who should have apologised.

The valley of fire below is a gripping scene. For a moment I forget reality while I gaze at it enchanted. The radio drags me out of my imaginary world. "Albert! I don't want to hear any more about blockages in the machine-gun. You've got kids at home. So have I. If the machine-gun won't work – we may not see them again. No, Amram, I don't know where we are now. In Syria, at any rate. Faster Abrasha, Ezra's calling for help. He's alone there, let's go."

Where have the Golani half-tracks come from all of a sudden? My God! They're getting hit. They're being torn apart. The half-tracks are bursting into flames one after the other. They've got a lot of casualties. A torn soldier is sitting in a burning half-track next to me. There's agony in his face, but he goes on desperately firing a machine-gun. His comrades who jumped off the half-track are waving their hands, signalling him to jump out. They're shouting: "Moshe, Moshe, jump!" He shakes his head and goes on firing the gun to cover his friends. Down there they can't see what I can see from the height of the turret: that man will never jump again – his legs are smashed.

Here's Dan Shilon. He flies from the half-track. Other men fly with him. A direct hit. Where? Hey, for God's sake, go to the mangled boy in the half-track. Get him out. Save him . . .

Here's a Syrian tank. Pay attention! Pay attention! It's green. The Syrian camouflage colour. Perhaps it's an ambush. "Albert, put an armour-piercing shell in the gun. Shimon, the moment I tell you, hit him." The Syrian's gun is twisted like macaroni. Somebody already got him. "Abrasha, pull over to the right! Don't leave the path, move, fast!" I think I can see barbed wire fences on the hill in front of us. It's difficult to say for certain. My eyes are tired. The sweat that's pouring into them burns. Something suspicious. "Shimon, be ready with the gun. I don't like the look of this place . . ."

6

What was that?

What's happening? What hit me so hard? A terrible blow. I'm falling. My neck's broken. I'm as heavy as an elephant. Blackness. Can't see anything. Must open my eyes. It's impossible. Yes, Dan, I'm spitting out the blood. Why are you laughing? I'm not dead yet. My brain's working. My name's Yaacov.

Where am I? Fog. A dream. Lying on something soft. My eyes are hurting. What is this – a nightmare? My head also hurts. There's something on it. There's also something on my face. Like a wet towel. My left leg's heavy. Tons of leg. As though wrapped in bandages, the whole length. Something's pressing on my right thigh. It's pressing hard. Something's pricking my right ankle. Something's pricking my right hand.

Now I know! Now I remember! I was wounded. They took me to a hospital. Where did they take me? I can't lift my head or open my eyes. I've gone blind. Ring my friends, Dan. Don't tell Yael. They'll give me a seeing eye dog. A blind man's dog. How that donkey got in the way, eh! . . .

Yael! It's your voice! You're here! With me!

How did she get here? Dan, the bastard, must have told her. Yael, your voice is wonderful. It's the most beautiful voice I've ever heard. Good that you're here. I can't see anything. I can hear you. Nearby. I feel good. Now I feel good. I can't talk to you. I can't get a word out. Yes, yes, "shalom". I'm sinking. I return to the black void. I must go there. I'm so tired . . .

7

I've floated up again. Now no more deceptive visions. My clouded brain has apparently completed its first digestion of the events leading to my wound. I am completely conscious now. I know where I am, and I know that Yael is alongside me. I begin dully to take stock of my limbs. My hands run over my thighs, my arms, my face and head – and I feel bandages, pipes and plaster. But I can only think of one thing: I am blind. I am overwhelmed with fear.

Yael sensed that I had awoken. She began to talk to me. I told her I would never be able to see her again. She – the doctors had told her about my sight – denied it vigorously, and asked me to look at her. I tried. I can't open my swollen eyes. Perhaps they are open, but I can't see anything.

I sensed the touch of a woman's warm hand on my arm. It's a very pleasant touch. Whose hand is it? Yael continues to urge me: "You see. Open your eyes and find out for yourself. I'm on your left and Osnat Rabin is on your right." With a supreme effort, and great pain, I open my eyes and distinguish a blurred image. I gather up the remnants of my failing strength and look to the right. It's difficult to see whether it's really Osnat. My eyes close. Osnat and Yael's voices fade away . . .

Again I awoke. My eyes are closed. I listen to the doctors' conversation by my bed. The content isn't clear. Visitors later come to stand at the bedside. My closest friends. My eyes open for a fraction of a second. I shake Eddi Zucker's hand. His daughter was born yesterday. They again vanish, and with them the whole world.

I awoke – with a clear mind. Strange, my wounds don't bother me. But the needle stuck in my vein to supply fluid, and the instrument to pump urine, are driving me mad. I complained to Yael and she rushed to tell the doctors. They came and stood by the bed. I gathered from their tone of voice that they were hesitating. I conversed with them in a faint voice. I bargained: promised to drink and perform my essential functions myself if they would only remove these alien elements stuck in my flesh. They finally agreed. I sensed that it was possible to make a deal with them. I added a request that they take off, or at least loosen the bandages over my right thigh. They're hurting me. This one didn't work. They explained that skin taken from my right thigh had been transplanted on my head. The bandage must be tight, so that the wound on the thigh will heal properly.

So what – I comfort myself – you can't win them all.

I felt much better after they took the needles out, and condescended to sip a few spoons of water. I didn't think about my wounds. For the time being they weren't bothering me.

After a few hours there was a change: I succeeded in opening my eyes for a few minutes, in distinguishing the blurred form of the room, Yael's nearby features, and – above all, I made the acquaintance of the ceiling directly above me. Yael turned to me. How much

34

time had passed? "Two days," she replied. I sensed that she wanted to make things easier for me, and was wondering how to do it: "What do you want me to do, talk a lot? Talk occasionally, or just be silent?" I smiled and didn't answer. My head was heavy. I wasn't capable of listening to chatter. Yael took the hint from my silence – and was silent.

She couldn't save me the torture involved in drinking. My body had to get fluids, and each spoon I swallowed was an achievement. It would later become clear to me that she was told to keep an exact record of every drop of liquid that entered or left my body. Her warnings that they would stick the needles in again did their work. I drank. But the "pissing" business didn't work. No matter what.

8

On the third or fourth day the room began to come alive. Till now its inmates were benumbed. Like me, they hadn't felt pain. Now the pains began to wrack our bodies cruelly. The burn cases began to scream. There is nothing more agonizing than burns. Their screams shook me. My leg was again squashed in a giant pincer. I itched to feel my wounds. To sense them. To squeeze, to pinch. But I was separated from them by the thick cast. I didn't shout. Embarrassed, apparently. They frequently brought me pain-killers. Like the liquids I swallowed, the pain-killers aroused waves of nausea.

Nature came to my aid, and occasionally returned me to a comatose or dozing state. A strange daily routine began slowly to take shape: there were good hours and bad hours. In the morning – bad. Afternoon – good. At night – worst of all. Many visitors collected round the door of my room. They weren't allowed in. Were the doctors wary of tiring me? Or perhaps they wanted to save the visitors from frightening scenes?

I finally began to take an interest in Yael. She had been by my bedside since Saturday morning, and had almost never left it. I was worried: she was a very small eater, and had certainly made use of the situation – to stop eating altogether. I summoned Yocheved Bina, the ward sister, and demanded that she feed Yael. Yocheved, who would later be revealed to me as an angel of mercy, seduced

35

Yael into going with her to eat. When Yael came back, she told me she was even forced to eat pickled herring, a food the mere thought of which normally make her shudder. I laughed. For the first time since I was wounded. Later Yael would reveal how happy she was that I had begun to worry about her health – a sign that I had some-what recovered – in honour of which she was even ready to guzzle barrels of salt fish . . .

We achieved a real conversation. We even held a stormy debate: I demanded that she go off to sleep – after three days of not closing her eyes; I insisted that she go home to little Tami, from whom her father had first vanished, and whose mother now abandoned her. I quickly sensed that I would lose this round. Her face-muscles tautened and she said: "Couldn't be considered!" I was weak. I gave in.

I wondered how she found me. How she had succeeded in reach-ing me. (I was the first casualty in the room to have a member of the family by his bed.) Actually Yael had been by my side since I was moved from the recovery room after the operations. I asked, but her answers were vague; either because she didn't want to say, or because I wasn't capable of concentrating. One thing I knew: Dan had betrayed my request not to say anything to Yael.

9

"I've got a great piece of news for you," Osnat told my wife, "Yankele is wounded!"

The hour was ten at night, Friday, June 9. Dan had kept his promise. He told my friends, and it was they who decided to break the news. Osnat, who we think of as a young sister, took it on herself to inform Yael.

Yael replied in the same coin: "I'm also happy." I don't believe that either was really happy. Each acted out her part for the other.

A suspicion began to take shape in Yael's mind: perhaps not only wounded? Maybe they're trying to soften the blow? Dan Shilon is our friend. If it's only a light wound they're talking about, why didn't he phone me directly? She didn't panic but began desperately to try to find out where I was. The confusion was so great that, despite the use of legions of journalists from *Ma'ariv* – my paper – and friends in different towns in the north, who searched every hospital – nobody could locate me.

The search continued for a few hours, perhaps the worst in her life. When she sensed that she was achieving nothing, she resolved to look herself in all the hospitals in the north. The fact that they hadn't succeeded in finding me, strengthened her suspicion that I had been killed. She phoned our friends, Odeda and Bubi Etzioni, and asked them to join her in her search. They immediately agreed and set the time of departure for early in the morning.

Very late at night the phone rang in our house. It was Bubi. "We've succeeded in locating him," he told her. "My mother phoned a friend in Haifa and he found that Yankele was taken to Rambam Hospital."

In the morning they went to Haifa. Our friend, Yaela Barker, who lives in Haifa, waited for them at the hospital gates. Yael's anxious hours during the night were nothing compared with the terrors that awaited her within the walls of the hospital, while I was in the operating theatre.

They arrived at Rambam, but could not locate my room. I wasn't on any list. The four of them dragged through all the wards and consulted the doctors and nurses who were rushing around the rooms and corridors which were overflowing with war-wounded. Each minute their hearts sank lower: the sights that met their eyes would have brought the inured to injuries to the point of collapse. They again returned to casualty reception – and were again answered in the negative.

Finally, a kind-hearted doctor advised them to try a last resort: go through each room, bed by bed. Bubi did.

Bubi would later tell me that he came close to collapse. He did everything in his power to stand fast, so as not to break Yael's spirit. In those moments – he related – he believed there was only one place remaining where I could possibly be: the morgue. He did not go there, but back to central registry. And now – wonder of wonders – they discovered that I was in the plastic surgery ward.

When they came to the ward, they were stopped by the ward sister – Yocheved. She at first refused to let them in. She feared the shock to my wife. But because she was kind-hearted, she could not be adamant enough. A moment before allowing Yael in the room, she told her: "Beautiful or not, injured or not – remember: you will have a husband!"

There was a good reason for Yocheved's hesitation: my appearance wasn't particularly appealing. In fact, it was so gruesome that Yael would not allow Bubi and Odeda to see me.

I would never want to be in the position of a woman, who a bare week ago had seen her husband hale and hearty, and now stood beside a broken shard. My face and arms were covered with congealed blood and burns – and spattered with black dots – splinters that had entered my body. My head, eyes and cheeks were bandaged. My left leg was in a cast. Yael pursed her lips. She later told me that she consoled herself with the fact that I was the only one in the room whose face had remained white. All the others, most of them tank crewmen, were as black as charcoal. They were badly burned. Their appearance was shocking. One or two died after desperate attempts to save their lives failed.

A few days later Yael was given medical reports on my condition, in a number of copies. She tore off a copy of each report, for she knew how curious I would be to see them in the future.

Neurosurgery: injured by shells. Upon reception, was conscious Moved his upper limbs and right leg. Left leg in splints. A broken bone visible in right temple, and skin missing. Similarly, narrow fracture of the skull in forward frontal area, and fracture in rear frontal area. Intra-brain splinter, which had penetrated from right to left.

Plastic Surgery: tissue missing on forehead, temple and scalp. Below the wound – fracture of skull-pan. A patch was attached to the skull to complete the missing tissue, and a transplant made on the area of the temple.

Orthopaedics: open fracture in ankle and shin. Infected wounds. A number of splinters in sole of the foot.

Eyes: right eye alright. Left eye quiet, but no signs of wound. The forward section is regular, haemorrhage within eye-socket. Details cannot yet be discerned.

In all, it seemed that my body had occupied a host of physicians on the day I was admitted to the hospital. The conclusions were not pleasant, but with a little optimism it was possible to regard the situation as not too terrible. It was only later that new and worrisome findings came to light, which were to upset these initial evaluations, as they appeared in the eyes of the layman.

At noon on the third day I was able to keep up a prolonged conversation with Yael. This was a great joy to her, but that evening I would levy the price of that happiness.

We exchanged a few sentences, and I suddenly fell silent. My face – so she told me later – took on a strange expression. My eyes, which were open wide, focussed on one point in the ceiling and would not leave it. At first Yael sensed nothing. Only when I didn't answer one of her questions did she look at me – and flinched. She began to talk rapidly to wake me – but I did not react. She tried the last weapon in her arsenal: told me she was going to eat, in the hope that I would encourage her as usual – but still I did not react. She shook my body – and nothing happened.

She immediately summoned the night nurse. She too was shaken. She checked my blood pressure and pulse; her expression turned ominous. She immediately phoned Dr. Doron, the neurosurgeon who had treated me. The doctor hastily gave me an injection. After a few minutes the state of unconsciousness was replaced by a more or less peaceful sleep. The doctor told Yael that it will be necessary to move me the following morning into the Neurosurgical Department. My condition had worsened, she claimed. The diagnosis frightened Yael. A nurse acquaintance who passed through the ward that night frightened her even more by announcing, with a mournful expresssion, that there would be no avoiding a transfer to the Head Department. The evening's deterioration necessitated it.

When I awoke in the morning I felt rested. Yael urged Yocheved, the Wailing Wall of the ward, to do all in her power to avoid a transfer. And after the doctors consulted among themselves, and in the light of my improved state, it was decided to leave me where I was.

That anxious night was the crucial one. My body was almost defeated in its struggle with general exhaustion, loss of blood, numerous operations, the wounds and the infection. But the will to live, with the help of that injection, triumphed.

My God! My God! Why must the bedding be changed every morning? I'm wounded and my body hurts. Don't add to my tortures. Every shifting of my leg is agony. Please, no. Without changing the sheets. I'm weak and you're strong. Don't exploit it. No! Don't touch me! To hell with explanations. Leave me alone! Leave

39

me alone! If only I had the guts I would curse you to your faces. Leave me be. Nothing will happen if the sheets are a little wet from sweat. The whole of last month I lay on the ground by the tank. It was much dirtier. No harm was done. Why are you so obstinate?

There was no escaping the rack every morning: a nurse approached with white starched sheets. I could see her come into the room, and already began to shudder. I bargained, begged, asked to delay the change by a day, an hour, ten minutes. But the nurses had to do their duty. At first they tried with a smile, and finally the smile gave way to a blank expression. Even Yocheved, who rushed to console me and divert my attention, couldn't reduce my fear and pain.

Doctors' rounds.

After the operations I was like a yeast cake in the oven: would it rise or fall? – meanwhile better not touch it.

The head of department, Dr. Bernard Hirschowitz, and his assistant the good Dr. Shmuel Golden, who always had a reassuring smile on his face, came in. I was the one who asked about his health this morning. "Not so bad," he joined in the game, "a little dizzy and some twinges in the broken leg."

"Never mind, we'll cure you," I said to him, "if you behave well." He passed on. The eye doctor followed. I always waited tensely for this one. My eyes worried me more than anything else. My fear of blindness plagued me, and nothing else would relieve my anxiety, even if I could already see quite well with my right eye (though I couldn't yet distinguish the headlines of my paper – *Ma'ariv* – it still appeared as one red block). The eye doctor, an attractive woman, was a little angry. She reprimanded me. According to her I am straining my eyes too much. She ordered Yael not to let me look anywhere except forwards – in other words, at the ceiling; and occasionally, to put a handkerchief over my eyes, so that they rest.

Yael would carry out the orders explicitly, despite protests and my contention that she put the handkerchief over my eyes especially during the shift of Erna Ordan – a beautiful and shapely nurse.

The orthopaedic surgeons came less often. The plaster on my leg was already sour from blood. The neurosurgeon looked in every so often, glanced at my head and mumbled something with satisfaction.

Then came the turn of the inexorable daily schedule: blood pressure check, taking of blood samples, injections, pills, pain-killers. "You must drink", "You must eat", "What about the urine?" . . .

I summoned up the courage to ask Yocheved for permission to smoke. I was sure it wouldn't be allowed. Permission was given, to my surprise – and I greedily gulped in the smoke. From here on I would steadily increase my daily cigarette ration up to five packs a day.

In a quiet voice Yael told me about my neighbour in the room. For the first three days Gadi Refen had lain next to me. He was a hero, Yael said. Not a single groan. Most of his body was burned, and his face like dough. He was the first to talk in the room, and the first to eat solid food. Yael fed him a few times.

Gadi – unlike me, with my total self-absorption – told Yael that it was worthwhile checking whether the toes of my broken leg would move. "If they move, it's a sign that everything's O.K." He was also the first to find the courage to look in a mirror, and didn't bat an eyelid at the sight of the horrible transformation that had taken place in his face. Relatives and comrades who came to visit, didn't recognise him. When they were finally convinced that it was he they were truly seeing – they were dumbfounded and weeping. He straightened up and declared that if they continued to react in this fashion, it would be best if they left the room.

When he was hit, his hand was torn off and hung by ligaments. The doctors, trying to grasp hold of any slim chance, grafted it back on. When he awoke after the operation and found that he had two hands, he smiled and sternly told the doctors: "Boys, stop surprising me. I remember that I came here without a hand – and now suddenly I've got one. So if you feel like taking it off, at least tell me before you do it . . ." He guessed. Three days later they amputated the hand again.

In the bed opposite lay Yaakov Horesh, another burn case. Very worried. His wife was due to give birth and he didn't know how she was and whether she had a child. Yocheved urged him to agree that she call his home. He refused. He didn't want to shock her. Eventually he was convinced. A few days later his wife arrived still carrying a full belly. She sat very close to him, and the two exchanged loving glances, like a pair of school kids. You couldn't tell who worried more about whom: the casualty for his charming pregnant wife, or she who had found a husband with changed and ravaged features. I wondered what was going through their minds as their first child was about to see the light of the world, and as he from time to time lovingly placed his hand on her belly to feel his son moving in her womb. (I was later told that Yocheved had worked and manoeuvred to arrange a place in Rambam maternity ward for the wife. She gave birth one floor above the room of her wounded husband, and two days later proudly brought her son to his father . . .)

Gadi was moved to another room. His place was taken by Yair from Kfar Menahem. Badly wounded. Condition severe. All the hospital staff, including Yael, were urging him to inform his family of his wounds. He refused. Finally, he made a condition: Give him a mirror so that he could see himself, and then he would decide. They were afraid to give him a mirror. They expected the shock to do damage. Finally, his family came to his bedside.

Eggs! The egg nightmare! Burn cases must consume immense quantities of eggs. Because of the burns their bodies lose protein incessantly. Their stomachs reject protein foods like meat and fish, but take easier to eggs. And they eat. Not two, not three or four eggs a day – but dozens of them!

Because I was lying in the plastic ward, they tried to ram eggs down me as well. None of my protestations that there was a mistake did any good. I'm not burnt! I can on no account stand the taste of eggs. They arouse in me waves of nausea, just like any other food does. Yael made use of the tactic that had already proved its efficacy: she threatened that they would have to feed me intravenoulsy again. I surrendered. I tasted a little and was about to throw up.

Meanwhile the gimmick that would make it easier for me to drink was found. Until now the difficulty had been that I couldn't lift my head. Now they had found straws and I could suck liquids from a cup that somebody held for me.

On another front I won a victory: on the verge of breakdown, Yael agreed to leave the hospital for a few hours every day. She hadn't yet even showered or changed her dress. It simply hadn't crossed her mind. Yaela was prepared to relieve her, despite the burden of looking after three small children.

42

10

Again. It's happening again!

Why? Why are they screaming so much? Mercy. Give them pain-killers. Sedate them. Now the one in the middle bed, facing me, is screaming. Now it's his turn. Then it'll be somebody else.

The exposed skinless flesh of burns tortures them. Their bandages are changed every two days in a special room. When they come out of sedation, pains wrack their flesh. They shriek, whine, weep. Even the nurses, accustomed as they are to pain and suffering, have terror-stricken eyes and walk on tiptoe. I'll faint soon. What's that? Tears well up in my eyes. I'm crying like a child. So many years have passed since I last cried. Nurse! Go to him, take pity on him, he's screaming! He's being tortured. Give him something. Give him an injection that will sedate him a little. If not – he'll die. I tell you – he'll die!

. . . Yuval, drive carefully. Watch out they don't hit you. Careful now. We had some good times during our lousy reserve service in recent years.

In the anxious days before the war, you showed me – the city oaf who knows only concrete and steel – the atlas of the heavens and taught me to name the flowers that peeped out in the shadow of the rock next to the tank. We spent hours trading stories about the cleverness of our daughters, who were born almost at the same time. Now we're at war! They're hitting us with shells! Be careful, Yuval! Be careful! They're getting closer to you, they're aiming at you. Put it down – your head down in the turret! They're getting nearer! Shove your head inside! They'll finish you off! They'll finish you off! They'll finish you off! Run for it!!! Run!!!

Idiot! You were showing off! You wanted to be a hero. But you're not. You're lying there inside the tank. You're gone already! That's it! All over! We won't meet again in the reserves. You used to laugh at me. Now, if only you could, but I don't care that I'm crying. I spit on the whole world, I spit, Yuval . . .

Somebody puts a hand on my cheeks. Who is it? Yuval? He's got a warm hand. More, more. It's pleasant. Now the hand is holding mine . . . Leave me! Can't you see that I'm weeping for my best friend? Yuval is dead! Leave me . . . Yaela, I hear your voice. Yours as well, Yocheved. Is it you stroking my arm? What are you holding there? My pulse is O.K. I'm alright. Nothing happened. Only, my friend was killed. That feels good when you stroke. Where am I? They pulled me out. They extricated me from the horrible dream. Nothing happened to Yuval. I only dreamt. That's it. I only dreamt . . .

"Just a nightmare! Poor guy!"

Who said that? Who's the poor guy? Yuval or me? It's hard to breathe. I'm wet, as though after a shower. Maybe sweat? What happened to Yuval? No, no Yuval. What happened to that boy in the opposite bed, the burnt one who screamed terribly as he awoke from the anaesthetic? How he suffered, poor bastard. What sort of a hospital is this? Are we living in the twentieth century or the Middle Ages? My mouth's dry. I can't drink. Only not that. Only not drink!

One morning the barber appeared and shaved me. Carefully, in order not to touch the wounds. It felt good. After him came some-body in a white gown who warned me I had better "pee". Ha! They talk to me as though I was Tami: "Now be a good girl and sit on your potty . . ."

"If not," the woman in the white gown said, "we'll have to put the catheter in again."

"Okay," I promise, "I'll try hard."

I really do try. But nothing comes out. Anything rather than have her keep her threat. She talked to me like to a mischievous child. As though it depended on me.

Yael, I recorded to my credit, made another concession. I demand-ed that she leave the hospital at seven in the evening, upon lights-out, and come back at eight in the morning. We made a compromise: she agreed to go only at ten. Between seven and ten in the eve-ning, I suffer bad pains and she wanted to be beside me during these hours. She already reappeared at four in the morning. It was still dark outside. I put on an angry face: Why so early? The truth: I was happy to see her.

Awake and clear-headed. I can see a nurse curled up in a chair at the end of the shadowy room. She watches over us during the night. I call quietly: "Nurse!" She straightens up, searches for the source of the voice, and comes over with questioning eyes peering through the darkness.

And I am silent. I don't need anything. I just called you. You've got good eyes and warm hands, a pleasant expression in the eyes and you're bursting with health. You can go back to your chair. Poor devil. Somebody fixed you. No sleep, no meeting your boyfriend – just listening to groans, waking up those with nightmares.

"Something happened?" she asks in a young, fresh and worried voice.

"No. Just . . . I just wanted to know what time it was."

An ode to the nurse. Last night I composed it – and she isn't even aware. But now it's a warm morning and my friend, Aryeh Nesher, a Ha'aretz reporter, brought me crimson juicy cherries. If only Yael doesn't use them for blackmail: "If you ate cherries, then at least taste the meat . . ."

Good Aryeh, falling over himself to say pleasant things. In his eyes the special expression of all the visitors who succeed in getting through to me, despite my wife's reign of terror. They say that I'm a hero. Nonsense! Really nonsense! I'm a soldier like any other, except that by chance I was wounded. Luckless – but not a hero. Just another Joe who didn't make it. Like all the rest lying here and in the nearby rooms.

Now I'll burst from emotion! Dan Shilon has come in. Tall, smiling, agile, but with anxiety in his eyes. Dan, my boy, we were good friends before the war. Nevertheless, now it's different. The friendship is cemented in blood and the taste of the water that you poured down my throat. And in fact, I owe you my life, because of that moment when you stuck your hand into my throat to remove the blood congealing there . . . The devil with it, stop playing games! I know exactly what's hidden behind your lightheaded chatter. Tell me, tell me, Dan, where was I hit? Nobody knows, and I must know exactly where. Tel Fahar? What's that? Where? I don't remember that we saw it on the map during briefing. I really got it there, didn't I! Scores did you say? Scores?! Many fell there, eh? You remember? A week ago exactly, on Friday morning, when I met you in Tal Grove, and we talked about the conquest of Jerusalem, I asked you: "Many fell there, eh?"

That same Friday our turn came . . .

It's an emotion packed day. Dan had only just left, when Nissim

45

Varsenau and Reuven Dangur came in. The first visit by my comrades from the company. They walk as though treading on hot ashes. Their eyes are downcast, avoiding mine. What is it, boys? What's happened? Nothing's happened to me. Only a little here and there. Thanks. It's nice that you've brought me a souvenir from the Syrian Heights . . . Why, in the name of God, are you so tense? The hospital terrifies you? . . . Somebody died? Somebody else was hurt apart from me? Why do you look at each other – and remain silent? Say something! Who? Ezra Barosh? He's here, on the floor below? He's lost a leg? Terrible! But, really, nobody was killed? Say something before I go mad! Michel Levy? Albert Amar? Yosef Molcho? Ephraim Epstein? The boys from the mortar half-track as well? God, how did it happen? I must – I must know!

I listen to them. Varsenau is a tank commander. A sturdy somewhat rough type. He finally opened his mouth: all night, all night after the battle, the company stayed together. They sat next to each other. Very close. Silent. They were dropping from fatigue but couldn't sleep. Chain-smoking – and silent. More: they thought of those who weren't there. It was the first time that the company had been bled. Eyes were red, and hearts torn. Seven dead. More than twenty wounded. "Ziva" was shrinking!

A few short hours before, on Friday morning, they'd chattered together gaily. Drunk cognac. If there will be a war – it must be marked by a drink. If there won't be – then it's also a reason to drink. By evening, seven were missing from the ranks of the living.

Ephraim, our communications sergeant, gone. A pleasant face. High-pitched voice. During the waiting period he was impatient. His plans to travel abroad were being foiled.

Michel gone! What a merry boy that was. Sunburnt with a full sturdy body. Always ready with a quip.

Molcho gone! Only two days before we went up the Heights, he asked me whether I could find work for him in *Ma'ariv* press. He was a first-rate printer, just as he was an efficient and quiet crew member.

Amar. Amar also gone! Driver of the command half-track. When on the second day of the war we had gone out to repulse the Syrian attack on Kibbutz Dan, he was somewhat bowed. After a while he recovered and turned his face to us with a broad smile, began to joke and distribute candies.

46

They had gone. Amar and Ephraim – a shell hit their half-track – and killed them. The Syrians had prepared an ambush for us.

Seven gone – and Ezra without a leg. What a tragedy! He'll commit suicide, that's for certain! Molcho jumped from the tank after he was hit, and began to run. A burst from Tel Fahar punctured his body. He staggered back to the tank, and fell. Michel – his tank was also hit. He got out of his compartment and said weakly: "Nothing happened to me, boys." And then – dropped and died.

The morning of the very day that we had drunk cognac and sang.

Varsenau, Varsenau – I talked to him in my thoughts – you don't know, but perhaps you are alive because of me. According to the original plan you should have been travelling in front of my tank. But when we ascended the Syrian diversion path I was overcome by a strange desire to get their first, to be among the first. I passed you and reached second place with my tank. "The second place", brought me the blow that landed me in this bed, and you – next to it.

Bastard! – I reprimand myself – what sort of filthy thoughts are these. What nonsense. I was meant to be wounded – and that's how it was. Every shell, every bullet has an address. My name was written on two shells, and the mail delivered.

The two continued to tell their story. Dangur has a nice smile that never leaves his face. (I would later find out how he heroically saved lives in the blazing hell of Tel Fahar.) They went on: four tanks hit. Mine was the first.

Seven gone – and Ezra without a leg. What a tragedy! He will commit suicide, that's for certain! Our tanks betrayed us. They didn't protect us. Their armour was like butter – and the shells ploughed through it.

I still don't know how my tank was hit, nor what happened to my crew; who was injured, and whose screams awoke me from my first coma – and who extricated me from the tank. According to my calculations I wasn't hurt by a shell that penetrated the tank. A fact: I was hit in the head – high above the turret. And so, if I was hit in the head, perhaps a shell hit the tank or close to it, and its splinters got to me . . .

Thomas. He was also hit because his head was outside. Not just his head – his whole upper body. He was a platoon commander and directed the movement of his tanks. That was in the Sinai Campaign, in the grand assault on Abu Ageila. Thomas wasn't

47

afraid. And then came the shell that hit the heavy machine-gun on the turret. The machine-gun pivoted on its mounting and cracked his head. Our first sight of death – and we were boys of nineteen. Thomas's death was different from that of the Egyptians, who were caught in the path of our charge. Thomas was our dead. They were strangers . . .

Thanks for the souvenirs, Varsenau. It's nice that you thought of me. But I won't smoke the Syrian cigarettes. I'll keep the Syrian officer's medal. When I'm a grandfather one of these days, I'll display it with the scars "that have healed years ago", as the song goes. My grandchildren won't be impressed. My war will already be obsolete.

Go now. I'm tired. Take with you the other visitors who've collected around my bed. Their expressions make me nervous. I know they mean well and are here because they like me. But they should stop looking at me with pity. Pity annoys me. And they should get rid of the guilty looks in their eyes. It's really unnecessary.

I know it's not pleasant for you: I'm lying here badly wounded – and you're healthy. I'm in hell and you'll soon be going down to the sea for a swim. It's hot in June, and a swim in the sea is refreshing; it's very hot in June, and the sheets under me are wet as though after laundering . . . And it's not you that's lying here. That's the way it is. Somebody has to lose in the lottery. So I lost. I don't care. If I tell you that you won't believe it. You'll think that your comrade wants to make an impression on you. And so – I'll remain silent. Go now.

11

Last night they hung a notice on the foot of my bed. Yael says that it's got "fasting" written on it. Must abstain from food and drink before an operation. They make me laugh! Even without the injunction I wouldn't eat. Food and drink have become my pet hates. Apart from the miserable pains, and the sufferings of my comrades in the room.

They've come to take me. I'm not excited. I used to hate hospital. Each visit was nauseating, frightening and pitiful. And now – I couldn't care less. An operation? – let there be an operation.

They place a gown over my naked body. So that people shouldn't see me. I lie all the time naked under the sheet. A pyjama won't pass over my leg, because of the cast. Now I wear something for the first time since they cut my clothes off, somewhere in some hospital or other in the field.

Ay! Be careful with the leg! Careful! You're hurting me . . .

If I was less apathetic to my surroundings, I would perhaps show some interest in this excursion into the corridor and in the nurses' rushing around. This is a part of my present home. See what respect they pay me! All the people in the elevator move over to the sides. They make way for me and look at me almost with awe. Get in, friends, get in. There's enough room for all. What are they? Courteous? Or perhaps they were shocked by my terrifying appearance?

I'm in a daze. They gave me an injection, like they do before every operation. The world passes by. People don't put their feet on the ground, but a little above it. The expressions of the orderlies are blank and frightening. They should smile a little. It's good that Yael is here with me. She's also tense, but tries to give the impression that her smiles are real.

The operating theatre. Why did you dress me in a gown if you immediately take it off? A woman holds me by the arm. Lady, are you the anaesthetist? Why are you so serious? If you knew how much a smile and a nice word are worth at this moment.

"Good night!"

"Thanks. Same to you!"

"Good night . . ." It reminds me of something. Somebody said it to me not long ago in similar circumstances. Good night, good night, good night. When? – when they brought me in. "Work for the Plastics." A woman's faint pleasant smile. "Good night," and then I fell asleep. I woke up to the voice of Yael who said "I'm here". Yes. I remember. Those were apparently the first operations that they performed on me. Yes . . . That's it . . . I fall asleep. Shalom. See you in the morning . . .

I woke up at one! They're tearing my body apart!

Hey, what's this? Where am I? People! They're murdering me! I'm dead! They're smashing my leg again. Mother! Mother! Mother! My leg! They're taking it apart. They're cutting. Don't hold me. Let me be. Why am I lying on a stretcher? You were going to perform an operation. Leave me alone, bastards! I want to fall on the floor.

49

To die! Leave me. I'm going mad. Yael, Yael! Where have you gone to? Save me! Save me! They're hurting me terribly. Don't hold my head. I must move it, and I'll do it as much as I please. I'll tear it out from its socket. Why have you abandoned me, Yael? Why did you let them do this to me? Oh! Oh! It hurts so much. Tell them . . . The leg! It's running wild! I'll kill you. Give me your hand, Yael. Give me your hand. Let me drown in your bosom. Your shirt's already damp from tears. Yael, they killed me – and you waited quietly outside. I can't control myself. I'm ashamed, but I can't. They hate me, everyone around here. You can see it in their eyes. They deliberately took me to torture me. Why, why did you let them do this?

 . . . How did I get back to bed? I didn't feel it. And I didn't see it. How is it possible that it can hurt so much, Yael? How is it possible? I'm now like the burn cases. They also went wild when they came out of sedation. Then it was their turn – and now it's mine. It's murder! Let them burn the miserable leg, and me with it. What is it, Yocheved? What do you want from me? It hurts me and I'm entitled to cry. Why are your eyes wet, and why are Yael's red? What's that syringe for? For me? Stick it in, stick it in. Do whatever you want. I couldn't care less. I'm finished – and I'm an idiot. If I hadn't spat out the blood when I lay in the half-track – I would be dead now. I would have swallowed it; and that would have been the end. What's this injection? A pain-killer? But it still hurts. A lot. Terribly. Why don't you do something so that I should pass out, and be finished . . .

Another syringe in your hand, Yocheved! It won't help. I know. Just as the first injection didn't help. Yael, don't you dare leave me. It hurts. It still hurts. What will I do?

Another one, Yocheved? Do they come wholesale? You've already seen that they don't work. You murdered me down there in the operating theatre. You simply murdered me. Now I'm in hell. Don't move, Yael, don't move from here. I need you. I once thought there was no hell. Now I know, I know there is . . .

Don't vanish. Stand here. You're not moving? Nevertheless, you're vanishing. Fading. Have you eaten anything today? Then go and eat. It's important. So that you'll have strength. Now it's a bit better. They gave me injections wholesale. It's better. I'm falling! I'm going. To sleep. They've cancelled out the hell. A reprieve . . .

50

When I awoke, I was weak and exhausted, but fresh and clear of any feeling of pain. Perhaps this is the way a woman feels after giving birth. I slowly woke up. My eyes turned outwards to the window.

It was already evening. The last rose tinge of daylight lit up the heavens. I moved my head a little and saw my mother and brother, who had come from Tel Aviv, whispering to Yael. Until now, my mother hadn't visited the hospital. Yael forbade it. She did well. For my old and sick mother the cup of mourning was almost overflowing. A few years ago she had lost her daughter in a road accident, and now – me.

They hadn't yet sensed that I was awake. My mind ticked over frantically. I must give the impression of being better. I must behave cheerfully and chat lightheartedly. "Mother," I called out weakly and smiled. She hopped over to me with a half scream, "You recognise me!"

I forced myself to chatter. To talk about unimportant things. "How's the neighbour on the third floor – the one who was ill when I was called up? Have they already repaired the hot-water boiler in the bathroom? . . ."

I succeeded in deceiving her. She was convinced that if I was capable of engaging my brain in such trivial matters – then the situation wasn't desperate. The anxiety had barely left her face, and she already began to take an interest – like any mother – in what and how much I was eating . . .

Visitors flowed in. On Saturday morning Micha Limor and Shraga Hargil from *Ma'ariv* arrived. I had resolved to summon up all my strength and not let anyone sense what was happening to me. My weakness and suffering were my own personal affair. I couldn't hold on and play-act for Yael, the medical team and the patients around me. But none of the visitors knew my secret. When I knew that I was totally incapable of putting a good face on, I would ask Yael to intercept them in the corridor. That was the way it was going to be.

Micha and Shraga brought me a present from the staff of the newspaper. A transistor. "Thanks. That will liven things up a bit. I can listen to the news." The truth was that I couldn't bear the voices coming out of the radio. The news didn't interest me. Any noise bothered me. My world only centred around all my aching limbs.

Oppressive moments. The two don't know what to say. Finally I ask Micha how he spent the war. He was in command of a torpedo boat. His eyes lit up. I had given him a subject. He talked – and I interrogated. Again – I was acting. His words flitted by my ears, without entering.

Yuval Gold came in. I had so much wanted him to come. The nightmare – of which he had been the hero – increased my desire to see him alive and well. There was no need to stimulate him. Because it was impossible to gaze at each other and remain silent – Yuval took the burden of conversation on himself. The company – he related – was stationed near Kuneitra. It was very cold. They were weary of being in uniform. It had been hinted that they may be released in a few days. They're living in a cinema hall. The boys had organised themselves very nicely. Here, take it! I brought you some photos of the Hule Valley. Work of Syrian Intelligence . . .

Yuval, my boy, you're the one who's faking now. You're acting. Not me. Your face is unmistakably pale. Your eyes are worried. You're an honest man. It's difficult for you to hide your emotions and real feelings. They told me that you sat a long hour in the corridor before coming in. You were afraid to enter. You almost needed medical treatment. The doctors were worried about your paleness. Somebody "leaked it" to me: your friend is almost fainting outside there. I suffered because of you in that nightmare – and you're now suffering for me. Go! Go now to your wife and daughter. Don't waste your short leave on me. It's good you came.

12

What is the order of importance of my wounds: Eyes? Head? Plastic surgery? The leg? Nobody in the medical staff has found the time to sit with me to explain my condition. It's a pity.

By chance I'm lying in the Plastics Department. They could just as easily have bedded me down in one of the other wards that's concerned with my wounds. The patches on my head are the most noticeable. But the leg hurts more than anything else. My one eye is closed, while the vision of the other is blurred. I was still unaware of the fractures in my skull, and splinters in my brain.

Yael would tell me later that she had enquired about my leg from everybody who could be approached. A young orthopaedic surgeon among our acquaintances reassured her that the situation isn't serious, and that at most I will limp slightly after I recover. A second doctor revealed that gangrene was beginning to set in. "But it's natural and expected. Not serious." A woman doctor acquaintance who came to visit from Tel Aviv, explained to Yael that I would need to undergo another three leg operations. They'll exchange the smashed bone for a plate, and everything will come to rights.

We were very optimistic. We didn't know what the future held. Now we smile when Yael relates how miserable she was when she was told that I would need three more operations, and would perhaps limp for the rest of my life.

The length of days is not measured by the clock. The intensity and duration of pain determines time. One day the plastic surgeons come and announce that they have finished their work on my body. They remove the stitches, paint the place over with iodine and turn me into a Red Indian.

They're followed by Dr. Yafa Doron, the neurosurgeon. A happy glint sparkles behind her eyeglasses. She says: "You're alright, dear. I have nothing more to do to you."

My uncovered eye clears up. In a rare moment of curiosity, I pick up a mirror and look at my profile. Well, my beauty – I say to my visage in the mirror – they say that scars add a sexy look to a man. In the Prussian Army every officer who respected himself bore some nice scars.

Only about the leg do they keep quiet. Why don't they tell me? Why do they leave me to wrestle with a thousand suppositions? The vagueness annoys me.

Miserable leg.

Today is Saturday, nurse. You've got a lot of work, and the team is small. Perhaps you'll forgo changing the sheets? Really, why must you? Yesterday wasn't hot. I didn't sweat, the sheets are dry. You agree? No? Let's make a compromise: You leave the sheets. We'll only change the pillow-cases.

It doesn't work. They're obstinate as mules.

13

I try to convince Yael to return to Tami, who has suddenly become "an orphan". I can manage by myself, Yael, go to the girl. We've abandoned her. Think of her. After all, I'm not going to die . . .

My efforts on this front fail. My friends are worried about Yael and the child. For some time I've sensed mutterings on the balcony. Their whispering, so that Yael shouldn't hear. Something's being plotted. Aharon Dolav, my comrade from *Ma'ariv*, visits almost every day. He's also a party to the plot being woven there outside.

Later, it will be revealed to me: they're attempting to have me transferred to Tel Hashomer Hospital which is close to our home. If Yael will be at home, she will be able to rest a bit, and the child will have a mother. At least for a few hours a day.

Ministering old ladies! Grandmothers with kind faces! You've come to make us feel better. You dragged that heavy basket full of bottles of orange juice from the city all the way here. Where do you find the strength? Thanks. Perhaps you also had sons in the war. "No, grandma. Thank you. I'm not thirsty. I'm never thirsty." If I see that juice in front of my eyes again, I'll vomit. "No, really. I've only just drunk two bottles. And I'm forbidden to drink a lot."

Oho! God of Gods! She rushed out and brought in, God knows from where, a packet of candy. "Have some sweets at least." I always hated sweets. And now – a thousand times more . . . She left. God be praised.

At the end of the room lies a tank crewman with first degree burns. He's very sad, Yael tells me. Nobody comes to visit him. And here – we need company so much . . .

One day Yael reports: There's a young boy sitting by his bed. He's wearing a Reali School uniform shirt, a curl lies over his forehead, he has pleasant features. The boy appeared one day in the ward and asked if anybody wanted company. They sent him to the lonely casualty. Ever since he's spent most of the hours of the day by his side. He chatters incessantly, gives him grapes and feeds him, brings him the "bottle". In short – a companion. What are they chattering about so volubly? Where did they find common ground

54

for discussion? What brings the boy here? A boy from the Reali.

A young angel! They're now putting gold stars next to your name up above in heaven.

Well, it was decided: I'm being transferred to Tel Hashomer.

It wasn't that simple. Such a transfer upsets all the arrangements. At first they refused, hesitated, and finally weakened.

Good Yocheved liberates Yael from the fatiguing work and the rushing around involved in collecting "medical reports" from all the departments that had treated me. She also brought my bag of personal belongings from the office of the military unit inside the hospital. The bag contains everything collected from my pockets when they tore my clothes off.

I carefully sift through the belongings and find the last letters from my dear ones, reddened by my blood. My identity tags, which I had improvised from a cigarette pack – painted scarlet. A wallet. A half empty cigarette pack. A small screwdriver. Little things. I'm looking for something else. Something that isn't here. Where's it vanished to? Everything is here but . . . – where is the leg of Tami's doll? The leg in which I placed my faith, the leg that kept my spirits up.

Nothing is missing. Even an empty match-box has been kept. But the leg isn't there! How will I find it? It will look silly to ask Yocheved to go down again to the military unit, and ask whether they have by chance found a doll's leg, the length of a thumb. She won't understand. They won't understand. It will seem idiotic. Hell, where's the leg?

I rifle through the belongings again with trembling fingers. But I suddenly have a consoling thought: I won't find the leg because it's already done its duty – preserved my life. After all, I didn't die. The job's done – the leg could go.

We part from Rambam.

At moments, I'm sorry: I've grown accustomed to the place. At other moments, happy: if I'll be in Tel Hashomer, close to home, perhaps it will be easier for Yael. I have a feeling that apart from a geographical move "forwards", this will also be a medical stride in the right direction. Perhaps in another few days I'll be able to see Tami, for whom my soul hungers.

I feel fine. Apparently in honour of the occasion. Clear-headed and fresh – and no pain. The sun dipping over towards the sea throws a strong clear light on the balcony. I lust to feel its rays on my skin.

Poor Yael. What hidden strength she has revealed. For fifteen years we have known each other, since we were youngsters of fourteen. Now I see sides to her character that I never saw before. It seems that it is true: women are stronger than men. This morning she drove in our car to Tel Aviv and to Tel Hashomer, to arrange the transfer. She later returned to Haifa – and now, again to Tel Hashomer. Where does she find the strength to smile, to chatter light-heartedly, to appear fresh? I wouldn't have managed it.

Now she's vanished. She's gone to bring the ambulance. I must say shalom to everyone. It's now afternoon. Pity. The doctors have already gone home. Most of the nurses aren't here. I'm sneaking out like a thief in dead of night. I leave behind me the tortured burn cases. Tomorrow they'll put somebody else in my bed. There are always clients. The beds stay warm. Like in a submarine.

The Italian orderly comes with a stretcher. That's it, we're going. How do you say in Italian: Lower me carefully? After all, if every slight movement in bed causes me terrible pain, the jerks of the stretcher are likely to become excruciating. Why, in the name of God, didn't I learn Italian – "Prego! Atenzione! . . ."

We cross the room. Shalom, boys. Be well. Shalom to you, waiting impatiently for your son to be born. Shalom, Hagelmud. A big and special shalom to you, whose name I don't remember. Both of us, you and I, were hit on that same stinking Tel Fahar.

Elevator. We're going down. Not to the operating theatre. Down. The entrance hall to the hospital. I've passed through here many times as a healthy man in the course of my newspaper-work. I always came in vertically. Now I'm going out horizontally. And without any material for an article.

People who came to visit their invalids close in on me with curious glances. You there! I'm not a showpiece. Move on. Move. Yocheved! Where did you spring from? I was afraid that I wouldn't have a chance to part from you the way I should. And here Erna is also running with an injection. Shalom, Erna. Shalom, Yocheved. Thank you. I want to kiss you.

"You see? He's kissing me, the old woman, and not you – the beauty," Yocheved says to Erna with shining eyes. Ha, Yocheved, Yocheved. The kiss is only a small part of what I owe you. For your

56

kindness, not only to us, the wounded, but also to our families. A few visitors come for me! You're late, boys. I'm moving out. Thanks. Namir, what's that, you've brought me? Syrian arak? Thanks, but now I can't drink alcohol. Shalom, David Friedlander. Dear David, take the grapes back home. Thank you. Ismarili! What are you doing here with that cast on your hand? Is that from the knock you got while we were waiting? You hung around the company and worked for three weeks with a broken hand – and didn't do anything about it. You're a donkey, with all due respect. War or no war, you can't walk around with a broken hand.

The ambulance is waiting outside. A whole procession forms up behind me. Even Dr. Golden has arrived. "What about that dizziness, and the twinges in your leg, doctor?" The ambulance is as hot as a baker's oven. Goodbye and thanks to all of you. If my eyes are dry, it's only because my tear glands aren't working properly.

14

It's three o'clock. In another hour and a half we'll arrive in a new world: Tel Hashomer Hospital. Driver, onwards. Careful, driver! Carefully, for God's sake! Don't fly. Don't jolt, please! Drive slowly. This is a first-rate urban road, and we're not in a half-track on rocky paths on the Heights. So why are you jolting us about?

What pains! What pains! Yael, say something to the driver! Every yard is like a mile, and we're only beginning. It's hot as hell. This is no ambulance. It's jumping like a tractor. Hot, suffocating and sealed. A box. No window. No air. My leg is bursting. I must hang onto something. Hold something. Grab some object, something that I can squeeze with all my strength. The sweat is soaking me, pouring into my eyes, burning them.

What! Where's he going to? He's taking the wrong road. Why isn't he travelling on the new road? Why has he taken the old road? Hey, you're making a mistake, friend. The old road is full of potholes. Go back! Go back! He doesn't hear. What is he, stupid? What sort of a driver is this? Chattering away in the cabin, and forgetting that he's driving an ambulance. An ambulance has priority on the road, comrade. You don't have to be courteous and move off the road onto the shoulders every time some private car comes from the opposite direction. If I could only get up – I'd let my fists loose on you!

So! That's the reason! A diversion from the main road, to take the passenger in the cabin home. If I could only lift myself up! With a clear conscience, comrade, with a clear conscience, I'd tell you: It's the first time that I wish somebody was in my place: you!

I don't care what the hitch-hiker, travelling behind with us, says. I can't stifle the groans any more. You won't laugh at me, hitch-hiker, will you? You're good to me, give me drinks all the time and light cigarettes one after the other. Yael's hands are busy. She's holding my leg and protecting it from the jolts.

Wonderful Yocheved. She apparently guessed what would happen, and equipped Yael with strong pain-killers, "if the injection isn't enough". The pill also didn't help, Yocheved. Nothing will help. I need a pill of another kind, for the driver.

I can see it in your face, Yael, that at any moment you'll get up and slap the driver hard. I'm sorry, Yael, for all my groans and squirming. I'm sorry for the tears pouring out of my eyes. I know that it hurts you, that you hate yourself for wanting to transfer me to Tel Hashomer. But I still can't stop them.

Yes, dolt! This is Tel Hashomer. Here! Here! An ambulance driver should know where the biggest hospital in the country is. It's now seven in the evening. We've been travelling four full hours, and a normal driver would have made it in less than an hour and a half. Yes, here – this is Tel Hashomer. Here! Here! Here! And I hate you.

BOOK 2

ATTRITION

1

What gaiety here! What a racket! What a difference! A real party!
I was astounded. My new hospital is a completely different world
from the one I left. As I entered I was already greeted by loud happy
voices, and the nurses ("My name's Yvonne," "My name's Bina")
smiled gaily. I was so taken aback that I even said shalom and
thanks to the ambulance driver as he parted from me.

Exhausted and completely washed out, I lifted myself up to look
at the new department. I couldn't believe my eyes. The patients
weren't lying quietly, as they were there in Haifa. They were sitting
or standing or moving around in wheel-chairs, and some of them
were chattering away cheerfully. I didn't discern that same sorrow-
ful expression to which I'd become accustomed in the eyes of the
many visitors here. Here and there conversations could be heard on
everyday matters. In one of the corners some of the wounded were
guzzling away fruit and cakes. Transistors booming out. It's gay
here!

My concepts of life in hospital are changing. There, in Rambam
Hospital, nobody said anything that wasn't necessary. Nobody
lusted after food, candies, flowers. Who would have been capable
of turning on a radio? The only music was groans and sobbing.
Nobody walked around, for no one was capable of getting up under
his own steam. The vision before my eyes somewhat alleviated my
fears of adapting to a new place. The "veterans" gazed at me curiously. Greeted me. They're nice guys. One of the boys rushed over with
a plate of fruit and candy. "So you won't be bored." He quickly
explains to Yael how things work: "You can visit all day. It's easy
to get on with the nurses. My name's Hilik. If you need anything . . ."

What a welcome. The faces of the veterans held more than pure
curiosity. I would only know the significance of the expression in
their eyes after a few weeks, when they found the courage to tell
me how shocked they were by my appearance, which had certainly
deteriorated because of the journey. On the day that I arrived, I
was the worst case in the orthopaedic hut.

Affairs are managed quickly and efficiently here. I don't even manage to absorb my first impressions, and the eye doctor, Dr. Bracha, is already by my bed. She examines me thoroughly, and rules: The left eye must be bandaged. She was followed by the Resident, Dr. Oliver, who blasted the nurses for leaving me in the "railway coach", as they nickname the beds that stand in the passageways. And they were already shoving in syringes with antibiotics and feeding me pills.

Eddie, my friend, comes to visit. I beg him to take Yael by force and "throw her" home. We part. Good night. A kiss.

First night in a strange place. Alone. I know no one. Not even the name of the nurse. My neighbour to the right is already snoring deeply. I will quickly drop into a troubled sleep. I wake from time to time in panic. Smiling faces come forward out of the mist. They're lit by the faint light of a night-lamp. The light dazzles me. "My name is Bina. If you need anything . . ." Sleep. Smiling faces, good faces. "My name is Bina . . ." Who are you? I don't know you. Where am I? Yocheved will soon come and feed Yael. Again – the smiling nurse. Her teeth are white. She's pleasant and charming. The light of her torch flickers over me. Her features appear and disappear, as though in a nightmare. "No, Bina, I didn't call you," I want her to stand by me and smile all the time. I also want her to vanish and not come back. Deep darkness.

At five approximately I woke to the touch of a soft cool hand passing over my cheeks. I open my eyes. A young nurse stands very close. I felt the chill of morning and trembled. A beautiful girl. "You must wash." In Rambam they didn't wake me. There seems to be a different schedule here. There, Yael washed me. Here – the girl. Such a young girl – and already a nurse!

A foamy sponge slides over my bristly face and chest. She handles me like one would a weak battered doll. It's pleasant to be washed. Yes. Her name is Zahava Giller. A student in the nurses' school. Third year. Full bosom, good legs below the gown. Quite a piece. I can't fathom: why does such a young girl have to look after the body of a dirty, unshaven, wounded and scarred brute of a man at such an early hour in the morning? I'm angry with myself. Because of me, she lost the best hours of sleep. It's a doubtful pleasure, Zahava. A girl like you should be asleep at this hour, or caressing her boy friend. She: "It's work. I'm a nurse, aren't I?"

An unpleasant moment: she's embarrassed and I'm a little shy.

I'm a strange man and she's a woman. It's her duty to wash my whole body. When she reaches a certain point, I stop her: "Give me the sponge. I'll continue – and you turn around, please. I want to know what you look like from behind." She agrees. Blushes. Turns her back.

Here come the laughing eyes that appeared at night. "You had a hard night."

"Truly?"

"I came to you a few times."

"A few?" Strange. I don't remember. Now go to sleep. You must be tired.

I also drop off again. My leg has granted me a short reprieve from pain. It won't be long before I will awake to the racket in the hut. I open startled eyes. Waking up is a matter of great ceremony here. At least ten transistor radios boom out in unison. Patients with tooth-brushes clutched in their hands pass by and glance at me. To my right a tall heavily-built boy stretches in his bed. He turns to me: "Good morning." I: "Same to you." He gets up from bed and brings up a big fruity belch from the depths of his belly. "Boys, just look what a wonderful morning! What can I tell you? Now I need three things – a shower, a big breakfast, and – as dessert – some girl to tickle a little here, and a little there."

Listen – just listen! A man, in my state, a casualty. What high spirits! He can walk, think of food, lust for a woman – and all this so early in the morning! I shrink back into myself. He turns to me again. This time he's chewing shelled almonds. We exchange courtesies. "I fell and took a bang on my back – God, what pains! Have some almonds? Eat, eat, they're very good. Come on, let's hear some music . . ."

Despite myself, my face contorts. The noise pouring out of his transistor pounds at me.

"Oh, sorry, I didn't know that it bothers you. But why don't you eat some almonds . . ." And to the others: "So what was I saying? Ah! The beautiful life. So what if I snored a little during the night? A man who doesn't snore isn't a man. If they don't bring breakfast, I'll die on the spot," the boy – his name's Moni – finishes his speech.

Yael comes. Happy to see the smile on my face. During doctors' rounds I ask Dr. Oliver what will become of the leg. He replies

63

that they must X-ray it. "A little broken," he says lightly. In three days time they'll take off the cast and check the situation. I bemoan the three days that will be wasted. I make a quick calculation that I will have to remain at least another month in the hospital – a frightening eternity.

Less than an hour goes by before the *Ma'ariv* boys stand around my bed. A gigantic basket of fruit. American cigarettes. Newspapers. Do you need anything? No, I don't need anything. Thanks for coming. Henceforward they will visit me every day. My companions in the room would nickname me "the spoilt one". "It's good to be a *Ma'ariv* journalist, eh? . . ."

Nearby lies a thick beard. Religious. During the days before the war an abscess grew on his arm. He was ashamed to go to a doctor for such nonsense. The war passed, and his hand swelled and got more painful. He only found time to look after it when the war was over. Then it became clear that the arm was badly infected, almost to the extent that it might have to be amputated – at best, it warranted a few operations.

2

Who thought, even for a moment, that I would find myself in hospital. During the days of waiting I thought of only two possibilities: death or return home unscathed. But not of any intermediate road. What do people who've never been hospitalised in their lives know about hospitals and what it means to be wounded? When they announce on the radio or in the papers some incident or accident, and follow with numbers of dead and wounded, we only pay attention to the dead. Nobody takes much note of the injured. I was no better than the rest.

It's a strange world – a hospital. A miniature world. It's all contained in the room where they put you. There's no status, or differences, between patients. A nurse is an angel. A doctor – a supreme being. You easily fall in love with the nurse, and esteem the doctor for every tiny little thing.

You're in a degrading situation in which everybody can give you orders. Your voice or opinion carries almost no weight. "A case" – not a man with senses, desires, a soul and pride.

You must wear the pale blue pyjamas, the uniform – I almost said convict garb – of patients, which blurs any sign of personal identity.

You must awake every morning at a fixed time to have your temperature taken, and nobody cares whether or not you sleep during the night, and have only just managed to doze off.

You must keep your mouth shut when the doctors probe away at the nerve centres of pain, and must bear their superior silence, behind which is hidden your fate, your hopes, your fears.

You're unable to fight the white prison. You are not the one who will decide whether your pains are bad enough to justify a sedating pill or injection. You are not the one to decide whether or not to eat the bland, uniform, unimaginative food. If you refuse to co-operate, they'll force you to "eat" by sticking a needle into a vein.

So there's nothing left but to bite your lips and keep reminding yourself that the purpose of these tyrants is to get you better, cure and return you healthy and in one piece to your home – to the life beyond the walls of the hospital.

"You must have patience," the visitors say. "We know how . . ."

Really? You don't know. You have no idea. The pain that no one sees. It's hidden under the outer layer of cast, bandages, the sheet, or the face you put on.

During many months I waged war with the nurses and doctors to increase their sensitivity to the suffering of the patients who are their charge. I sometimes listened unnoticed to the conversation of nurses who were angry with me because I prodded them to help some patient. For those who have already had hundreds pass through their hands, the patient is just a nuisance or an extra liability. This apathy was not, thank God, the lot of many among the hospital employees. It could perhaps be understood. A man gets used to everything. But it should never be forgiven.

2

Second night. Again a conveyor belt – wakefulness, lucidity, fever, blurring of the senses, restless sleep, horrible dreams. Bina whose eyes are wakeful: "Do you need anything?" and again Zahava, come to wash from my body the sweat glued to it from the previous day. I begin to like her. She heralds in the morning.

This morning, it seems to me, I have to comfort her. Her eyes are almost extinguished: "I feel terrible." I stroke her hand: "Perhaps we should change places? I'll vacate the bed – and you rest on it. If you behave nicely, I'll even wash you . . ."

She's very pale, but manages to bring a smile to her lips. She wags a threatening finger: "Lecher!"

This idea of changing places tickles my fancy. For the first time I play around in my imagination with the possibility that I will be capable of standing on my legs, walking, driving, living a semblance of life. But the joy is momentary. I'm still far from all that.

They take me to the X-ray department on the other side of the hospital. I make the stretcher bearers swear to move carefully. Despite their caution – groans escape my lips. After a time I begin to take interest in the tour.

I see new landscapes. The little worm has come out of its apple for a moment. I see other patients, the nurses' station, relatives waiting in the lobby. And even the blinding end-of-June sun. For the first few seconds it's pleasing, but it soon hurts my damaged eyes. Its cruel rays beat down on my tightly closed eyelids. I cover my head with a sheet. Suddenly a shudder passes over me: with my whole body covered, people will think they're carrying a corpse on the stretcher. I'm not dead. I'm alive! I lower the sheet, but the sun again defeats me, and I no longer consider what people will think.

If I am ever rich, if I ever make the big time, the first thing I will do will be to send a donation to Tel Hashomer, so that they pave their pathways properly. Each little stone, each pothole, emits waves that pass like a current through the wheels of the stretcher, and flow into my legs.

No. Not pave paths. I'll simply buy them ambulances to transport the patients around the hospital pathways. That way they'll get there quicker . . . Meanwhile, I'm not rich and the road to the X-ray department is long and sunswept . . .

Perhaps because of lightheadedness, perhaps because of the dizziness caused by the hot clean air outside, I don't remember the long pageant of X-rays that explored every limb of my body. When I awoke, I found myself in a new room. The nearest to the entrance of the hut. This is for those who merit special attention. In other words, the serious cases who are best kept as close as possible to the doctors' and nurses' rooms.

When I recover somewhat, I will discover Ron Avitan's right profile on my left side. Badly injured. A land mine. The two of us will lie side by side for many days. It will be many weeks before we see each other in full face. Neither of us are capable of rising or turning our heads. Both our legs are in casts. A friendship of silence is woven between us. Most of the hours of the day and night, we lie quietly gazing at the ceiling. As though we are carrying on some undeclared competition to see who will be the more successful in silencing his pain. It seems to me that he won . . .

Visitors flow through in their masses. I am still resolute in my decision not to reveal my suffering to them. I play a game along the lines of "Provoke them into talking – and delude them into thinking that I'm also participating in the conversation". It's difficult for me to talk.

My cupboard is filling up with stacks of boxes of chocolates and candy, fruit, books, cigarette packs, flowers. I only enjoy the cigarettes.

Visitors subdivide into two categories: those who are close to me, with whom I can remain silent, or who are sensible enough to talk to me without expecting a response. And the distant acquaintances. The latter tire me. I don't want to appear impolite and remain silent in their presence, and so I must exhaust my brain searching for subjects for conversation. The situation is especially embarrassing when about ten visitors from different circles all stand around my bed. I must chatter with each one on a different subject. I exchange a few sentences with one – and immediately turn to another so that he won't feel ignored. So I become a player facing many "opponents" simultaneously, in a game of incessant exchanges.

Yael would occasionally come to my assistance by taking on the burden of conversation. She would sometimes stop the visitors at the entrance to the hut. I rebuke her: People take the trouble to come to the hospital in obedience to the old commandment of visiting the sick – and you block their way?

Every evening Yael and I draw up an account: the number of visitors rarely falls below thirty. We sometimes even reach forty or fifty. A nurse with pursed brows occassionally comes over to warn that she will forbid so many visits. I protest vigorously: "Don't dare . . ."

Prolonged lying on the back without moving for many weeks causes unpleasant side effects. One of them: bed-sores at the end of the spine. I tell Dr. Oliver about the pains that I have there. He immediately orders the nurse: "Turn him over, on the stomach." The thought that they will turn me over shocks me. It will hurt! Luckily the nurse forgets to carry out the doctor's order. I don't remind her of it. I occasionally put out my hand to the painful place and feel the dampness of an open sore.

With time it will become clear to me that an invalid must also bear other kinds of side effects. They trouble him no less than his battle wounds. Moreover, they're doubly annoying: "This I don't deserve." After the operation in Rambam they plastered my leg very tightly. The edge of the cast was as sharp as a knife and cut my flesh. I complained to a doctor, and he, without examining me, contended that this was nothing but pain from the fractures in the leg. One day I felt the place with my finger. As I pulled it out, it was sour from blood. I again turned to the doctor. This time he checked, wrinkled his forehead and said that the cut wasn't caused by the cast, but was one of the mortar shell wounds which the doctors had not spotted before. He put a light bandage to separate the sore from the cast. Nevertheless, I wasn't convinced by his explanation. The following day I summoned Atara Briterdot, a nurse I trusted. With special scissors, she cut off the upper part of the cast, and I felt relieved. To this day, I bear a deep scar to remind me of that side effect.

Hate the old man or take pity on him? He's wrinkled and his face is covered with the bristles of old age. He has difficulty breathing and there is a rasping in his throat. From time to time he spits on the floor. On the one hand I'm sorry for him and on the other he nauseates me.

I'm now in the waiting room at the entrance to the operating theatre. They put a screen beside me, and brought me this miserable neighbour. We are both laid out like trussed offerings, ready for sacrifice in the operating theatre. Before bringing me here they plastered my body with a plethora of local anaesthetics and sedatives. I have been given pills since last evening. Before we set out, a nurse injected the "premedication" that muddles us and turns us into drunkards. Since midnight I have been fasting. Not eating is a delight for me. But the thirst is troublesome. The June nights are stifling. The hut is hot, burning and suffocating. Your body, unceasingly pouring out rivulets of perspiration, empties of its fluids during the night. By the time you reach the operating theatre you may be likened unto parched scorched earth. Your tongue is heavy, and your brain clouded over.

Add to that the special atmosphere of an operating theatre, where everybody moves around on tiptoe and talks in whispers. All are dressed in sterile green garb, and too busy to glance at you. You suffer from nausea, are sorry for the old man alongside, and wonder whether you will come out alive from the surgeon's knife. If only they would let you smoke. I can't even peek at the medical secrets hidden in my personal file, left by my side, because I'm not yet capable of distinguishing letters. The minutes drag by slowly, with no way of measuring them. They also took my watch and ring away from me.

I'm waiting here for an operation on my leg and for a change of the cast. The doctors want to know what is new under the white envelope. I'm not afraid of operations. For some reason I have a naïve faith that every change and operation brings forward the date of my leaving hospital.

I awoke. I am back in the hut and astounded that I have no sharp pains like those that accompanied each operation. Yael caught my attention and revealed that not only my leg was operated on, but also my eyes. They worked on me in parallel. I hadn't felt any difference in my eyes. Anyway, I was also bandaged before the operation. Yael adds that Professor Stein himself carried out the operation. He pulled out of my left eye a splinter the size of a dime. The splinter showed up on the X-rays taken a few days before. Though they don't usually remove splinters unless it's really essential, the professor believed that he could do it using the attraction of an electronic magnet. And he succeeded. Has he saved the eye?

I remembered that before the operation a man in civilian dress had annoyed me by coming over and beginning to probe my eyes. Now the memory made me blush: the man was Professor Stein – and I behaved so rudely!

I played around with the splinter that Yael handed me, and

marvelled: how such a large foreign body could find a resting place in such a sensitive place as an eye socket, without my feeling it. I was still thinking about it and unconsciously scratching my unshaven chin when "bristle" came unstuck. I looked at it curiously, and found that it was a splinter that had been moving about under my skin. By scratching I had unwittingly helped it out. The discovery amused me.

At that moment Menachem Talmi and Moshe Dor of *Ma'ariv* entered. Their faces were dismal. The transition from the hub of Tel Aviv, where "business proceeded as usual", to our room was not the most inspiring. I was sorry for them. Because I was in a jolly frame of mind, I tried to keep up a light conversation with them, boasting of the rich iron lodes spread around my body, and quoting . . . Jabotinsky: "Learn to laugh – and make steel." They smiled – and I felt good. A few days later Yael read me a moving and heartwarming piece that David had written in *Ma'ariv*. A description of his visit to the hut.

If only our days were without nights! How I hated them! Unending nights of sleeplessness, technicolor horrors madly unreeling. Grotesque visages. You must think of something. Must think of something. If I think, thoughts may disperse the throbbing pains. Time will perhaps also hurry on its way. Perhaps a miracle will occur – and day will dawn.

Good nurse, don't just pass me by. Be not only for others. I need you. Stay a moment. Say something to me. Anything. Without rhyme nor reason. Just words to break the shapeless silence. If your patient is stretched out by the door, and doesn't call you – it doesn't mean that he doesn't need anything.

I will slowly go mad. My hands quiver. My body trembles. I'll collapse at any moment. All the match-boxes that I prepared before lights out for the night's chain smoking – have fallen. I've got nothing with which to light this lousy cigarette between my fingers.

I must think. Of what? Of what? Give me a subject, give me a subject. Let me but grab the tail of a thought and I shall ride it to . . . I don't want to break . . .

4

. . . At first the letters arrive. The Tel Hai School in Kiryat Shmoneh discovered that a company of tanks is parked in the shade of the grove by the town. The teachers initiated a letter delivery to encourage the "brave soldiers that defend our lives". These were the last of the days of waiting.

The company clerk one day brought a thick package of letters. "Here's the goods, boys! Who wants a letter from kids?" I hastened over to him and took the package. My colleagues did not display such zeal.

It reminded me of similar letters that were sent to us eleven years earlier, when we were a company of young tankers drunk with victory, parked by the Mitle Pass in Sinai. Then I also picked out the most beautiful letters from the bundle. I even kept up a prolonged correspondence with one girl. I now sat on the stump of a fallen tree and went through the letters. In the Sinai Campaign I was eighteen. The children who then wrote were ten. Now I am twenty-nine, and they who then wrote are twenty-one. Today they are soldiers like me, and are receiving letters from ten year olds. Are the children who are now writing also condemned to be warriors, receiving letters from their younger brothers?

I hated the war and loved the children of Kiryat Shmoneh. But not their letters. They were decorated with too many sketches of different forms – the sentence: "Go, hero soldier, and kill all the Arabs."

I held the letters in my hand and looked at the Syrian Heights which threw its silent and hostile shadow over the Hule Valley where we were. The Syrian positions couldn't be seen with the naked eye. But in my mind's eye I could see the soldiers sitting in them. Hell – I thought – they want war as little as I do and are scared of it just like I am. They undoubtedly also have small children waiting for them at home. There is no doubt that they would abandon their positions, if they hadn't been forced into war by their hate-maddened leaders.

I picked up my pen and tried, tried hard, to translate my thoughts into the language of children. I was afraid that I would fail. I am indeed a writer – but I'm accustomed to writing for adults. Since I couldn't answer each of them separately, I addressed my letter to their teacher, Edna, with a request to read it to her pupils.

I tried to explain to them that none of us wanted to cut heads off, and that our country is spacious enough even without Damascus and Cairo. The war was forced on us, and if we must fight, conquest would suffice without murder. That a beloved little girl called Tami waits for me at home. That even Ahmad who sits up there on high, above Kiryat Shmoneh, has a little dark-eyed Fatima or Said. And so on and so on.

The following day the company tender brought a group of teachers to while away the time of evening with us around the camp-fire. They asked for me and found me. It turned out that my letter had been read to the pupils, and the teachers had also read it. I was happy when they told me that the pupils had understood.

Something warm was created between me and those teachers. Especially between me and Edna, to whom I had sent the letter. The clear air around the camp-fire was full of the depression of the eve of war. We tried to cover it up with inanities. Our conversation had a special taste and preciousness which I still keep alive and fresh in my heart.

When the teachers arose to return to their homes in the town, I also got on the tender that was to take them. We said almost nothing. Our hearts were full of the deep feeling of parting. We all knew that this was no ordinary camp-fire at which we had "killed" an evening. It was quite possible that houses in Kiryat Shmoneh would be shelled the following day, and that we would go out to a war from which we would perhaps not return. Edna's shoulder touched mine. She was trembling. Perhaps because of the chilly air. Perhaps because of the dread in our hearts. When she got off, I held her hand a little longer than usual, and she left her hand in mine a little longer than usual.

Four days after the war, as I lay half shocked in Rambam Hospital, I discovered Edna standing beside me. I almost swallowed my tongue from emotion. How did you arrive? How did you find me? I loved her for standing beside my bed at that moment. She told me that she had heard of my injury from Dan Shilon.

On that fateful day, Dan had burst into the emergency head-quarters of Kiryat Shmoneh. A number of the teachers were employed there in different capacities. Dan's clothes were sticky with blood. The shocked and stunned teachers asked him what had happened on the Heights. He exclaimed impatiently: "Leave me alone now. My friend, Yaacov Haelyon, is dying – and you ask stupid questions!" The teachers who knew me rushed to tell this to Edna.

Edna, whose heart – in her words – froze, would not believe that I was dead. She traced me to Rambam. I wasn't capable of talking to her for long in the hospital. But when we parted, we shook hands. Again – for somewhat longer than usual . . .

5

We must crack it. We must hit the tank bursting out from behind the house. Hit it before its shells will peel the armour off our tank. "Armour-piercing, 500 yards on the tank ahead. Fire! Fire! Fire!" Fire!!!

I dreamt. Again. Why does she rush to me, the nurse, with a lighted match in her hand? Hanna, little darling! No, no, I wasn't asking for a light for a cigarette. I was dreaming. Right, right, thank you. I really couldn't light the cigarette. All the match-boxes that I had prepared had fallen a long time ago onto the floor. I'm sorry that I shouted so loud. Yes. Maybe I woke somebody. I'm sorry. Would you like a cigarette?

At first I see a waist. Then my eyes ascend upwards and identify its owner. I used to regard doctors and nurses as mortals like me. Today they are the commanders, and I their subordinate. I like the nurses in Hut 25. They almost all share an aura of patience and goodwill. Each in her own way. Fair Bina Palgi; dark-skinned Hanna Eliahu with her white teeth; Aliza, the masseuse, her magic hands soothing aching backs; Yvonne Goldschlag; Hanna Kolkovski; and Rahel Eliahu – the head nurse, who runs the ward with an iron hand. There's also golden-haired Rivka Bott. I call her the "madonna". From my angle of vision, she doesn't walk but floats. She's soft, smiling, talks with a soothing voice that diffuses an atmosphere of tranquillity around her.

Morning, and she arrives with another nurse whom I don't know, to change my bedding. I lift myself up to help them. A blinding light suddenly pierces my brain, accompanied by a kind of blow. Waves of weakness engulf me. I began to dive towards the floor. The

73

"madonna" didn't panic. She caught me just at the last moment. I lay in her arms, half unconscious and gulping in air with difficulty.

Slowly she returned me to a lying position. With cool hands she began to stroke my arms, murmur soft words. I was incapable of answering. I was grateful. Tears began to well up in my eyes. I couldn't stop them. After a while I regained control, but not over the well-spring of tears. I was utterly ashamed and despised myself. I tried with all my will to stop the sobbing and flood of tears. Rivka continued to soothe me. When my attempts to calm myself failed, I bit into my arm almost to the point of drawing blood. The second nurse warned, "If you continue to bite yourself – we'll tie you". This was the most irritatingly inane comment that anybody could make to me at that moment. I buried my head in the pillow. When the nurses were convinced that I had calmed down, they left my bed and went to the other patients. I remained under cover of the pillow for another hour.

When Yael came I was so exhausted that I could not even greet her. From her anxious face I understood that some damn fool or other had already chattered about what had occurred. I didn't open my mouth except to exchange a cigarette-butt for a fresh cigarette.

Yael tried to stimulate me to talk. I finally managed to open my mouth. I said: "Turn the hospital inside out, go to the director, to the head of the ward, to the psychiatric ward – and find something against insomnia. I can bear the pain more or less with dignity during the day. But I haven't the strength to bear the terrible agony of another sleepless night. I'll lose my mind. It's not possible that the science of medicine hasn't yet found something against insomnia. If they know how to carry out open heart surgery, transplant kidneys – there must be a way of overcoming this as well."

Yael nods her head in agreement and promises to move worlds. Meanwhile she tries to distract my attention with the help of our daughter Tami's witticisms.

In the evening they doubled the sedative injections and added sleeping pills. But nothing helped. I can't fall asleep. Why? Because of my pains? Because of emotional tension caused by war and injury?

It is only in the mornings that I manage to doze off for a quarter of an hour or half an hour, until somebody opens the transistor at full blast, or someone else passes by my bed and shakes it by accident. The agony of being jolted projects me "through the ceiling".

74

The new cast is very tight. I feel like somebody putting on a shoe three sizes too small. The doctor promised to relieve the pressure. The sawing of the cast is done by a young doctor, a volunteer from abroad. He passes among the patients with a similar problem, and cuts the plaster with an electric saw and special scissors. I follow him with my eyes, and notice that he is about to leave the room without attending to me.

"Hey, Mr. Carpenter," I call to him, "have you forgotten me!"

He stops, looks at the list in his hand, and says with a smile: "You're right. I forgot. Apart from that, I'm not a carpenter. I sweated for seven years to get my doctor's diploma." I apologise and point out that the saw is clearly a carpenter's tool . . .

The cutting of the cast only eases me a little. The pains continue. I'm battling a medusa: you cut off a head, and immediately seven more mouths bite into your flesh.

We're informed that the nice Dr. Oliver is leaving the ward. A new doctor, Dr. Weigel, takes his place. I complain to him about my pains. He nods his head as though agreeing, and orders the nurse accompanying him to give me a "Vilan" pill.

Meanwhile he bends over my leg wrapped in its cast, and sniffs at it. The junior doctors also sniff, and nod their heads comprehendingly. I wonder: What have they got to sniff at so much?

The "Vilan" is a strong drug. A few moments after I swallow it the room becomes blurred and the figures in it move about in a strange way. I manage to say to myself that I now feel something like a drug addict, and immediately fall into a deep sleep. I will awake from it an hour and a half later. A gift of ninety minutes.

6

This afternoon – so Yael promises me – they will bring Tami to see me. I am delirious with joy. I miss her so much. I long for patting, kisses, frolics on the carpet, her bright remarks, to tell her stories and to sing her the traditional lullaby when she is put to bed.

A long time before the hour set for her visit, my heart beats with emotion. I feel like a young girl waiting to be presented to the hero of her dreams. I try to comb my hair. At the front, my head is shaven – while behind, it's so wild, tangled and dirty that the teeth of the comb won't pass through it. Rahel, the ward sister, solved the problem. She brings me a white hat to cover my head.

I looked in the mirror at least a dozen times. I was filled with anger at the sight of the deep scars on the right side of my face and forehead. They were painted with a gaudy red iodine. I couldn't hide those. I at least tried to camouflage the leg covered in plaster.

When the preparations were completed, I was left waiting as tense as a spring: What will happen during my meeting with my thirty month old daughter? Time and again I ask my neighbour and the nurses whether my appearance isn't too shocking. They reassured me. I put a bar of chocolate next to the bed, ready for anything that could happen. Perhaps I'll have to win her heart with candies. My eyes constantly flitter to the door. When will my little girl come through it?

Three days before the outbreak of war, in the course of a telephone conversation I leaked a hint to Yael of our location. Yael promised to come the following day, Saturday, with Tami.

By my calculation, Yael would arrive at ten in the morning. At eight, I was festooned with water bottles, and shaving carefully. While still shaving, one of the boys in the company ran up to tell me that my wife was waiting by the road. I dropped the razor, wiped my face hurriedly – and rushed to meet them.

Tami held Yael's hand tightly and as I erupted from among the trees in a camouflage uniform, I reached out my arms towards her. She clung to Yael and followed me with frightened eyes. She didn't recognise me. It was only when I came nearer that she identified me and ran into my arms, wondering at her transformed father.

Something fluttered in my breast as I saw my toddler come through the room in low gear, throwing surprised glances at the rows of beds, and asking in a clear voice that reached me: "What is this? A shop for beds?"

My eyes feasted on her, on the plump legs sticking out under the white summer skirt, on the face that I loved so much.

I already wanted her beside me.

When Yael said: "Here's Daddy!" she straightened up on the spot. Threw me a glance of apprehension and terror. I saw that she didn't identify her father lying in bed in this monstrous form, and gazing at her with damp eyes.

It was only after much persuasion that she came near. I stuck out my hand. She recoiled. She looked at me hesitantly. Suddenly her gaze fell on my watch and the wedding ring on my finger. She always used to play with them. She put out her hand very slowly and fingered them, mumbling to herself: "Ring . . ." "Watch . . ." "Ring . . ." "Watch."

What was going on in her soul? What would win out? Would she recognise me? Would she reject me? Am I her father or a strange frightening grotesque man?

I felt my strength ebb away. The tension and emotion that preceded the child's visit, and now her alienation and fear – weakened me. I asked Yael to take Tami out. I couldn't bear the tension. In my imagination I had pictured a totally different meeting. They all went outside and left me alone with myself. The bar of chocolate remained, orphaned, on the low cupboard beside the bed.

I didn't ask them to bring Tami for additional visits. But, after the first – when I was as a stranger to her – she began to demand that they take her to Daddy. Her fears did not vanish in the coming visits, but each time she grew a bit more bold. Each visit she first checked to see that I was wearing my "identity card" – the watch and ring. She never forgot to bring some small present – on her initiative: a lollypop, a rubber elephant, or some cookies in a nylon bag – the most precious gift that I have ever received.

One day she came to my bedside with a very self-important expression on her face. She asked our friends, Riba and Micha Dotan, for the "paper", took it, climbed on a chair, and turned on me the eyes of one who knows how to read. She began to recite:

"Tami loves Daddy,
Daddy's leg hurts badly
Tami kisses Daddy today
Daddy's pain goes away."

I turned stricken eyes on those around me. It soon became clear that the performance had been staged for me by Micha and Riba, who had improved the recitation on the way from Tel Aviv to Tel Hashomer. The little one absorbed it quickly and even understood that it would be much more impressive if she acted as though reading from the paper.

If she would only have let me, I would have hugged her. But, when she finished the recitation, she descended from the chair

77

and formally demanded chocolate. I sobbed silently without tears. I was as proud as a peacock. No, not a peacock. As a father.

On the morning of Tami's first visit, Mr. Dr. Carpenter had afforded me some relief by sawing off a little of the cast. After he left the room I felt a strange discomfort and coolness in the infected area between my thigh and the cast that encased it. I didn't attach any importance to the matter. If I dwell on every minor discomfort, there will be no end to it.

That evening, before I parted from Yael, my fingers moved down to the bothersome spot. I felt something, a sort of strange object lying there. I fingered it curiously. I sensed that I was touching a lump of metal with two rings on its end. I grasped the rings and pulled carefully. I pulled and pulled and still hadn't extracted all of it. I stopped for a moment: a lot of things had been done to my body by the doctors without me knowing about them. Perhaps I was destroying something? I asked Yael to take a look under the sheet. When she straightened up, there was a broad smile on her face: "Pull it out, pull it out!" she said, with no explanation. I pulled hard and it came free. I burst out laughing. They were – no less and no more – the plaster scissors that the doctor had used in cutting away. The scissors were about 30 centimetres long and as thick as crude metal workers' pincers. Mr. Carpenter, you said you sweated over your medical studies for seven years? . . .

More than thirty casualties were bedded in our hut. But the doctors' rounds were mostly devoted to three: to Yaron Dolav whose condition was the most serious; to Ron my neighbour who bore his suffering in stolid silence; and to me.

As far as I was concerned they repeatedly for some unknown reason made most use of their sense of smell. Again I was puzzled: What is the delicate perfume that emanates from my leg? No answer. It appears that even a doctor's heart may be perplexed, though less bemused than mine. The electric saw was again brought, and they cut a square "window" in the plaster above my ankle. Dr. Weigel lifted the window, bent over, looked carefully, and proclaimed: "You've got an ugly sore."

That's nothing new, doctor. In my opinion it's also very ugly. I shrugged my shoulders and said: "Is there such a thing as a beautiful sore?"

78

A thought crossed my mind: perhaps I can gain some profit from this conversation: I'll ask again for the redeeming "Vilan" pill.

A hallucination. The first vilan put me to sleep. This time I'm hallucinating. Neither awake, nor asleep, neither dreaming nor day-dreaming. My eyes are closed but the room swirls around in a dervish dance. Images rise up: to surface for a second – and disappear. Your sore is not at all beautiful. If it's not beautiful, then it's ugly, if ugly – that's a bad sign. I'm afraid of bad signs. Afraid. To fear – so many synonyms. Anxiety, apprehension, terror, dread, dread-dread-dread. Fears. Worries. Horrors. No! – fear. Mother, I'm afraid that the pigeon will bite me. Your sore is not very beautiful – and I am very afraid.

Why all of a sudden? I'm not afraid of sores. The first aid station in Maze Street once pulled a finger-nail without anaesthetic, and I didn't bat an eyelid. "Why do you always come without Mother?" "Sssh . . . Mother doesn't know about it." A sore under the cast, perhaps it's really ugly? I always envied my colleagues at school who broke a hand or other limb, who walked around in plaster. They were the day's heroes. I never broke anything. Ordinary bandages didn't count. Now, too late and not really necessary, my childhood dream had come true.

The room whirls round and round. The bed is a seat on a ferris wheel. Some are scared of the giant wheel. I'm not. I tasted my first kiss on the ferris wheel in Jaffa Amusement Park. She was fifteen and I – fourteen.

I first felt fear creep up on me when I received the call-up notice. Something in my heart whispered that this time it's war – and I took the doll's leg as a lucky charm.

The second time, it descended on me as I rested on a concrete floor, in a gigantic ammunition dump in the north of the country. We had finished loading twelve trucks with shells. We were tired after a sleepless night, and keyed up for the first morning news bulletin. The announcer said that Nasser had closed the Straits of Tiran. We looked at each other. Anxiety showed in our eyes.

Henceforward fear accompanied us every time we assembled before going out to battle. Our departure was delayed many times and the pre-departure briefings were many.

Yuval and I spoke to each other about the fears gnawing at us. We both knew that we would overcome them at the moment of trial. We tried to silence others who gave vocal expression to their fear, so that they wouldn't awake the grey worm in their comrades.

I thought that I would be killed. I worried about my small family. In the faint light of a pocket torch I wrote last wills and testaments. One for my friends in the Rabin family – and the second for the Editor of *Ma'ariv*.

I reported my debts and my property, and expressed the hope that should something happen, they would know how to look after my wife and daughter.

As I licked the flap of the envelopes to seal them, a sudden thought: How stupid I will look if I return home in one piece, or if there is no war.

That same evening, I wrote two more letters, to Yael and to my parents. I swore to them that I was in a safe place, and that the chances of my being involved in war, if it does break out, are very slight.

7

So-me-th-ing is pier-cing my annn-kle!!!

I shout and scream and rant, and don't understand what's being done to me. That lousy vilan. I can't open my eyes. Somebody's taking my bones apart. The room has stopped spinning. I shake my head violently and my eyes open. There, at the foot of the bed, my gaze encounters the doctor's eyes.

"So why is he complaining about insomnia, if he sleeps all the time?"

That was a cruel remark, doctor. You gave me the Vilan yourself. Why did they put a screen around me? Where's Yael? When I fell asleep she was next to me. Why do the doctors and nurses surrounding my bed seem so stern? Why are they so angry, all of them?

No! No! Doctor, what are you about to do to my ankle? Don't jab me again. He doesn't even look at me. He bends over the sore exposed under the "window". It stinks! A bad smell exudes from it. What sort of a smell is this? Rot? I'm beginning to grasp! I understand. Stinking flesh is a symptom of gangrene. My flesh is gangrenous. Aaah!

Doctor, mercy! You're killing me! You're shaming me! This is the first time I've screamed during treatment. Nobody has yet squeezed a scream out of me. I only yelled after operations and anaesthetic. Under the influence of anaesthetics, a man loses control of himself. The screams were torn from my lips. Stop! Stop! Stop! Rahel, the nurse, passes a bandage to the doctor. The features of the second nurse are frozen and severe. Stupid bitch! Instead of standing like a statue you could hold my hand. Then I wouldn't be so alone among this cabal of devils who perpetrate their hidden acts behind a screen.

"I know it hurts, but we must finish," the doctor said dryly. Sure you know it hurts, but you haven't even the first idea of how much, you butcher!

They finally left me alone. Closed the "window", thank God. They surprised me. What agony! The screen and the expressionless faces. When will they finally realize that I'm not a "leg case", a "head case" and an "eye case"? When will they understand that behind these damaged limbs – is me? You dolts.

They took away the screen. I look around surreptitiously: Did they hear? Ron turned his head and asked: "It hurts a lot?" I nod my head. They heard. Why couldn't I control it? Here's Yael. Her eyes are red. They betray her. She also heard. She sits next to me. I reach for her hand. "It was bad, Yael, it was bad."

I can already see well enough with my eye to take a quick glance at the pages of the newspaper, covered in black funeral frames. So many pages with so many similar notices. Small and big, 3 inch, 10 inch – all depending on the bulge in the wallet of whoever placed the announcement.

My small world suddenly opens wide. I now begin to digest the other significance of victory: the price. So far I had only thought of myself. At most, the wounded from my company. These pages cast up many names. Hundreds! Any of my acquaintances among them? – my enfeebled eye can't decipher the names.

I had two visitors today. Both, strangely enough, made similar remarks. The first was my comrade Yigal Simon, an officer, who fought on the West Bank. This was his first visit. He looked at me with sad eyes, and as though unwittingly lets drop the words: "I knew that something would happen to you. I even told my wife a day or so before the war . . ."

After him comes Yuval Gold. This time, he seems more at ease than during his first visit. He says: "I was afraid all the time. I remember the moment we parted, as we left Tal Grove for war. I then knew for certain that you would not come out of it whole . . ."

Our friends, Gershon and Tova Zvitlasky, are vegetarians. We forgive them this eccentricity. On earlier visits, they had already beseeched me to maintain a vegetarian diet, which in their opinion has the virtue of rapidly curing wounds. Meanwhile, I couldn't care less what I eat. But the little devils in me incite me to tease them. I announce – I am a "luster after flesh" and I don't intend to be redeemed.

This evening, Gershon has brought another wonder drug with him – this one against pain and insomnia. Gershon contends that he tried it on himself successfully. The name of the medicine: muscle relaxer. I must remove the pillows from under my head, and lie as loose as possible. If I follow instructions – he says – I may be relieved of my pains – perhaps.

The hut has already emptied of most of its visitors, and a pale light now prevails. Yael went out to escort some of my friends. The nurses prepare themselves for the end of shift. Quiet. I lie loosely. Gershon began to talk in a low voice, almost a whisper, mentioning the names of every muscle from the soles of my feet to my head, and commanding me to relax them. I obey. Something similar to a process of slow sinking overcomes me. The pain has almost vanished. I begin to doze.

I suddenly heard the panic-stricken voice of a nurse: "What's going on here?" They're not used to seeing me sleep at such an early hour. "Nothing," Gershon pacifies her, "think he's falling asleep." As soon as she departed, he continues to whisper his instructions to loosen up. We were interrupted again. Yael returned. She was shocked to see me without pillows, with a tranquil almost vapid expression on my face (in the process of loosening up, the lower jaw drops). She had a moment of anxiety. I sensed Gershon's embarrassment. He didn't want to look like someone mumbling Kaddish over the dead, or a witch whispering incantations over a brew. I took pity on them and opened my eyes. I regretted the failure of our "exercise" . . .

Gershon was compelled to go about his affairs. Before we parted, we decided to repeat the experiment on another day. After all, here was somebody – not a doctor – doing what no drug had yet achieved: sedating me, and making me forget the pains. I now needed that, more than anything else. I relied on doctors to return sight to my eye, and put my head and damaged leg back in their former state. What bothered me was the pains and the insomnia. Who would help me overcome them? – I didn't care who: if doctors weren't powerful enough, I was prepared to place all my trust in Gershon.

My thoughts continued to flow: There are doctors and doctors. Those I trust, and others whom I prefer to see pass my bed without stopping. Those who cloak themselves in the raiment of gods and, on the other hand – those who display human warmth and friendship.

When I get out of here, I will ascend the podium in a medical school lecture-hall, clear my throat, and pound into the medical students' ears the following advice: Dear boys, please! Remember, repeat and remember: Before you treat a sore, before you diagnose a disease – find a way to the patient's heart and soul. One smile, a nice word, a wink, a shrug of a shoulder, patting of a head – are worth many medicines!

I clear my throat again and add: "Don't relate to the patient as a 'case'. Remember: there, lying before you is a terrified, bewildered, exhausted, helpless being. He sees in you a human edition of the Angel Raphael – and that's a lot. Encourage him, give him security and faith – only after that, then roll up your sleeves to your medical work."

That's it. My speech is over. And now: go forth and practise what I preach . . .

Doctor Yitzhak Parin inspired trust from the very first meeting, and a faith that would bear much fruit.

Hut 25 was improvised for war-wounded as an orthopaedic ward to supplement the existing ones. Senior orthopaedic surgeons would occasionally visit, in order to keep au fait of our condition.

One day Dr. Parin arrived and began his rounds at the other end of the hut. When he reached me, he stopped, smiled a broad smile and said in a pleasant voice: "How are you, Yankele?" I was surprised. Not one of the doctors had yet addressed me by that nickname. Where did he know me from? To this day, I hadn't seen him. From whence this personal address?

No matter, my pleasure was immense. I returned his smile, and was happy when he told me that the patients in Hut 25 would soon be divided among the orthopaedic wards. I would be his "client".

From that meeting I sensed that I could place my unreserved trust in Dr. Parin. Even during the most difficult treatment under his hands, I felt no extreme pain. I regarded him as a kind of "trustee". Long after I left the ward, I still benefited from his good advice, directly or indirectly.

Cora Moskowitz is a woman of about thirty, tall and erect. Beautiful features with aristocratic and tranquil lines, black eyes – and I hated her on first sight.

It would later appear that I sinned in passing hasty judgement. Cora was a nurse. I saw her the first time when she stood near me in the "screen incident". I wanted her to hold my hand, and she stood there with a frozen face, not hearing nor understanding my heart's murmurs.

A few days after that painful treatment, she asked whether, by chance, I had any relative with the same name in the United States, working for Zim Shipping Lines. I replied that the man, Haim, was my brother.

Cora – so she told me – was a veteran nurse in Tel Hashomer. A few years ago, she left the hospital and went to study in the States, where she met my brother and became friendly with him. After a while, she was offered a research fellowship in Brazil and went there.

Came the Six Day War, and the heart of a sister of mercy awoke under her researcher's regalia. Without a second thought, she abandoned her research, and flew to Israel. She reached Tel Hashomer and was posted to our hut.

I revealed that I had hated her as she stood so coldly during the "screen incident". She blushed and, with an apologetic smile asked forgiveness: that had been her first day of work as a nurse – after a very long break. She was still upset and horrified at the sight of the suffering she saw all around her. The doctor suggested that she watch my treatment. My groans and the sight of gangrene shocked her. "I had to fix my eyes on a certain spot on the screen, to stop myself from breaking into tears. Until everything was over . . ." she said.

We decided to forget the affair. During the coming days, she would make amends. I became her adopted patient, and we were quickly fast and close friends. This friendship was of short duration. She soon went back to Brazil.

8

We went to war a big gang. Most of us, thank God, returned home safely. Some of us had to pay the tax to a varying degree. Some were condemned to death, others badly injured and still fighting a bitter fate, and some were lightly injured.

I lay in bed and surveyed my comrades. Some would go home in a week or two, with no evidence of bodily injury. Others – would drag out their suffering for many months. Perhaps years. Perhaps their whole lives.

I imagine that each individual only thinks of his own suffering. A man with toothache gets no consolation from the fact that a cancer patient is in far worse pain. I'm no different from my comrades. I also think only of my sorrows. This, though I am told time and time again of others whose suffering is greater than mine. In other words: Don't show off! You aren't the worst off. Go and explain to them my feelings. My sorrows leave no room for consolation because of the greater sorrows of others.

Yaron Dolav was wounded in many places. His injuries are ugly: his belly is open, and both his legs are broken. A whole system of pipes and bottles hangs above his bed. From my place, I can only see his feet. From the voices that pierce the darkness of the room at night, and from the probing beams of the nurses' flashlights that come and go frequently, I understand that he especially suffers greatly at night. As I look towards his room my ego is deflated to a certain degree. Something latent, somewhere in my breast, reprimands me: shame on you – it says – look at Yaron, and be silent!

One day, his energetic wife who, like Yael, spends most of the daylight hours beside her husband, comes over to my bed. She told us that Yaron's problem of insomnia had been solved. Somebody somehow got the idea that they should approach a psychiatrist. The doctor talked at length with Yaron, and prescribed special drugs that succeeded in putting him to sleep.

I listened attentively. Perhaps the lifebelt had been found. It was worth a try. A try won't hurt. During morning doctors' rounds, I demanded a psychiatrist. The doctor knew my problem, and agreed immediately. I was happy. Actually, there was also some resentment in my heart: why does the idea have to come from me? Why didn't the doctors think of it?

The following day, Dr. Floro, an attractive, pleasant woman, appeared by my bedside. She said that she had come to discuss insomnia. I told her, and fixed hopeful eyes on her. In her opinion, I was suffering from mental tension as a result of the war, and incessant pain. She promised to order new drugs, to relieve tension and put me to sleep. I doubted her powers. After all, all her medical colleagues had failed.

That evening I tried to fall asleep without the psychiatrist's drugs. Some sort of personal pride. My spirit occasionally rebelled, and I tried to prove to myself that I could control my body by willpower alone. After a few hours of battle, I raised my arms. As night begins, I stand firm. But as the moments pass, as the hours pass – I lose self-control.

The lifeline hangs above my bed. At the end of it – a button. You press the button. This lights a lamp above the doorpost of the room. From the light the nurses learn that one of the patients needs them. Then you quickly catch sight of their blurred visages, illumined by their flashlights.

It was difficult to find the night bell. My hands fumbled around until I finally grasped it. A few seconds passed, and the nurses, Yvonne and Hanna, stood by me. Smiling. It was good to see the two of them. Two good angels. "That what's its name that the psychiatrist prescribed for sleep," I announced. The something or other had a medical name. But I am totally incapable of pronouncing it. They went out – and came back with rubber bottles and pipes.

"What's that?" I was shaken out of my torpor. "An enema?! They promised me drug, not this disgusting thing."

Since I was wounded, I had been waging a battle to "preserve my dignity". I am not capable of exposing my whole body to the nurses' eyes. I know they are used to their patients' nakedness and are to a certain extent indifferent. It's just part of the job. Nevertheless, I am adamant.

"I will certainly not agree to an enema," I declare vigorously.

They shrug their shoulders and giggle. Apparently they haven't understood me. They seem convinced that I'm afraid of the enema, and don't understand that I am simply shy.

"But it's not an enema. The drug is so bitter that it's impossible to swallow through the mouth. It's more bitter than anything you know, so it's worth your while to agree."

I shake my head: "Never. Unable. Simply unable!" They plead with me, but in the face of my obstinacy they give way and leave the room.

I was left alone with my solitude and wakefulness. I have foregone an opportunity to sleep.

I understand how it's possible to break a man's spirit. How they succeeded in brainwashing the strongest, most obstinate and toughest. How they brought men, considered giants, to degrading confessions in the purge courts of Moscow and Prague. They compound a recipe of two ingredients: intense pain, and acute insomnia. Who can face those?

I surrendered. The white rope. The night bell. The nurses in the flickering lights of their torches. "O.K. I'll agree. Only quickly, quick'y. Let it be an enema. If it only lets me sleep a little."

I lie still, and they – the nurses – fuss around with their tools and my body. My teeth gnash away at my lips in rage. I'm angry at myself. They giggle and go about their work. When they finally finish, they wish me a good night and vanish. My sheet was a little damp. A little of the liquid medicine had spilled from the bowl. The nurses hadn't worked well by the feeble light of torches.

It's not comfortable to lie on a damp sheet when you're naked. No, certainly not comfortable. Babies cry when they wet their bedding. But tonight I prefer to lie on it till morning. I cannot bother Yvonne and Hanna again. And in any case, it would be better to walk barefoot over hot ashes, rather than go through the process of changing sheets.

The wet sheet bothers and irritates. If it wasn't for the lousy leg – God only knows, I'm beginning to hate it – I could move to the other dry half of the bed. The bed is on wheels. When somebody bangs into it inadvertently, it slides to the right and left easily. Like a small boat in the water . . . Right and left, left and down, left and right, row. Row! Up and down, rise and fall, bow butting up above the flowing waters. The bow rises, the stern sinks. Water flows into the boat bottom. Water sprays on the back and spills over the trousers. The waters are cold, a pleasant touch to this terribly hot body. A stream, a little rivulet, a brook, a tributary. Clear water.

You can see the bottom. A brook like those you see in illustrated stories. In Tami's stories. We don't have any brooks like these. It's a pity. It does you good to look at them.

None? No! – there are! I saw for myself. Once when the war to expel the Syrians was at its peak, and my tank dropped into an anti-tank trench, I swished my legs through the clear waters of one of the Dan tributaries, at the foot of Tel el Kadi. The drug they just gave me is so bitter – no ordinary man can stand its taste in his mouth. The River Dan waters were sweet. You can drink. Not just to quench your thirst. You are overcome by desire to fill your belly to the brim, to bursting point. And then your instincts impel you to fall, soak and wallow like a hippopotamus. They're pleasant, good and tempting.

9

The June sun in Upper Galilee rises at four in the morning. We were accustomed to awakening at this hour to cover the tanks with camouflage net, so the enemy eye won't spot them. On the morning of June 7, the day after war began, we were awakened earlier. We were called out from our sleeping bags to the bitter cold and the darkness. Still befogged with sleep, we didn't grasp what had happened. We forgot that somewhere in the south, bitter battles were raging. We only knew: if we are awoken – then within a minute or two, the tank engines must be turning over; our rolls of personal belongings must be packed; the radio must be working, and the driver must acknowledge the tank commander's orders.

"Driver, do you hear?"

"Yes. Driver hears."

"Driver, roll it!"

Our armoured column was already moving, its tracks crushing the asphalt road leading northwards, towards Metulla. I was still puzzled and bemused, rubbing the crusts of sleep from my eyes, making sure that in the darkness my driver won't approach too close to the tank in front.

We were travelling northwards, our limbs stiff from cold, and battling between the obligation to watch the dark road and avoid accidents – and the lust to soak in the landscapes of Upper Galilee and the Golan Heights, slowly unfolding as night peeled back, layer after layer.

As we reached the first houses of Metulla, the tanks ground to a halt. A short pause, and then we began to manoeuvre o n the narrow road. Back the way we had come.

What had happened? What was this? A morning limbering up for tanks? I bent over the turret and asked my comrades directing the manoeuvring tanks from the ground: "What's going on here?"

There is an explanation: There was Intelligence information that the Syrians intended to attack Metulla. Our company bears the burden of protecting the "finger" on the map of Galilee. Now there's no need for us, for the information was found to be misleading. We return therefore to the grove facing Tel-Hai. As we move south from Metulla and descend the mountain slope, the heavy tanks race forward quickly, with almost no possibility of braking. An immense mass of tens of tons. There's a bend in the road in front of us. Abrasha doesn't notice it. My God! We're sliding into the abyss. We brake at the last moment . . .

"Hey! Abrasha! Are you mad? You almost had us down there!" I roar.

I shouldn't have been angry with him. The tank slipped across the road like a man on a banana skin. Abrasha has children at home. Albert has children at home, I've got a child. Shimon and Amram are still bachelors, but we all want to return home.

We returned home. To our tank park. Nets over the tanks. The cold penetrates bones, but I'm keeping the bottle of cognac for tougher moments. Perhaps we should go back to sleep, but who can now? Anybody who makes us a cup of hot coffee will be doing a great favour.

The radio begins to spew unpleasant news. Elyusha Lishinsky, who is sitting with his company at Tell el Kadi, is the speaker. He relates that the Syrians are trying to attack Kibbutz Dan. We must go to her aid.

We will repel the Syrians. The task is ours. We moved out quickly along the Security road. The Syrians had begun to bombard settlements along the road. Heavy thunder and clouds of smoke gathering. Burning fields. Over the radio we hear almost desperate cries for assistance. The tanks can't travel faster. A plump woman comes out of a house by the road. She raises her arms and face to the heavens. I knew: she's praying. She's praying for us, to heavens grey with smoke. Thank you, lady. Thank you.

We move off the road onto a clover field, spread out under the eyes of Syrians in the Ramat Baniass, Tel Aziziyat and Tel Hamra emplacements. The clover is green and fresh. Now there's a war on. We can't help but mash and crush it. Our apologies to the kibbutz-niks. We're not destroying your work deliberately, maliciously.

We're spread out and moving in a line abreast across the field. "Ephraim, is your machine-gun down there loaded?" I cock mine. Amar, the driver, hands candies around. Poor Amar. Poor Ephraim. Is something telling you that you're on the threshold of death? That you have only three days left?

My sheet is damp. I wonder how many hours have passed since they gave me the sleeping drug . . .

Whispers. The light of the nurses' torches. Yvonne and Hanna: "The medicine helped a little, didn't it? We've been to see you a few times and noticed that you were lying quietly." Yes, girls, I lay quietly and my eyes were closed. But I'm not really sure that I slept. Perhaps I only dreamt while awake. Now, I'm awake again. Awake and fresh, and not waiting impatiently for morning to come . . .

10

Two days later they took me to the operating theatre again. The leg. Again the doctors don't explain what they are about to do. Perhaps I don't show any interest or ask.

I was worried and frightened. I was afraid of the agony when I awoke from the anaesthetic. I was afraid that again I would have no control over myself, and would scream.

. . . I awoke. I'm in my bed. No more pain than usual. Dry mouth and rough tongue. The effects of the sedation haven't yet passed. My head is heavy. I'm having difficulty opening my eyes. I must do it: to drink, I must look for somebody and ask for water.

How fortunate! Yael and Osnat are by my side. They'll give me a drink: "Water, water. A lot, a lot of water. Bring me water. I'm very thirsty."

My head fell back on the pillows and my eyes closed. It was clear

90

that Yael would now rush to carry out my wish. She will bring water. She knows how thirsty I am. In a moment she will touch me and hold the cup to my lips. I must drink. Must. She knows this, so I'll drink in a minute. Immediately. Another moment . . .

How much time is needed to fill a cup at the nearest tap? None! None? So why aren't I drinking? Why is it taking so long? Apparently she went to take cold water from the fridge in the kitchen. The tap water is insipid and tepid. She probably wants me to enjoy it more. That must be it. I'll be drinking clear water. What now? Where's the water? Water. Yael, you're not behaving properly. I'm terribly thirsty, and you're slacking around!

I must open my eyes to see whether she's approaching with the cup. What is this?! She and Osnat are standing just like before. They didn't even move from the bed. They don't even intend to bring water. "Where's the water? I asked you for it!" What are you saying about being forbidden?! By what right is it forbidden? I'm thirsty! My mouth, my throat, my stomach, my head, my whole body – and you say it's forbidden? Why are you looking at me that way? What do you say? The doctor doesn't permit? Forbidden after sedation? I couldn't care less about choking, I spit on what he told you. I'm thirsty – not him!

They don't want to give me water. They simply refuse. They're conspiring against me. I must drink. I must. My belly is screaming for water and it knows what's permissible and what's forbidden far better than the doctors. I couldn't care less about choking. Couldn't care less about anything. "Bring me water, I told you, bring me water!"

I've turned into an animal.

I'll get up, off the bed and go and drink by myself. That's it. That way. Aaah! My body is wracked with pain. Lousy leg betrayed me. It's against me. On the side of the doctors and Yael and Osnat. "You sadists. Do what I ask of you, or to hell with it – I'll start a riot."

I can already feel my face contorting. If my mouth wasn't so dry, I'd already be foaming like a mad dog. I'm going crazy. Persecution complex. Everyone's against me. Orderlies! Orderlies! Bring a strait-jacket! The patient is going wild! Electric shock, hot baths, sedative injections. I couldn't care less, Osnat, that you're angry. I know: you're against me because of my anger at Yael, who's torn between my suffering and the doctors' orders, to hell with them. Water! Water! Water! No – forbidden! By order! An order from above. The lousy doctor. Water! Give me water! Taps. A noisy shower. River Dan. Oceans. Beer straight from the barrel. Gallons of soda. Juice . . .

No! I don't want that cotton-wool that you dip in water. It disgusts me. Let the doctor suck it. Parasite! I almost vomited because of him . . .

I must get them out of the room. When they go – I'll find water. Yael, go to the doctor. Perhaps now he'll permit it. Perhaps now it's alright. Osnat, please escort Yael. I want to be alone. I want to rest . . .

That's it! They've gone! I won! Now, grab the first visitor who enters the room, make a supreme effort to rise, give him the empty cup off my table. "Excuse me, perhaps you're prepared to bring me some water from the nearby tap? Yes, it's very hot here. We're all very thirsty. It's hot inside the huts. There's no air. We're sweating."

It's lucky that he doesn't know about the prohibition. Swallow all the water in one gulp. Aaah! Wonderful. "Maybe I can ask you to fill it again? Thank you." I've no time to talk to him. My body's lusting for water. "Thank you, and again?" Another cup. Now the fourth. The man looks at me with suspicious eyes. "Are you sure that what you're doing is O.K.?" – "Why not? Of course it's O.K. We must drink a lot."

I like this stranger. He has eased me. "Shalom, thank you!" The devil with the doctors and their prohibitions. I didn't vomit, and there was not even a shadow of nausea . . .

Yael and Osnat come back disappointed. The doctor didn't agree. I'm no longer angry, though I could drink another litre willingly. Now, if you'll forgive me, I'm going to doze for a bit. I've no doubt you'll welcome this sleep. You'll probably think I suffer less this way . . .

I hadn't been in Hut 25 for more than a few days, but it seemed like months. I had a similar feeling in Rambam Hospital. The parting had been difficult. Hut 25 became my home in the course of time. As soon as I was able to identify faces, and know from which direction visitors enter, and where my cigarettes and paper-handkerchiefs were.

Now I know all the doctors and nurses, and have made up my

mind about them. I was also well acquainted with the vague land-scape that could be seen beyond the net windows. I adapted to the burning heat of the hut, and knew all the essential details. I was familiar with the daily schedule and knew when the nurse carrying the "horse syringe" was coming to me, and when she intended to stick it in somebody else. I could guess when the flow of visitors would wax, and when it would wane. I knew at exactly what hour Tali, the young girl volunteer from Kfar Hayarok, would come; When Hagit Yaron, with her beauty spots, would come – and what was the state of mind of Ron, lying in the next bed – even without talking to him. I hated the worst hours of the day, and loved the good cheerful ones, when my agony was somewhat alleviated.

So it was only natural that I would be saddened when, on a Friday, Rahel the ward sister told us that I was being moved to another hut. Number 16. I feared the need to adapt again to a new home.

However, it didn't depend on me. I don't decide matters of this sort. They decided I must go – so I must go. A few words of farewell, a glance backwards at the memories that I would take with me, a warm handshake to the nurses, and low and depressed spirits. My heart prophesied the worst. I didn't know why.

11

If Hut 25 was a happy place, compared with the plastic ward of Rambam Hospital, then Hut 16 could be considered a ballroom or discotheque. When my bed was wheeled in, I was astonished at the hubbub and uproar, the booming of transistors, the patients' shouts and cheerful cries from one end of the hut to the other.

There were no more than three or four patients in my room in Hut 25, and all were quiet through most of the day. Here, on the other hand, the room was very big. Eighteen or twenty noisy and rowdy patients lay in it, shouting at the nurses – who replied in kind. Some of the casualties walked around between the beds, others sang or noisily nibbled away at fruit.

Very cheerful, but I need quiet. Noise rattles me and grinds away at my nerve ends. Rest. Rest. Quiet! My bed is the outermost, but the density is so great that any move by my neighbour to the right vibrates through the cupboard between us. The cupboard moves my bed, and with it – my leg. The slightest movement by my neighbour, and I'm already writhing in agony. Silence! Quiet! Please, don't make so much noise! My head is bursting.

In Rambam, I was a king, and in Hut 25 they spoilt me like a baby. Here they hardly even look at me. I feel lonely. Yael must do something. She can work miracles. Yes, she can. She tries but it doesn't work. There is no way of making things easier for me. Nobody will be impressed if she tells them: see, gentlemen, my husband is wounded and cannot bear this racket. There are no special rooms marked "For the Privileged Only". Perhaps I'm only a grumbler. Why should I get special treatment? Maybe for Yael I am the whole world. For this institution called a hospital – I'm just a patient like any other.

So, there's nothing left but to be angry and nervous. I have no urge to hide what I feel. Yael is also annoyed, though she tries to conceal her anger and distract my attention.

Soon after I arrived in my new bed, two doctors appeared beside me: "I am Dr. Kuzari, head of the neurosurgical ward, and this is Dr. Bornstein, head of the plastic ward."

Charmed to meet you. They probe at my head and forehead. Perhaps you can tell me, gentlemen, what all this probing is about? No, they don't explain. It seems that they are discussing how to operate on my head, in order to remove the bone splinters that have penetrated the brain.

My head injury hasn't bothered me much. My other injuries have taken my attention away from the head. It hadn't troubled me especially, apart from the aesthetic defect caused by the deep furrow in my forehead.

It was only months later that one of the doctors would tell me, in a chance conversation, that the team believed that the pressure on my brain was causing intensified sensitivity to pains in my leg, and it was even possible that this injury caused the fogginess in which I found myself for at least a few hours every day.

While I didn't give much thought to the matter of a brain operation – Yael was very anxious.

Now, I was listening to doctors' conversation, a conversation in which the fate of my head was being decided. They agreed that the operation would take place on Monday. "Figaro", the Tel Hashomer barber, was ordered for Sunday, to shave my head in preparation. When they concluded their discussion, the doctors informed me that

I would be transferred from the operating theatre to Neurosurgical Hut 40. I was very pleased. I wanted to move to a new place. More than anything else, I wanted to abandon this terrible Hut 16. I didn't believe that anywhere else could be worse.

Enough. Enough of thinking about myself.

Must see who my neighbours are. I don't like Asher, who lies facing me. He kicks up an unbearable bedlam. Doesn't stop shouting, arguing with the nurses and bewailing his injuries. What's he got altogether? Lieutenant Colonel Chaim Tamir also lies facing me. Aggrieved face and amputated leg. Could be an ally of mine. He's also incapable of bearing the merry atmosphere of the hut.

I can't see the face of my neighbour to the right. A pitcher full of tall flowers separates us. When will visitors finally understand that you send flowers to maternity cases? There's no place for them here.

My neighbour's leg is in a cast. I can hear his voice. I make a note for myself: later, I'll try to match a suitable face to that voice.

Hey – look here: what's this? An installation or a man? Both. A strange mixture: a sort of large hanger on wheels. Like those you see in a barber's shop or a doctor's waiting room. There's a hand in plaster, not quite hanging, and not quite tied to the hanger. It belongs to a young dark-complexioned boy, who spreads smiles to right and left. Very cheerful. Strange. Who can decipher the stratagems of a hospital? They've probably mixed the psychiatric and the orthopaedic wards. Anyway, I will apparently also need the services of psychiatrists, if I stay here.

Sad. Friday night. There's no hint of Sabbath eve. Everything's normal. Like any other mundane week-day. Even those who aren't religious look for something special, something festive, as the Sabbath draws near. There's no difference between a week-day and a festival in hospital. The pyjamas are the same pyjamas, the nurses rush around as usual, the cleaning woman cleans the floor, and the food is as bland and dull as ever. This evening differs in one respect only: the hut is empty of visitors. They've all gone to their homes, families, Sabbaths.

The hut is silent. I'm overcome by a feeling of bitterness. The strains of an accordion, and of voices singing, can be heard from outside. A special appearance by a troupe of musicians. All patients and casualties capable of walking on their own feet, or moving in

95

wheelchairs, have been collected in the space between two huts. The distant strains only increase my bitterness.

The room remains quiet and somnolent. Nothing is said, except what is essential. It seems that not only I, but also my colleagues, are waiting for something to break the silence and the routine. Suddenly, a fresh, smiling and cheerful spirit bursts into the hut. A guitar over her shoulder, and freckles on her face. Nehama Handel.

Ah, Nehama, Nehama. If only you knew how you warmed our souls that bitter Friday night in July. What your voice and music did for us. You brought us the festive and the Sabbath. You helped us for a few moments to forget our daily sorrows. You stood in the middle of the hut and sang as though in front of an audience in a theatre. The first time in a long time I straightened up into a sitting position, so I could see you. Even after my pains got the better of me, and I lay back, I continued to listen in rapt attention. You finished. You were about to leave. I stopped you and said: "Thank you." You replied: "My pleasure", with a warm smile. You made our week-days into a Sabbath.

I was still pondering over Nehama's appearance, when two very welcome visitors arrived. Dina and Aharon Dolav. He is a quiet, serious boy, and I am grateful to him for having helped transfer me to Tel Hashomer. She is the opposite – bursting with life and energy under a crown of golden hair.

Before my injury, my relationship with Aharon was one of routine work. I had only seen Dina a few times. Since my injury – the two had displayed unqualified devotion. Aharon didn't miss a single visit. He made a habit of appearing in my room, even upon his return from long trips for his journalistic work. Often, Dina came with him and made me happy with her laughter, her light-hearted stories and cheerful and pleasant chatter. My wounded comrades recognised her and were also quickly spellbound by her stories. They soon began to ask me when she would come again.

This evening, Dina was also overflowing. I felt like a little boy thirstily drinking in tall tales. The clouds of gloom that covered my first day in Hut 16 were dispelled. We didn't sense the passing of time, until the nurse arrived to throw visitors out and turn off the light.

That same evening one of the wounded disclosed that our hut had once served as . . . a stable. Tel Hashomer's original purpose –

then it had another name – was as a rest home for soldiers who served in Palestine during World War II – so he told me. So that these soldiers wouldn't be bored, they brought riding horses here and housed them in this hut. "Now we are the duty horses," my neighbour said.

The appearance of the hut was indeed most miserable. The paint on the walls was peeling, and what remained – was very dirty. It did not have even the most elementary arrangements needed for the care of a patient. A night-bell to summon the nurse, for example. The ventilation was faulty, and by the early hours of night the vacuum of the room was full of heavy motionless air. More than thirty patients lay here, almost shoulder to shoulder. I wondered what the horses would have said if they had been packed in so closely.

12

Saturday. Late morning. Scores of visitors enter the hut. They crowd in around the beds. Standing. The few chairs in the hut have already been taken. The endless parade passes by my face. I can't even identify some of my visitors, since my acquaintanceship with them was brief and superficial. Nevertheless, when they heard of my injury – they bothered to come here. To say a good word, or even to stand and say nothing.

They didn't come specially to me. They came to the wounded. By chance they caught me. Perhaps we met once, or maybe they know my name from the pages of the paper. To the same degree they could have stood by the bed of any other casualty. I think they wanted to give me the feeling that I hadn't been abandoned.

The situation in the hut this morning is most amusing. Most of the patients are creating pandemonium as usual. The visitors, on the other hand, come in cautiously on tiptoe, the behaviour of healthy people who've fallen into the jaws of a hospital. When they encounter the great rejoicing and din of the hut, they're astonished. You can see that they are wondering how to behave. The expressions of participation in sorrow that they had fixed on their faces before entering, now seem a mockery.

As midday comes round I am completely washed out. Entertaining such a large number of people after a sleepless night, my last drop of strength ebbed away. What's better? Visitors or no visitors? On the one hand, to a certain extent they make me forget my bodily pains, but on the other hand they don't allow me even a moment of rest. There are times when I pray for them to leave me, and for tranquillity. I don't dare tell them this. My close friends berate me for this. It's your right – they say – to rest whenever you need rest. I nod my head as though agreeing with them, although of course I have no intention of behaving as they say. To be on the safe side I conclude with Yael that when I pinch her arm lightly, it's a sign that I have reached my furthest limit, and she should take on herself the unpleasant job of getting rid of the visitors. I don't remember that I made use of this code on any occasion.

"Relax the leg-muscles. Slowly-slowly, concentrate. Now the soles of your feet. Right, left. Relax your ankles, relax. Thighs. Now your knees. Go on. Right thigh, left thigh, pelvis, every muscle. You must concentrate as much as possible. Your belly. The whole length of your back. Each disc, one after the other, from the bottom to the top. Another disc, and another. Loosen every muscle, think about it – and loosen up. The chest. Breathe slowly, deeply, slowly. All your chest-muscles. Now – the neck . . ."

Gershon came at noon, when all the visitors had been cleared out. We decided to repeat the experiment of loosening up the muscles, which had almost succeeded before. Now, especially, I needed it: tired to death – but I know that I will be unable to sleep. Gershon's ponderous voice by my ear has an almost magic influence. He's hypnotising me. He succeeds in doing what I would never have believed could be done. The miracle is happening. The lower half of my body is relaxed, and the rigidity that oppressed the bones of my broken leg has slackened off. I almost don't feel it.

". . . Have you slackened your neck? We move to the palms of the hands. Right hand, the palm, the lower arm, the upper arm. Left hand, the palm, the lower arm, the upper arm. Slacken the jaw. It should drop downwards by itself. If you succeed in loosening up your whole body – perhaps you'll sleep. You want to sleep a lot, don't you? The muscles of the right cheek. Slowly, slowly, concentrate. The muscles of the left cheek. The forehead, back of the neck, your whole head. Now you are slack. Don't move a single muscle. You are loose, relaxed, loose."

Right, Gerhson! I am slack, slack, slack. Breathe quietly. My body seems to float. I don't feel pains. I breathe easily. The air is coursing through me. I've succeeded! I've succeeded!

"Yankele, Yankele! – get up!"

The cries pierce my dense and distant brain. As though they come from a long way off, beyond a thick wall. Somebody's calling my name, but I am sunk in deep sleep and cannot answer him. I also don't want to answer. It's good to sleep. It's good to be distant from everywhere. Not to be anywhere.

"Yankele. Yankele!"

Oh-ho! The boy's obstinate. Let him come later. Let him come tomorrow. And if he doesn't come at all . . . Now I feel good. Now I've got no time for him. If I wake up now, I won't be able to return later to the cotton-wool in which I'm sinking.

That's it! He's awakened me.

I slept well and deeply. There were a thousand layers of sleep – and I was below all of them. And there were no dreams. Not a single one. Nothing interfered. The torpor of a baby. But he, he had to come with the "Yankele – wake up." What does he want of me? What have I done to him? I will open my eyes. I mean, only one eye, because the second is bandaged. Why is it bandaged? What's happened to it? Who's calling me? Hallo, who's calling me?

It's . . . it's . . . it reminds me of the Vilan. Now the room is also revolving, like a big ferris wheel that spins in front of me at immense speed. No, not in front of me. Inside me. Stop! Stop! I'm your driver. I tell you to stop. That's better. It's slowing down.

I begin to discern shapes. They're unclear. They're blurred. I'm in Hut 16. Men are lying on the beds. This is a hospital. My eye is bandaged because I was wounded in battle. They're trying to rehabilitate it. That's why it's covered.

"Shalom, Yankele."

It's him again. The one who called me. I have difficulty in identifying him. It's not one. There are two of them. They didn't give me Vilan. Yet, I'm drunk. He is two. There's a man, and alongside him a woman with long hair. Hell, who are they? There's a bitter taste in my mouth. I slept. So what? A man sleeps a little – must he be so hazy? So, a man and a woman – a couple? A married couple? Why don't they lie down to sleep? It's Saturday afternoon! Why don't they lie together and enjoy themselves? After all, a man and a woman do sleep together occasionally, don't they? Be fruitful and multiply and fill the earth. Perhaps it's not a woman at all, but a man with long hair. Aaah, that means they're musicians! Let them dry up. Why did they wake me, in God's name, from such a pleasant and sweet sleep? . . .

"I'm sorry, Yankele, that we woke you. We've sat here for twenty-five minutes without disturbing you. We got short leave from the Heights, and felt we must visit you. The boys are worried about you, and hope that everything's turning out alright."

Now I know who you are. I recognized you by your voice. You are Aryeh Goldstone, my comrade from the company. I'm sorry that I thought what I did of you a moment ago. It was simply difficult to drag myself away from the good sleep. I slept so heavily. Yes, Aryeh, who's the girl next to you? Happy to meet you. Very happy. You talk to me, please. I'm not yet awake enough. What's going on up there, on the Heights? You're being screwed? When are they going to let you out? What time is it? What do you say! I slept so long?

Oh-ho, see who's come in. Almost the entire company. How are things with you, boys? How are our other casualties? What are you? Fools that you're wasting your leave on me? What's it like to look at the Hule Valley from the east?

Cora, the nurse, breaks through the wall of men, angry and excited: ". . . How can you fall on him like that? He's badly wounded. He must rest. Did you all have to come at once? Do you think he's got the strength to look at all of you and talk to all of you? I ask you to leave immediately. Within a minute."

O.K., Cora, O.K. I'm a little bit on your side in this. I really haven't got the strength. But these are my good friends. They're giving up valuable hours of leave to see me. You can't just drive them out like this. Give them a few minutes. No? O.K. – you're the boss. It's a pity. If I've already woken up, I could be with them for a little bit longer. At least with a few of them. So you're going back to the Heights? Give my regards to everyone personally. If by any chance you meet the teachers in Kiryat Shmoneh, to them too.

Hey, Cora! Don't be cruel. Let them answer . . .

They've gone. Driven out. Now I remain alone. Try to reconstruct the nice taste of sleep that Gershon gave me today.

13

For a few days, and especially nights, I play around with an idea that has come to mind: to write. By turns, I am enthused and then dejected, according to the mood of the moment. The war's over but everybody's still thinking about it and involved in it. There's almost no other subject that people talk about, at least those who stand by my bed. Most of the reserves haven't yet been released.

My colleagues, the journalists, visit me often, tell me that they're still working – as reservists or for the paper – writing about war subjects.

I was jealous of my colleagues. I was sorry that while everyone was writing about the war in which I was wounded, I was lying a helpless block of meat, without lifting a finger.

One sleepless night, in the thick darkness of the hut, I suddenly realised that I also have a story of my own. The story of a soldier wounded in the war. I knew they would write about the casualties, and try to picture their feelings, sensitivities and needs. But I had the great advantage of a journalist: personal impressions! I was lying on a bed and therefore – I was convinced – I could depict this subject directly.

I didn't know whether anybody would be interested in the story of how I was wounded. Perhaps people preferred the drunkenness of victory, without its by-product called: the price. I couldn't blame those of my acquaintances who, a long time after I left hospital, came in a self-justifying tone, and apologised for not having visited me: "We're not capable of seeing things like that. It shocks us . . ." I sincerely didn't get angry with them. Of course, I would have preferred them not to say what they did, because they forced me to put on a bright face and tell them hypocritically: "It's alright. I would probably have behaved just like you."

But, in the difficult and depressing atmosphere of Hut 16 I sought a lifeline. Something to grab hold of in order to escape the hostility that I felt for the small world of the hut. For the cheerful people who hurt me by their cheeriness. For the incompetent orderly who somehow could never succeed in placing the bandages over my eye. For the heavy depression that I felt from the moment I was brought into it.

That Saturday I resolved: the story will be written! I immediately told Yael, and she readily agreed. This was exactly what she had so desperately looked for: something that would draw me out of my introversion. In a flash she had a pen and paper in her hand: If you are unable to write – she said – you can dictate.

I was on my back with my eyes fixed on the ceiling, or perhaps not on it but rather on the fresh memory which had been completely retained in my brain. I dictated rapidly. The words flowed from my mouth as though ready and waiting for the moment when I would release them.

I suddenly felt my depression dropping away, and my bitterness at Hut 16 fading. I was totally immersed in dictation. My pains made themselves felt from time to time, and then I was forced to ask Yael to wait a while. Then I would close my eyes, clench the metal bed-posts and beg of my body that at least this time it would stop sending waves of pain through me for an hour or two.

I was restricted by the arrival of Saturday night visitors. As soon as they left I went on dictating to Yael. When I finished, I felt easier. The article I had written was like a valve which allowed me to release the pent-up steam inside. I didn't ask Yael to read it back to me. I was afraid I would find that it was bad. Osnat arrived. I asked her to read it. Osnat knows how to be critical. She is honest and doesn't hesitate to be destructive when it's necessary. If she was in favour, then it would be a good sign. If Aharon would come this evening, I would ask him to take it to the editorial board. If they want to – they'll print it. If they don't – too bad.

On Sunday Dr. Parin again came with his assistant, a young smiling doctor whose French origin could be seen in every gesture and expression. His name was difficult to pronounce – Dr. Oroshovsky or Choroshovsky.

Dr. Parin: "What's new, Yankele?"

I: "It hurts a lot, doctor. Especially down there, around the ankle. Perhaps you can do something so that the cast won't press?" I remember that I had another leg operation coming, and asked that it be done on the same day as my head operation. As they had done some time ago: a leg and eye operation together.

No, it wasn't possible. They checked. The senior surgeon didn't agree. A brain operation is too dangerous a matter to allow the "appendage" of a leg operation. Pity.

Meanwhile they must examine the reason for the terrible pain in my ankle. Dr. Parin bends over my leg. It seems to me that he is also sniffing, just like his predecessors. He pulls at the plaster with which they closed the "window" in the cast. My body was tense with dread, and my heart fluttering, simple as it sounds.

"No, doctor! I forgo it. There's no need. It doesn't really hurt me. I mean, it does hurt, a little, but it's alright like this. I don't want to scream again."

You miserable coward! He gives me a reassuring glance: "This time it won't hurt!"

I don't know whether to believe him. How can he prophesy how much it will hurt me. My pride is victorious. I hide my fears behind a smile. Draw courage from the expressions of the two doctors and the nurse, who stands by the trolley of bandaging materials. She is not indifferent. They smile and chatter amongst themselves light-heartedly. Yael is also standing by me this time.

The doctor ties a sterile mask over his face, lifts the window and puts a hand on a dressing that is stuck to the sore. Now is the most difficult moment. My body tenses up like a piano string. To be on the safe side, I grip the bed-posts. In a split instant Dr. Parin pulls at the dressing and tears it off the flesh. A terrible sharp pain passes through my body for a second. But the red dressing has already been thrown on the trolley. The doctor looks at the sore, cleans it with a caustic material and lays a new dressing on it. The window is closed – and it's over! "You see that it didn't hurt too much? We didn't do much, but we'll probably be able to ease it during the next operation. The important thing is that it didn't hurt too much now . . ."

I nod in agreement. My body is still tense and my muscles haven't yet slackened. The doctor kept his promise. What was this, the act of the true expert? Then why in the "screen incident" last time, did I feel as though all the devils of hell were prodding me with their pitchforks and beating me with their sledgehammers? What was the difference? The doctor's trained hands? His agility? His sensitivity? Perhaps the most important thing: his warm personal relationship?

Dr. Parin seeks my opinion: "And so, how would you define the treatment: terrible? Very painful? Just painful? Not at all?"

His terms offer insufficient choice. I look for another definition: "Let's make do with – felt!"

103

Man's ability to withstand pain never ceases to engage my thoughts. This is one of the greatest challenges that man can face up to. How strong is his spirit in overcoming his bodily and mental agonies? I would research this subject for many months to come. Mostly seeking the opinion of medical men and psychiatrists. First of all, I wanted to know how I had stood up to the test.

"The thing that differentiates us from the animals, is no more than a thin shell," Dr. Parin would tell me. "Very severe pains, the daze that follows sedation, break through this shell, and then we are no longer guided by the brain, but by our feelings, and especially by our instincts."

And a psychiatrist would tell me: "Pain is a subjective feeling, and it cannot therefore be measured in absolute terms. A man's reaction to suffering is the result of his education, culture, ability to control his feelings, customs and even his approach to life."

I was convinced that this was the truth. I have seen grown and strong men blanch with terror in the face of an injection. On the other hand, I have seen a man having his toe-nail pulled out without batting an eyelid.

Dr. Parin left with his assistant. I now felt well enough to ask my neighbour to remove the vase of flowers that separates us, so that I could see his face. He accepted the suggestion readily. The flowers also oppressed him. One of the visitors was asked to put the vase aside.

His name – the neighbour told me – was Jean Claude Melamed. A tank crewman. Gunner. His tank took a direct hit that penetrated his compartment. His leg was smashed.

We quickly found a common language and a sense of affinity. When I found out that he was a tank crewman, I already didn't see him as he now was, pale and in pain, in a blue pyjamas. My imagination fashioned him into his previous image: tank crewman's helmet on his head, grease and petrol-stained overalls, and a dusty face. I see him as a tank gunner, with two deep black pools around his eyes, the marks of the rubber telescope sight, with which you lay the gun. One of the boys.

He also found it difficult to bear the noise and uproar in the room. His leg was completely smashed. He apologised for the fact that every little movement of his caused pain to my leg. I responded with an apology in kind.

Jean Claude and I agreed that the hut was hell for the severely wounded, and an entertaining place for the convalescent. Asher, for example, is one of the few who can walk around freely and wash at the basin without needing a nurse, and can therefore allow himself to sing in a high voice, revile the nurses for not finding him a pyjama that flatters his figure, curse the chefs who "feed us stinking compost", and complain that the wound with which he was blessed wasn't . . . aesthetic.

Will I ever find myself in his shoes? Will I also have the strength to speak so much about things that now seem so unimportant? Will I be able to wash myself, feed myself and allow myself such a free attitude to the nurses? – I find it difficult to believe.

Morning. A man in a white gown comes in, a small suitcase in his hand. A nurse directs him to me with hand signals. The man comes over to my bed, pulls out a wide leather strip and attaches one end to the back of the bed.

He takes a small shining object out of the case. In one hand he holds it, and in the other grasps the end of the leather strip. No more than a second passes, and a shriek of agony escapes my lips, without my understanding why it hurts so much.

"Hey, Figaro! What are you doing to him? Are you mad? You're murdering him, man!" Asher, who is idly strolling between the beds, exclaims.

How do I look? I've never been shaved bald. I'm very curious – and the mirror's in my hand. To look or not to look? Curious, but also frightened. No! A moment. We'll wait a while. What are you afraid of, you fool? After all, you're as hideous as the Six Day War could have made you. Ha, bald! I threw the mirror away disgustedly. My hand darted for the drawer where I'd hidden the white cloth cap which they had once given me to hide some of my scars from my little girl. I covered my baldness with it. My shame. The cloth cap gave me back a little bit of my confidence. After all, it was better to look like a chef – and not a monster . . .

In my heart I prayed that visitors wouldn't come. For the first time I stopped seeing my injury as something self-explanatory. I was still wallowing in my sorrow, and now I could hear Jean Claude quietly proclaiming to me: "That's how it is. It takes one second to get hit – but you can suffer from it for months. Perhaps your whole life."

I quickly take hold of myself. Yael is smiling. She contends that baldness suits me. She's a good girl. Trying to encourage me. I'll co-operate with her. I respond with a smile, and we decide together that I should continue to have my head shaven from time to time.

Tami comes to visit. She's not happy with the hat on my head, and demands that I remove it. No, daughter. This time I refuse you. You've seen enough tough sights here. You're not going to see my scarred bald head today . . .

14

What's your opinion of the news this morning?

I am a journalist, and everybody is convinced therefore that I can evaluate news items. Which are reliable, and which should be taken with a pinch of salt. I'm in a good mood. I participate actively in the conversation.

Today we're discussing the question of withdrawal from the occupied territories, which is being demanded – so the journalists tell us – by our enemies in the UN. The air is filled with questions: What are we? Imperialists swallowing territories? A small state that set out to defend its existence? Of what importance are the discussions taking place in the United Nations? What happens to the large Arab population that has been added to Israel's borders?

We're holding a lively discussion, and my remarks are accorded special weight. I wend my way slyly through this conversation. The truth is that I haven't read a newspaper for weeks. I don't listen to the radio. All that I know is absorbed from snatches of conversation between visitors around my bed.

We're still chatting, when my eyes catch sight of the bright lights of the operating theatre hanging over my head. I'm astonished: God above, in a short while they're going to carry out an operation on my brain. They're going to pierce it and probe it; I face the danger of death or madness. And meanwhile we are placidly discussing political problems.

Yesterday my friends' parting from me was almost routine. Almost. I saw the anxiety in their eyes. I knew: this time they're going home, nursing a grain of fear for my fate. It seems to me that even the nurses are more friendly in their behaviour to me. In preparation for this operation – the seventh or ninth or tenth – all were more tense than usual, and especially Yael, who would turn to stone every so often.

Everybody was afraid – except me. From whence complacency? Had I become too stupid and dimwitted to understand the full significance of what awaited me? Or was this another heritage of my indifference to my head wound, which had never bothered me as much as my other injuries?

What's happening here? Am I the one who's lying on the operating table? I carry on a light banal conversation with Dr. Kuzari, Dr. Feinsod's assistant and Adina, the nurse. What's happening here? My second identity, the one that watches events as though from the outside – is astonished. The operating theatre always appeared a mysterious place to me. Frightening, dangerous. Today I see it with different eyes.

I examine the room carefully. On the wall, facing me, is an illuminated X-ray of my skull. The surgeons will be assisted by it during the operation. Alongside the table where I lie there is another table for the tools of the trade: the instruments, the scalpels, the sutures, bandages, and other paraphernalia. I will soon be dazzled. They'll turn on the lights above my head. They'll stick a needle in my vein. I'll fall asleep.

I was given sedatives before I left Hut 16. I can already feel their influence. Dr. Feinsod, a young friendly boy with a hedgehog haircut, looks at me out of the corner of his eye. He proclaims with a smile: "A little scared, eh?"

"Why should I be?" I respond insulted. "Of course not! I rely on you."

The needle goes in. "Good night." "Thank you." I dive into the pleasant anaesthetic sleep, but manage to note to myself that, by comparison with the other huts, the operating theatre has an advantage: it is equipped with air conditioning and kept at a pleasant coolness.

I'm suffocating! It's the end! I should have known that this would be the end. I'm suffocating! I've got no air to breathe! My hands are heavy and I can't move them above my throat. Something's blocking the air there. I'm going to another world. A brain operation. They did a brain operation on me. You can die of it. I've got no air! No air! If only I could shout so that somebody would hear. My voice has betrayed me. This is exactly how you die of suffocation. They suffocated me. This is how I felt when I was once tugged into a whirlpool in the sea, and almost drowned. I'm going to die. I'm afraid. I don't want to die. Something's blocking my throat, like a cork. I can't cough it up. I can't see anything. Darkness.

Aaaah . . . Aaaah . . . aaaah . . . aaaah . . . Air. There is. They pulled out the cork. I can breathe! I can breathe! I'm saved! Safe! (Days later, I would discover that the feeling of suffocation was caused by tubes placed in the throat to ensure regular breathing. In my case, they were late in taking them out – and when I awoke from the operation, the tubes caused suffocation.) My body eases up. Ugh! How frightened I was. I can already hear faint voices around me. It's cool here. They're calling me by name. Should I open my eye? Perhaps they need me. Two faces bend over me. Smiling. I know you. They ask me to tell them their names. Why do they want me to name them? Don't they know? I mumble with difficulty: "You're called Dr. Kuzari. You, Dr. Kuzari, operated on me. And you – Misha." What is it? Why are you smiling. He's called Misha. That's his name. Perhaps they don't know: in the hospital he's known as Dr. Moshe Rakovchik, head of the urological ward. He's a friend of the family. We call him Misha. They think that I didn't recognise him. It's very cold. How cold. This air conditioning can freeze a man.

Why did I have to identify you? Why did you ask me for your names? A moment! I'm beginning to understand: a brain operation. When you perform an operation – how cold it is – a man's senses can leave him. O.K., mine haven't left. I recognised you. Thank you, nurse, for covering me with a blanket. I'm very cold and tired. I'm very cold and tired. They take me from here to some other place. Let them take me. I'm already asleep . . .

Where am I? Strange place! I've never been here. Nurses rushing up and down. People lying, like me, on stretchers. Almost all are sleeping. Where am I? Excuse me, hey nurse, what is this place? "Here," she says, "this is the recovery room." Thank you.

Nurse! Wait! Don't go away. Please, don't go away. Give me your hand. Your hand's warm. I'm like a baby, I need your hand. You seem to me tall and smiling. Tell me something. Why are you smiling? I'm wounded, did you know? From the war. I took a couple of bangs . . . My wife, my wife. She's waiting outside. Worrying. I've got a cute little daughter, Tami. I saw toys in the entrance to the operating theatre. It's strange, isn't it? Why toys in the operating theatre? My daughter's called Tami. I already said so? She's very cute. Comes to visit me and gets frightened, poor thing. In the beginning, she didn't quite recognise me. A lot of people died in the war. A hell of a lot. When I will be fit and well, we'll have a brother for Tami. We'll call him Uri. Uri? – yes, I'm sure we'll call him that. It's a nice name. No! It won't be a daughter! We've already got one, and now we need a son. Hey, where are you going?

Pity she left.

15

I fell asleep again – and when I awoke, I found myself in a small room with three beds. I'm in the middle. Wonderful! What a difference. Compared with Hut 16. Nobody's screaming and there are no transistors booming. It seems to me that Aharon Dolav is in the room. Yael is discussing flowers with him. Yes, he's going to get them. Same as always after sedation. Sleep, awake, mumble something! And sleep again . . .

"Yael, I'm hungry!"

She smiles. What's amusing her? Her man is simply hungry.

"There's no food now," she says.

Great pity, because my stomach's rumbling. "There's no food in the entire hut? Nothing?"

She smiles. I'm tormented by my hunger.

"Hey, I know! There are some biscuits in our car. We once took them for Tami to chew on the road. They remained there, I think. Bring a few. Why are you laughing?"

Yael was content. Hunger is a good sign. But after an operation, and especially a brain operation, they don't allow food. Yael doesn't need to go to much trouble to make me forget my appetite. I sink again into sudden sleep. When I awoke, for God knows which time, Yael gave me a note from a member of my company, Gershon Cooper, who had come to visit me: "At long last, *Ma'ariv* has a journalist with an open mind . . ."

I laugh and fall asleep.

They check my pulse, blood pressure and temperature every half an hour or so. I'm burning. The first time since I was wounded, the mercury in the thermometer climbs above 101. Yael is anxious. I'm sleepy.

I'm not comfortable. They forbade me to put a pillow under the head, and forbade me to move it right or left.

When Dr. Kuzari comes back from the operating theatre, he will summon Yael to his room. He will explain to her what they did to me. There was a bone splinter in my brain – and they removed it. They also straightened, as far as possible, the skull bones that had sunk inwards when they broke. As far as can be seen now, everything is O.K. and there's nothing to worry about. No. He regrets they didn't keep the splinters. He threw them away. Yael is sorry. She wanted to add them to the rich collection that we now own.

She calmed down after her conversation with the doctor. Now she could reassure the visitors flowing into the hut, who were not allowed to enter my room, and those who were phoning all the time to ask how I was.

A cool hand comes to rest on mine. The pleasant touch awakes me. Who is it? My eyes open with difficulty. I identify the editor of the paper, Aryeh Disenchik. He says: "Shalom, Yaacov, it's Chik." No words come out of my mouth. As he reaches the door to the room, on his way out, I manage to murmur a weak "Shalom" to his back.

A few hours later I awoke. In the darkness of the room – only a weak light penetrates from the corridor – I distinguish the figure of a man slumped on a chair by my bed. I ask him what he's doing, and he explains that he was summoned to keep a private watch over me. He is a medical student and sometimes medical orderly. After difficult operations the patient must be watched over constantly. From time to time he checks my pulse and blood pressure.

Our sparse conversation is joined by Lulak, my neighbour to the right. He was also operated on today. We chat leisurely. I suddenly want a cigarette. I remember that somewhere, sometime during the day, I heard a doctor's voice, or perhaps Yael's, forbidding smoking. But the lust is greater than logic. And not only mine. Lulak also wants to smoke. The orderly hears our conversation, and declares that under no circumstances will he allow us to put a cigarette in our mouths. We decide to boycott him. Lulak surreptitiously passes me a lighted cigarette. We both enjoy a concealed smoke, while revelling in the deception. Stolen waters are always sweeter.

110

The night passes slowly. The leg – thank God – isn't causing any bother. And when Yael comes, at dawn, I receive her brightly. I feel as though a ton has been added to the weight of my head. It's also buzzing in a constant monotone. But apart from that I feel good here. A silence that revives souls. Only, I can't understand why a fast is decreed for patients in this ward. Yael informs me that I will be receiving no solid food for a few days. When during the late morning hours they bring me a plate of yoghurt, I fall on it ravenously. And, of course, remain hungry. Dr. Kuzari makes his first visit just before noon. He doesn't stop by me. It's still too early to take the turban of dressings off my head. He is followed by the first visitors. Shalom Rosenfeld from *Ma'ariv*. He, Chik and other *Ma'ariv* people worry about me as though I was their son. He brings me the Life edition on the war. He tells me that it contains a vast treasury of combat photos from the six days – but meanwhile I'm incapable of even glancing at them.

In the evening Yael introduces me to Avramiko. Private watchman. Why are they giving me such a watchman on the second night after the operation? Nobody tells me. The truth: the boys from *Ma'ariv* "seduced" Yael into resting at least at night. They took care to have somebody to fill her place.

I silently follow Avramiko's movements. He's wandering around the room as though it belongs to him. He's only just come in, and he's already begun to make changes: he's getting rid of the fruit and flowers. "So that there should be a little air here." He washes my face and body. He orders me to put the cigarette out, because if I don't "he will finish me off". The boy's tough . . . The room sparkles with cleanliness. I am exhausted and too puzzled to explain to myself why, for God's sake, do I obey him in such abject surrender?

Less than an hour passes before I get to like Avramiko. It's not difficult to see that he's carrying out his task devotedly. His job doesn't require him to clean the room, to wash me and take care of me. His duty is limited to careful watch over my state of health – and calling a night nurse if something happens. He chats with me lightly, and even occasionally sprinkles some cologne over my face, "to freshen you up".

We while away a whole night together. I'm grateful to him for not only looking after me, but giving the same degree of attention to

Lulak. It's not pleasant to be privileged. This time Lulak and I don't succeed in deceiving him over a cigarette.

In the morning, he compels me to shave, picks up the sponge and washes me thoroughly, as no nurse has ever done. Yael will have a pleasant surprise when she arrives soon. I almost don't feel anything when he changes the bedding under my body, by himself. This job is usually done by two or three nurses, and then less successfully. I like the look of this guy. He's not the sort of worker who is always looking at his watch. The end of his shift comes and goes, and he's still hanging around looking for things to do, so that my day should be more pleasant. Yael turns up and makes morning tea for us.

At five in the morning Dr. Kuzari comes into the room. He hints to Yael and Aliza – Lulak's wife – to leave the room. We fall silent. Even Avrom our neighbour, who hasn't stopped chattering, falls silent.

Today they take off the dressings for the first time. Dr. Kuzari and Dr. Feinsod unravel the bandages from my head. They bend over the forehead, and mutter something in a satisfied tone of voice. The implication – there's no infection. "Ether," the doctor ordered. It must be cleaned. Brrr! The ether is as cold as ice and burns like acid. My face screws up and the shriek of pain is choked in my throat. A cute young nurse stands to my right. Her name is Yael Zulser. Her eyes wrinkle up as she watches my agony. Something unexpected is happening here. Her hand whips out over mine, takes hold and grasps tightly. The wave of warmth across my chest was enough to melt the burning ice of the ether. I tried to catch her eyes to express something of my gratitude. Her eyes were downcast.

Meanwhile, the doctors finish treating the wounds, and wind on the bandages again. Dr. Kuzari says with a smile that my brain is "completely alright". I turn to him and ask him as "one man to another", to co-operate with me and warn my wife that "because of the operation, it is absolutely forbidden to annoy me henceforward, because it may damage my brain". He refuses. "Whose side are you on, doctor?" I toss at him . . .

Avrom is drowning in a sea of hair. His thick beard flows out over his chest. Tangled ear-locks mingle in the long beard. The hair on his head, on the other hand, is almost completely shaven. He is a member of a religious settlement, who was called up for reserve duty as a cook or kashrut supervisor. While travelling on a command car he met with an accident in which he was seriously wounded. At first he was in such great danger that they didn't believe that he could live. Yet, Avrom was amongst the lucky ones. He is the veteran in our room. He lies on my left and talks non-stop. He's not even silent when he falls asleep. His appearance and longwindedness, which is more a muttering in his beard than real speech, entertain us. We tease him and he easily falls into the traps that we lay for him.

The first few days he made things difficult, because he demanded that I look at him when he was talking to me. I did so out of politeness, but turning my head towards him increased the buzzing and ringing in my ears. I finally had no alternative but to stage a heavy attack of "headache". This was the only way to convince him that I could hear him without looking at him.

Avrom doesn't stop marvelling at two things: the miracle that saved him from almost certain death, and the fact that his wife is about to give birth. In my naïvety, I was convinced that he was talking about a first child. When he heard this thought, he burst out into hearty laughter. We already have five. So why? You must rejoice over every additional child that the Lord, blessed be He, brings into the world, as though it is the first.

He is the only one amongst us who can walk. Throughout the daylight hours he scampers back and forth to the kiosk at the gate of the hospital to buy delicacies for us in honour of the anticipated happy event. We eat little. And are compelled to refuse. We can't eat much. He is insulted. He turns aside and falls silent. After a few minutes he softens and tries to tempt us again with the delicacies that are piled up on our table: "Eat, eat something." Then we have no alternative but to urge him to rush and to phone, from the nurses' station, to the hospital where his pregnant wife is awaiting to give birth. "You should. Perhaps there's news." Avrom is tempted and rushes out. We feel for him that he can't stand beside his wife, but are also a little happy. At least he'll let us rest for a while . . .

16

They've come back. Exactly at eleven o'clock they sent their first emissary. He approached hesitantly, like a spy, feeling his way and when he found me unprepared, rapidly set to work. I felt as though my body was being torn to pieces. My hands of their own volition reached for the bedposts and gripped tightly.

What was that? In the name of God, what was that. Why all of a sudden? After such a respite.

The first pain rushed back and crowed to his comrades: "You can come!" And they came. One after the other, cruelly and constantly. One goes and another comes . . .

The lulls are mere bridges of terror and anticipation: "They'll be back straightaway!" I'm afraid. Afraid to breathe, to move. Only to grasp the bedposts with all my strength; to tear them out of their sockets!

Don't scream! Don't shout! I have pains like a woman in labour. I'm not a woman – and therefore I won't scream. Tears well up in my eyes. Should I turn my head to the cupboard so that they won't see me in my agony? No, Lulak. I don't need anything. Nothing. Don't call the nurse. Don't do anything. It will pass soon. And don't look at me. No – go to hell, Avrom, I don't need anything! Why don't you leave me alone? Hell, Avrom, leave me alone!

The pain slowly dies down. The attackers have retreated. It's still difficult to breathe. I'm exhausted and will soon sleep . . .

Forbidden to smoke! But we're dying for a cigarette. We can't deceive our lusts. But the doctor – that's another thing. In the morning he did indeed catch Lulak and me sinning, and warned us that God help us if he catches us again. He even asked Yael and Aliza, Lulak's wife, to inform on us if we don't obey his orders. "I'll know how to punish them."

The only lesson that we learnt from this incident was that we must simply increase our wakefulness, so that Dr. Kuzari won't trap us again. Each time we light a cigarette, Lulak takes responsibility for "the corridor sector" that faces the door of the room. I supervise the "window sector", from which we can see anybody coming towards the hut. Each time we discern the figure of the doctor, we rush to stub out the cigarettes and scatter the smoke with our hands. Even Yael was trained to co-operate, after she despaired of getting me to give up smoking. We have a password. When she says "Kuzari's casting an eye" – it means: Danger threatens.

17

Two events excited me today:

My wife's class from school visited the hospital. Yael had abandoned them, following my injury, before the end of the school year. The kids recruited a number of parents with cars, and came in a big gang to the lawn beside the hut. They brought me a present – a flower-pot – and Yael placed it on the window sill. All the windows of the hut look alike from outside. Now the flower-pot was the trademark of our room, so that she could look through the window as she came to me in the morning.

Later, Yechiel Avraham – Abrasha, my tank driver, arrived. This was the first time that one of my crew had come to visit me. He hobbled into the room leaning on a cane. I turned puzzled eyes on him. I didn't remember that he had been wounded. Since my hospitalisation I have been cut off from the crew and have heard no news of them.

Abrasha sat on a chair by my bed and turned a sad look on me. He was silent for a moment and then decided: "Do you know, the important thing is that you're alive!"

Why did he choose that as an opening for conversation? I smiled at him: "Why all of a sudden do you say that now? I've been fit and well for some time."

He sadly shook his head: "Nobody saw you in the state I did. It was terrible."

Again I look at him curiously. I don't remember that we met after I was hit. But now he will reveal to me – in his simple way – details that I hadn't known up to now:

"I didn't sense you were wounded. I didn't know anything at all. I continued to drive along the path that you told me to stick to. After a few minutes, I was puzzled by the fact that I didn't hear your voice. I looked back to the turret compartment and saw that Shimon Epstein, the gunner, and Albert Sarosi, the loader-radio operator weren't inside. I didn't understand what had happened. It was difficult to see anything because the turret was dark. I suddenly noticed your legs. The trousers were red with blood. I stopped the tank. I knew: you had been wounded and perhaps even killed. I couldn't grasp what had happened to Albert and Shimon. I opened the driver's compartment and climbed out. What I saw outside was

– horrible! The Syrians kept on pounding away at our tank. I jumped out quickly. I saw you lying on the turret, as though dead."

Abrasha is about thirty. Father of two children. He looks Slavic and talks a lot about Bulgaria, his homeland. I liked him best of the tank crew, because he was the most energetic and stable among them. During the long days of waiting, he talked a lot to me about his troubles. His profession – frame carpenter for construction concrete. During the boom he had got himself deep in debt by buying a new flat ("to build only for others – it's not good, it's not. You must build for the wife and children as well"). Along came the slump, and his source of income dried up. I tried to console him. I told him that the slump is a passing phase, and that if he is a good trades man – as he says he is – he will manage.

I hoped that after our release I would be able to use my contacts to find him a decent place of work.

He now sat and told me.

"I knew I must get you out of there. Because if you're not already dead – you would be killed within seconds by the bullets that were striking the tank all the time. I called out: 'Yankele'. You didn't answer. I ran over to the machine-gunner's compartment and shouted to Yoram Amram that he should come out quickly, to help me get you out of the tank. I left him down below. I climbed up and began to drag you out. To this day I don't understand where I found the strength to lift you. You didn't co-operate and didn't say a word. You were soaked in blood.

"Amram was waiting on the ground. Meanwhile, the equipment on the outside of the tank began to burn. I was afraid that we would also catch fire. I told Amram that we must hurry. The two of us dragged you a safe distance away from the tank. We laid you on the ground and took the steel helmet and tanker's helmet off your head. What we saw underneath was so terrible that we decided there was no point in bandaging your head, and that it would be best to leave the helmet in place. We also returned our first-aid kits to our pockets. We didn't know what to do, and we lay down beside you.

"Heavy fire from light weapons and mortars was dropping on us all the time. Perhaps also artillery. But we had nowhere to run to. I suddenly heard terrible thunder. A mushroom cloud of smoke spurted up two yards away from us. It happened so quickly. I felt something tear into my knee, and began to scream. A second later you were also screaming. This was the first sign that you were alive.

"I didn't know what was happening to me or what I was doing. I began to walk. I don't remember where. My ears were buzzing. What happened to you, I don't know. I was certain that you would die."

Many days passed before he heard that I was alive. He was hospitalised in Nahariya. He'd only just been released and allowed to walk. He came to visit me a short time after returning home.

He shrugged his shoulders: "I'll no longer be a frame carpenter. I can't climb the scaffolding. The important thing is that we came out of it alive. What will happen now? – let's wait and see. We'll manage somehow."

Abrash arose and left. I needed a visit like this. Before I had managed to digest it, Micha and Riba arrived carrying a fan. They heard yesterday from Yael that I was suffering from the heat, and rushed to borrow a fan for me. The devotion of our close friends was so great that Yael and I simply decided not to mention in their presence the things that we lacked. Odeda and Bubi once heard that the cleaning woman had broken the thermos in which Yael brought me cold water. They immediately went out and bought one with their own money. Alexander Rabin once saw that I had run out of matches. The following day, he pulled an expensive lighter out of his pocket. This kind of attention moved us deeply.

Close to five in the afternoon I was again in the throes of an attack of pain similar to the one that had battered me in the morning. This time, Yael was beside me. I squeezed her hand tightly. A quarter of an hour passed. The pain weakened.

Avramiko came again in the evening. Like yesterday – the epitome of efficiency. His hands were not still for a moment and, of course, neither his tongue. He thoroughly checked the temperature and pulse chart that was hanging on my bed, washed, cleaned and in the midst of all this told us about his dog and pressed Yael to go home.

And to me – "Have you got your pills?" "Have you had a bowel movement?" "Can I bring you something?" "Listen, I don't like the look of your face, it looks just as though we didn't shave you this morning." "Perhaps we'll change your bedding?" "No, I'm not prepared to bring you another Optalgin. You'll get drunk on them finally. Too many drugs – it's not healthy! Better that you overcome the pains without using them." "You're wheezing from cigarettes. You smoke too much – you're not going to get even one from me this evening."

At night I'm very tired. As usual, I don't sleep. Insomnia continues to besiege me. Avramiko rose from his chair and promised me "the best possible thing for sleeping". He returned to the room with a pill in his hands: "Listen. If you don't sleep with this – then you're not a human being. This is a bomb! Not just a pill." I swallow the pill and thank him gratefully. After a few moments I drop into a deep sleep from which I awake only a few hours later.

"That wasn't bad. Where did you get the pill?" I asked him when I awoke.

He shrugged his shoulders: "Professional secret. I won't tell you."

It was only after a few months that I discovered his "professional secret". Avramiko simply deceived me. He didn't give me a sleeping pill, but a vitamin tablet! No more and no less! . . .

Since we were awake, it was possible to organise a tea party in which Lulak also participated. We didn't share with Avrom. He was, as usual, deep in the sleep of the just. By the light of the torch in his hand, Avramiko's eyes seemed bloodshot and tired. I encouraged him to go out of the room and rest for a while on an empty bed. He refused. For as long as I am awake he is beside me, ready to lend an attentive ear, as well as to fetch drugs and sleeping pills. Night nurses, taking a few moments off from their work, occasionally join in our party.

In the morning Yael went to see to Dr. Kuzari. She demanded that an orthopaedic surgeon visit me. The treatment of my head was devoted, but in our opinion the leg was being neglected.

Dr. Kuzari agreed with her and invited an orthopaedic surgeon. Hours passed, and he didn't come. I went through the morning attack of pain. I would certainly not agree to another attack like this without the help of sedation.

Meanwhile Dr. Kuzari had finished his business and left the ward. Yael went in a towering rage to search for an orthopaedic surgeon in the various wards of the hospital. It was difficult to find them. Eventually she met Dr. Parin, and told him what was going on. He mentioned the name of a strong drug that I could take to silence the pains. Yael returned to the ward and approached the ward sister. The sister shrugged her shoulders: she is not permitted to do anything without a personal order from Dr. Kuzari, who had already left the hospital.

According to hospital rules, only the ward doctor is allowed to give a "drug prescription". On the other hand, in my particular case the ward doctor is unable to do so too, because he deals with my head and not my leg wounds. Dr. Kuzari cannot write a prescription for a sedative, because he isn't an orthopaedic surgeon; Dr. Parin cannot order the ward sister to give me the drug, because she takes her orders only from her ward doctor. The situation is even more complicated because both doctors have already left the hospital, and can't even deliberate together.

Fortunately a friend who is also a senior staff doctor came to visit. Yael asked him to influence the nurse. At first he refused. It isn't allowed. Finally he agreed and the nurse condescended "on your personal responsibility".

The injection had a beneficial effect. The evening attack wasn't so serious. As it waned, I could good naturedly accuse Nurse Cora, who had come to visit me, for having abandoned me: She hadn't transferred with me to Hut 40, as I claimed she should have done.

A day after the affair of the sedatives, Dr. Ernest Shapira, head of the orthopaedic ward, came to visit. His visit was preceded by a long, detailed conversation between him and Yael, the contents of which I would only know after a few days. I received him with joy, but he responded with a sombre look and opined that the leg injury was so serious that it wasn't possible to ease the pains. I must bear them until the operation, which will take place when Dr. Kuzari decides that I am ready.

All that could be done meanwhile: sleeping pills. The pills helped me to sleep three or four hours each night. The remainder I would spend smoking or light-heartedly chatting with the nurses. At first, they always pretended to be angry: "You should sleep, shouldn't you?" But after a few minutes, they were already so deep in conversation with me that they would provide a cup of tea or something to nibble.

Ten days after the brain operation, Dr. Kuzari rolled off the bandages, pulled out the stitches, and said cheerfully: "From my point of view, you are almost well." I was glad to hear it. I was pleased. The turban was removed from my head and replaced by a small dressing that covered only my forehead. I happily felt the stubble that was beginning to grow on my bald head. After a few seconds

119

I was again in the throes of terror: if I'm already healthy from Dr. Kuzari's viewpoint – I will be returned into the hands of the orthopaedic surgeons. If I'm returned to them – they'll transfer me into that terrible Hut 16. It will kill me. I begged Dr. Kuzari not to send me out of his ward, at least – not before the operation that was planned for my leg. He smiled and said: "I'll see what can be done."

A few days later it became clear that he had indeed taken pity on me and left me in Hut 40, though I should have been returned to Hut 16.

I urged Yael to bring *Ma'ariv* from the kiosk. I longed to know whether they had published my story about the injury. Yael brought the paper – with the story headlined "Thus I Was Injured". I was very happy. It was good to see my name at the top of a newspaper column. Five weeks had passed since the day I was called up for reserve service. And now I was again a *Ma'ariv* correspondent. As usual. At least, almost as usual...

My mother-in-law almost broke down under the burden of the many phone calls that Friday and the coming days. In one single day she recorded that she took sixty-three phone calls. People read the article and on impulse phoned to express their opinions. Others, among my more distant acquaintances, only heard about my injury for the first time from the article.

These telephone calls were no more than a prelude to the scores of letters which began to pour in from strangers and acquaintances, who folded into their letters much love and anxiety for the wounded of the Israeli Army.

The nurses began to grow accustomed to my light-headed attacks and chatter. These attacks manifested themselves when I wasn't besieged by pain. I even succeeded in astonishing Nurse Lisette: as she was giving me an injection, I declared that it wasn't antibiotics that I needed but wine, women and song. The nurse, of English origin and educated to good manners and restrained behaviour, for a moment froze. In Hut 40 patients do not often come out with declarations like that. She recovered, put on a stern face and said that at best she could do something about the wine. As for the dance, she wasn't convinced that I could dance well enough for her – this with a glance at my leg. Women – she wasn't the one to solve that problem. She was now on duty – and regulations forbade ...

In the afternoon I was visited for the second time by my friend

120

Major Yigal, who was then serving in Hebron. It is common knowledge that a brain operation is very dangerous. Apart from that, the terrible scenes in the hut were enough to augment his anxiety. Yigal's astonishment was immense when he found the patient singing at the top of his voice.

I was singing simply because I didn't have anybody to talk to. I was overcome by a strange desire at the time. Any inhibitions my tongue might have had loosened up and I couldn't stop talking day or night. When Yigal – a man with a pair of ears – came in, I had found a perfect victim. After the exchange of the usual courtesies, my tongue embarked on a long stream of pointless remarks, which I couldn't control. I was as though drunk.

I made a speech about the important fact that "Hebron has another name. A name that for the moment I cannot remember. My forgetfulness is completely justified. The circumstances in which I now find myself give me the right. In my state, I'm not obliged to remember everything. I'm allowed to forget. I'm prepared to bet any amount of money in the world that Yigal, a man now serving in the town called Hebron, which as I already said has another name – can't answer this difficult question. Is he prepared to be the second party to this bet? No. He's not prepared. That's what I thought. Hebron has another name, and the faster he checks out this puzzle, the better it will be. This phenomenon only goes to prove that the average Israeli's knowledge of the geography and history of his country is astoundingly wanting. All the People of Israel should be ashamed. And especially so my friend Yigal who is serving in Hebron. I am embarrassed for him. I placed such high hopes on him. No? He doesn't remember? What is the other name? Why then had his parents endured such financial hardships to send him to school, if he hadn't learnt anything? What did he know if not the other name of Hebron? The town where the patriarchs are buried. Kiryat Arbah? Yes! That's it! Kiryat Arbah! I remembered. I remembered – not him. Kiryat Arbah – that's the other name for Hebron . . ." And so on and so on.

I noticed the expressions flickering over my friend's face. Now I also know what he must have been thinking during those moments. The joy with which he had heard me singing when he came was now replaced by wonder. The wonder – by astonishment. The astonishment – by shock, and the shock – by pity: the boy's going mad.

Yigal parted from me sadly, even though after the opening diatribe I had subdued myself and conversed more conventionally with him.

18

Sabbath Eve. Night has already cloaked the hut. The visitors have all gone. In our little dark room, Aliza, Lulak's wife, and Yael still remain. The two couples speak quietly, each engrossed in their own affairs.

That same evening, a special atmosphere pervaded the hut. Hut 40 had never been a hub of vitality or noise, but tonight it seemed as though even the nurses were walking on tiptoe. Outside the hut, through the windows, no movement could be discerned and no voice heard.

Suddenly one of us began to hum a tune to himself. Someone else joined in, and another, and another. Within seconds all four of us were singing. With gusto, though in low voices. And there was, in this soft, vibrant communal singing, an uplifting of spirits.

We sang intently. We held onto each word and bar of music with our very souls. Without sensing it, our voices gained force. The nurses hastened to the door of the room, and looked at us with astonished eyes: singing had never been heard in Hut 40. Instead of reprimanding us for causing a disturbance, they joined us in humming the tune.

Very late at night. Lulak and my new neighbour to the left (Avrom had been released and returned to his family) are snoring faintly. I peer into the dark. The wonderful flavour of the song had not yet left me.

As I lie alone in bed, I ponder what it is exactly that gives a song the deep force and power of expression? I have recently stopped telling Yael about my agony. Instead, I sing about it. I borrow a tune from one of Naomi Shemer's songs, like "My Soldier's Come Home", and add my own words: "Yael, Yael, Yael; it hurts me terribly. Hoy, hoy, terribly; what what what what; what what what what; what to do? this lousy leg; this lousy leg I hate it!".

And so on and so forth. Yael's answer, with a sad smile, is that I am out of tune as usual.

122

"Say mother, Uri, say mother."

A woman's voice coming from the nearby room tears at my heart. I know that this is no young mother teaching her baby child to speak. The speaker is Uri Rosenman's mother, and he is already past twenty.

"Say mother, please, Uri, say mother."

Uri Rosenman can't say "mother". He is silent. He can't speak. He is barely able to move, as he drags one leg behind him, with his hand limp at his side.

I sometimes see him hobbling along the corridor. Sadness and despair never leave his dark eyes.

A bullet in his head during a battle in the Gaza Strip, and he was brought to hospital unconscious and paralysed. After Dr. Kuzari operated, he regained consciousness, but seemed to refuse to establish contact with the world around him apart from a wave of the hand that indicated: "let me be".

It was difficult to feed him, wash him and change his clothes. It seemed as though nothing would redeem Uri. Nevertheless, they did not give up. They had to move his body to prevent its deterioration. The burden of treatment of this paralysed and dumb youngster was placed on Micky Cohen, the physiotherapist. She couldn't raise any reaction either. Uri fixed her too with his bemused look. But she stuck to her guns and, during her visits, kept up long monologues with him.

One day he surrendered. With her help, he rose from his bed, put his healthy leg on the floor, and then something happened that astonished Micky: the paralysed foot somehow reached the floor. Uri stood on his two legs.

His face remained expressionless.

After many exercises in bed over the course of a few days, she dared to place him between two parallel bars, and tried to make him walk as his healthy hand held one of the bars. Uri, supported by Micky and the bar, stuck his healthy leg out. The physiotherapist pushed the paralysed leg, and – he walked! They repeated the exercise a few times.

Micky was encouraged – and Uri silent.

They kept up these exercises for a few days – and then, wonder of wonders: before entering the parallel bars with her assistance, he released himself for a moment from her grasp, and took one step without her pushing the paralysed leg. Only one step – and no more. A partially paralysed man – walked!

This paralysed boy who had drawn a screen between himself and the world around him could not express his emotion in words. He burst out crying, heaving sobs that wracked his whole body, and did not quieten down for an hour.

The details of this event were known instantly throughout the hut. The astonishment was general.

Micky exceeded the obligations of her work – motory movement. She wanted to stimulate him. During each visit she tried to break the silence that he had enforced on himself. She appealed to him, almost begged him to say something. "Yes", "No", "Mother", "Father", "Shalom".

And as time passed she sensed that Uri too wanted to speak. But he couldn't. The speech centre in his brain was damaged. His throat only emitted stifled sounds. But Micky and others, in particular his mother, who never dropped the encouraging smile from her face while close to her son, did not despair. Again and again they begged, cajoled and pleaded: "Try to talk! Say something! Try!"

"No!"

Was it the long hand of coincidence that the first word broke out of his lips in Micky's presence? She doesn't remember what brought out the forceful "No". Her astonishment at hearing it rung down a curtain of forgetfulness over the cause for that "No".

This was the third in the series of wonders. The fourth – the second word that he spoke: "Micky."

In the course of time Uri learnt to voice more words, and was capable of walking the length of the corridor, although in great difficulty, and supported on somebody's arm. And then we discovered what had previously been unknown: Uri had lost his memory.

That same Sabbath eve that we sang so zealously, to express by song our victory over the hell in which we found ourselves, I dropped my eyes for a moment from the ceiling to the door, and saw Uri standing there.

He nodded his head awkwardly in time with the tune of the song and when light from the corridor fell on his face, I saw in his eyes – for the first time – joy.

The neurosurgical ward's veto was removed. Dr. Kuzari was convinced that I could now withstand an additional operation at the hands of the orthopaedic surgeons. In telling me of this, while busily examining my forehead, he promised he would not abandon me completely. Should I so decide he would be able, sometime in the future, to straighten the deep furrow in my forehead, for the sake of aesthetics. I was resolute that my head should henceforth be left alone. I would be able to manage in life without an alabaster forehead . . .

The cast around my leg was pressing tight. I felt as though it had been pushed into a shoe that was several sizes too small. The evening before my leg operation, I hastened to write a letter to the orthopaedic surgeons. In this letter, which I taped to my injured leg, I wrote: "Dear doctors! If you do not adjust the dimensions of the cast to the dimensions of my leg – I will have no alternative but to cut off all my contacts with you, and to call on the services of another shop, where it is customary to supply clients with shoes and/or casts of the correct size."

In the morning, as my stretcher was being wheeled along the corridor of the hut on the way to the operating theatre, one of the nurses happened to cross my path and read the note. "No. Never!" She was shaken: "What will the doctors say? Take the note off!" I waved her aside. It was difficult for anybody working in that terrible ward to have a sense of humour . . .

Upon arrival in the operating theatre, I saw Professor Shapira and Dr. Parin, who were going to perform the operation. Dr. Parin's eyes fell on the note. He smiled: "O.K., we'll try to satisfy your requirements, though without ultimatums." The others also read it and smiled. The smiles lifted my spirits even further. The operating theatre nurse captured my heart. Smiling eyes, a round beaming face, and eye-glasses astride on her nose. She waved a threatening finger at me, indicating the note with a nod of her head. "My name is Tami," she said, "Tami Lipschitz, and you're a rascal."

"I read your column about the injury. I even read it twice," Dr. Parin told me, rubbing his palms together as he prepared for the work ahead. His opinion of the article interested me, although I didn't succeed in hearing his remarks to the end. The anaesthetics had put me to sleep . . .

I awoke half drunk. I knew that I had never been in such terrible

125

pain. None of the agonies that I had so far suffered were more than a hint of what I was going through now.

I screamed with all my might. I sobbed, I moaned and I swore in the filthiest possible terms. My leg was only the centre and focal point of the pains. The agony pierced all my other limbs as well. I could sense great activity around me. It made me dizzy. I was toppling over and over down black chasms, and then flung into the heights. It seemed to me that there were people around my stretcher. They talked. I couldn't absorb what they were saying. I deciphered blurred images in white. Yael's visage from time to time emerged in front of my eyes, and vanished again. I continued to rave, rant and scream – and I don't remember what I said. The images began to push the stretcher towards my bed. I waved my arms in the air like a madman. From time to time I could feel them pounding soft flesh. But I didn't care. On the contrary. In a murderous rage, I was pleased every time my fists beat on flesh. I think that I screamed that I would murder anyone who tried to touch me in order to move me to the bed. I heard Yael's voice asking for Miriam Oren. She believed that because of my preference for that nurse, I would calm down and agree to move into bed. Somebody went to get her. Somebody else said that I should be given an injection of Patidin as sedation. Then, Yael's angry voice could be heard: "Why wasn't he given Patidin in the recovery room?!" My arms continued to wave round like the sails of a windmill. "I'll murder you! All of you!" I beat on the bedposts with all the strength in my fists. The skin on my hands was damaged but I didn't feel any pain. No pain could compete with the agony that I already suffered. Despite my rage, they transferred me to the bed. I continued to hit out wildly at anybody who tried to approach. I felt strong arms grasp me. I don't know whether I fainted, or whether the injection in my arm did its work.

19

The following day after lunch, Professor Shapira and Dr. Parin came into my room. I was still lying spent and empty. I was a little surprised at the high-powered delegation. Why had they bothered to come together? Had they heard of my hysteria last night? And if so, what of it? I've calmed down now.

126

Dr. Parin stood to my right and Professor Shapira to the left. Yael stood at the foot of the bed. All three wore gloomy expressions. There was a long moment of silence which chilled me. Finally Professor Shapira opened his mouth. His voice was quiet and somewhat strange.

"During your operation yesterday . . ." he said and paused. "In your operation yesterday, it became finally clear to us. Your leg is in very bad condition. In fact, you almost don't have a leg. The bones are completely smashed, and some are missing. Muscle, flesh and ligaments are missing. The blood vessels are damaged. There's a lot of skin missing. Infection and gangrene are spreading."

Why does he tell me all this? Why does he say all this with such a gloomy expression? I know my leg is badly damaged. I sensed that the situation is bad. Sensed – for five weeks, I have known it. Why the details? Why did they both come, he and Parin? What happened? What's the celebration? The operation didn't succeed? Another one? They scare me! Parin dropped his eyes when I looked at him. And Yael. God! I'm afraid! They're ashamed of something. They're hiding something.

"There's something called a cosmetic leg. Perhaps it would have been possible to try it on you. At first we thought so. Now, I don't think that a cosmetic leg is the solution. In my opinion, it would be worse than any other solution. It means pain for your whole life, limping, restricted movement. Long rests after every few paces. Pains with every change of weather. No, I don't think that's the solution. You will suffer from it more than from anything else."

What's a cosmetic leg? Why is he suddenly talking about a cosmetic leg? What's this something else? What does he mean when he refers to "anything else"? I don't understand a word. I can't grasp what he's saying. Where is he leading? To what? To what? They're talking as though to prepare me for something. Slowly – slowly. Like an announcement of impending death. But no one I know has died. I never heard of a cosmetic leg. And I don't even know what's this "anything else". Why are Parin and Yael silent?

"Believe me, we hoped that we could save it. That we could return it to a reasonable condition. In yesterday's operation we reached a decision. There's no other way. If we want to avoid a year and a half or two years of hospital, and torment for your whole life – there is no avoiding the most drastic and suitable thing under the circumstances . . ."

My God! Am I completely mad? I don't understand. A year and a half, two years in hospital? I thought that the whole business would be over in months. Why can't they return the leg to a "reasonable condition"? I've seen many men with broken legs, and they were soon back on their feet. What's going on here? I'm bewildered! I'm totally confused.

"We are not the ones who can decide. The decision is yours. We only want you to carefully consider the possibilities: the one – that we try, with very slight chances and a considerable amount of suffering, to go on treating the leg, and the second – that we amputate it!"

Or we amputate it!!! Amputate! Amputate! An invalid. A cripple. A wheelchair. Why amputation? Why must I decide? I'm the junior, an ignoramus who can't succeed in grasping what's happening to him. How can I decide? What do I know? Am I capable of judging? To consider and coolly decide? I'm in shock. After all, we're talking about a leg that was mine. Yael, tell them something! Why are you silent? Why don't you help me? Parin, whom I like so much, also says nothing. Let him say that it's true, that there is another way. That I'm dreaming. That it's a nightmare. That I'll wake up and see that it isn't reality . . . "Or we amputate it . . ."

God above, help me say something. They're waiting for me to say something. I must say something. I must decide.

"A cosmetic leg . . . Change of weather . . . We tried to save . . . There's skin missing, bones missing, blood vessels missing . . . A year and a half in hospital . . . Or amputate it . . . Very slight chances and a lot of suffering."

I must snap out of it! Cool down! Behave like a man! They gave me the opportunity to consider – and time has come to decide. And if I say no? If I don't agree? – I'll be in terrible pain. More terrifying operations like yesterday's. Perhaps I'll try my luck again? Maybe they'll take it back? No! They said what they had to say. Now, I must be a man. Not a weakling. The devil with it! Decide! Now!

"Doctor, I understand that my answer is only a formality. For the record. In practice, it's already clear to you what the decision must be?" My voice trembled. Something was choking in my throat.

"No! The answer isn't a formality. We will accept your decision and behave accordingly," the professor answered.

He's thrown the ball back to me. Not fair! Why must I decide? It would have been much easier for me if he had simply said: "Listen, we're amputating your leg. We must and that's it." He's forcing me to take the responsibility. If I take it – then to the devil – I'll take it to the end!

"Doctor, amputate!"

BOOK 3

"WELCOME TO THE FAMILY, COMRADE"

1

. . . Awake. Unfamiliar objects appear for a moment then vanish. New shapes. Different smells. Unrecognised images. Bewilderment. Thick torpor. Where am I? My mouth is parched. Water! What place is this? It's hard to keep my eyelids open.

Somebody familiar is bending over me. It's Yael. Once, a long time ago, generations back, she had leaned over and said: "I'm here." And I answered: "Shalom" and slipped back again into the unconscious. Like then, like then . . .

The leg. That's what it's about. The leg. They did something to it . . . Or they were supposed to do something . . . Yes, I remember. Something about the leg. No alternative, they said. Can't be saved, they said. You decide, they said. They also said something else. I don't remember what. Only that it wasn't pleasant to hear. What were they supposed to do? I'm tired. I'll soon fall asleep. But, what was it about? It bothered me. The thoughts drift away, are lost in the fog. I can't catch their tails. Connect up . . . Somebody said – perhaps I said it myself – that I must be brave, and I decided to be brave. It's easy to decide, difficult to be.

It was a serious matter, most important. The leg. Something about the leg. I'm certain. What happened to it? Yes, something happened. It's different, not like always. Very heavy. Not heavy like a leg in a cast is heavy. Different. Strange, alien . . .

Sleep . . .

"We'll amputate tomorrow. There's a limit to suffering."

. . . I didn't want them to let visitors in. I didn't feel like visitors. I had problems of my own. Just for once, it's permissible. Let me be. I don't want anybody. Time to settle accounts. Not with the soul. With the leg. It too has an account that must be balanced. Leave me alone!

They left me alone. This is to be my last conversation with it; with the leg. A farewell speech. Before it – what remains of it – goes on its way. The last time. My dear, twenty-nine years, a little more or less, is no insignificant period. We grew attached, we travelled many roads together. I wet you when I was a baby. I dragged you along with difficulty when I began to crawl. You trotted along on hikes in the Scouts, I can't complain: you did alright. You were muscular and strong. You carried me on the tough route marches of boot camp. Later, you sprawled in a tank, lazy so and so. It was a bit difficult to find shoes to fit you, but that was a reasonable failing. I'm prepared to forgive you that, leg. Now's not the time to be petty. After death – we are all martyrs. It's you I'm addressing, sainted leg. You – you that intend to leave me.

Why this bad run of luck? Why didn't they put you – I mean, me – a yard to the left or a yard to the right of the place where I lay wounded when the mortar shell burst? The one whose splinters ripped one after the other into your flesh. Like white-hot pig-iron thrown in cold water.

Why did Abrasha, lying next to me, only take a slight wound in the knee? Why didn't I get a dose like his?

Since then I have hated you, leg.

Now, as I weep for you, leg, as I make this little speech that only you and I can hear – you're very close to my heart. But before sentence was passed on you I actually hoped they would take you from me. I couldn't bear the agony any more. The professor himself said only a moment ago: "O.K., we'll operate tomorrow. There's a limit to the suffering and tension that a man can bear". Even he was against you.

But now, suddenly, I desire you. I don't want to be without you. They deluded us that everything would be alright. They said – if I can move my toes, everything will be O.K.! Another genius doctor declared that one operation, or perhaps two, a few pins and some irons inside, and you would again be as agile as a deer.

But tomorrow you leave me. Adieu, leg. One more night together. How are you going to behave tonight? Will this be a night of agony? A night of love? Tomorrow, they execute you. I grant you the privileges of the condemned's last night. My doll's leg. My doll of a leg. A doll's leg that got lost in Rambam Hospital, and they couldn't find you there. Then, I was very worried and I didn't know why. Now I know.

134

2

I don't remember the last morning in Hut 40. I don't remember when they took me away. All I remember of the operating theatre is Dr. Parin's face. It gazed at me through a thick fog. He is the one who is amputating my leg. This time he didn't smile. He was serious and deliberate.

Six hours later they returned me to the old unloved hostel – Hut 16. Hours passed before I opened my eyes for the first time. My teeth chattered from cold despite the many blankets they piled on me, and the July sun burning outside.

Faces passed by one after the other – inquisitive stares, anxious stares, curious glances. Like figures that appear in a dream, but have no connection with its plot.

Yael later told me that I tried every so often, while in dubious consciousness, to rise up and reach for the leg that wasn't there. Each attempt ended in a dive back into the pillow in total exhaustion. She also told me that only once I opened my eyes in full consciousness, and asked: "Is everything over?" When she said yes, I again fell asleep, this time for a good hour.

"You've got visitors," Yael said.

With an effort I opened my eyes. A figure in a wheelchair rolled towards me. It looked very purposeful. It spoke deliberately. I couldn't concentrate enough to understand him. I didn't grasp who he was and why he had come to me in particular to talk, question and explain.

A social worker, or something similar. He said there were forms to sign. You are a cripple. You must submit a claim to the Ministry of Defence, and be recognised as such . . . I've brought you this book – read it! It tells you all about your rights. A car. Medical treatment. Everything will be alright, there's no need to worry. Sign the forms. If you have problems – there are no problems. You can always ask me. I work here. Sign now, please . . .

He turned the wheelchair and was off. Within moments I forgot him and was asleep.

When I awoke, his image floated foggily back into my memory. The memory was accompanied by a bitter taste. He – there was hate in my hazy recollection – welcomed me as though with joy, too much joy, to the family of cripples. Welcome, new comrade, to the family. Welcome to a family that I wanted no part of.

"Good morning, Yankele. How are we?" Micky Cohen, the physiotherapist. It's not morning now. It's already noon. A damp and sticky noon. An old man stood next to Micky. White-haired, long shorts down to the knees, and high stockings. He said something about being a colleague of mine.

That means – also an amputee.

"I want to prove to you that what happened to you isn't so terrible. You don't need to worry. You'll be able to do almost everything. Even take a swim in the sea." On the spot, he pulled down his stocking and showed me what an artificial leg looks like. It was the first time I had seen an artificial limb: pink, rigid. Strangely like a leg. But the colour's different.

"Now, look what you can do with it," he said and began to jump up and down. I was apathetic. I couldn't relate the show he was putting on to anything that concerned me.

The following day they began to make unwarranted demands of me. They said I must wear pyjamas. Up to now, I had lain naked under the sheet. The thought of wearing pyjamas nauseated me. I don't know why. My whole being revolted against this order. In anger I declared that I didn't want to hear anything about any kind of dress.

Then they tied a web strip to the far rail of the bed, and gave me the other end. They said that I could use it to pull myself up to a sitting position.

I again revolted. How will I be able to sit? I'm not capable of forming my body into this posture. I'm not allowed to move! Any movement wracks my leg with pain. That's how it has been in the five weeks that have passed since my injury. I'm not prepared to lift myself. It will hurt again.

"But the leg that hurt isn't there," somebody said.

I wasn't convinced. I lay frozen in that same posture I adopted the first time that I found any movement, however slight, meant excruciating agony. I was afraid of the demands they were making of me. I wasn't prepared to listen to the explanations of the nurses, and of Yael herself, when they said I must sit up – it's important for me. Not just in general, but especially because of my head operation. I was petrified every time I was compelled to withstand their pressures, and weakly but forcibly announced my refusal. The thought

136

that they would compel me by force to comply with their demand –
chilled me. I knew they were capable of winning.

Of course, they did win. This time. Yael was also on their side.
I was hurt and insulted. I regarded her as a traitor. I hated her.

I tried to rise and fell back helplessly. I tried a second time and
vomited. I tried again and was overcome by a terrible dizziness.

"I want, I want, but I don't succeed," I whispered helplessly.
They saw that I really couldn't make the effort and let me be.

Somewhere inside I knew that I must obey all their orders. They
meant well. But I simply didn't have the strength.

At night the day's events unreel before the mind's eye. The man in
the wheelchair, the man in the long shorts ("Shalom, colleague");
the doctors, the nurses and Yael – and their demands: do this,
do that. I hated all of them.

Leave me alone, social worker, leave me alone. You say I'm disabled, me? Look at yourself; you're the cripple. You're sitting there
in a wheelchair, not me. I don't want to submit claims. I don't want
rights. I don't want you to solve my problems. I didn't invite you.
After a difficult operation I need to rest. I've got no strength for
your nonsense. What's your haste? What is it? Are you getting a
percentage, a commission on every claim that you submit in our
name? Get out! Go! Buzz off! End of reel . . .

"You can even swim in the sea. The technique of producing artificial limbs has developed very nicely. You take off the leg you use
for walking, and change it for a special leg to swim in the sea. It's
water resistant. Water-proof. Seventeen carats. No problems.
Consider, you simply change a shoe for a shoe. At night, if I want to
go to the bathroom, I put on the leg just like a slipper. No
problems. Look how I jump."

You too, "colleague", leave me alone! Where do you all come
from? Leave me alone. What are you to me? You have no leg – and
me . . . Yes, it's true! I don't either. Good, so leave me alone for a
short while. Come later. In another week, in another month. Not
now. I've no strength for you now. I'm very tired. Later.

Please, I can't rise. No, I won't wear pyjamas, under no circumstances. If I rise, my body will be wracked with pain. I mustn't.
It's forbidden. Why are you tormenting me? Get rid of this miserable
web strip. Why don't you let me rest a little? A week. Two days. An

137

hour. I'll rest a little and then carry out all your orders. Now, I'm not capable. Simply, I can't. My head is spinning. In the name of God, let me sleep. I didn't sin, I committed no crime. It's not my fault I was wounded. I didn't plan it. It happened. It would already be worth dying, just so you shouldn't torment me. Let me sleep . . .

3

In the morning I opened my eyes and discovered the hut. I had seen it earlier, but this time it seemed brighter, whiter and cleaner. A new world opened up before my eyes – a more beautiful and rosy world. I was lightheaded. My lunatic cheerfulness had returned and I began to speechify. I smiled to myself and found a subject. Bedpan: the "pot" used by bed-bound patients.

"Gentlemen, dear comrades who have collected here from all over the country, lend me your ears: The subject for today's discussion is, what is more preferable: a metal bed-pot coated in chrome, or its colleague, a plastic bed-pot? Though we are all of us well grounded in the subject, though we are all wise men, the matter is too difficult for us to give an unequivocal answer. You say the metal bed-pot is preferable? Good, you are right. Its form is far more pleasing to the eye than that of the plastic bed-pot. But, my friends, this is a mixed blessing. Have you not considered the pleasant touch of a plastic bed-pot as opposed to the ice cold feeling of metal on your flesh? No, gentlemen, you cannot make a hasty and superficial decision, which would only indicate lack of seriousness. Both have their good traits and characteristics. Both have disadvantages. Please only make up your minds when you have the full picture before you . . . And since I notice that a delegation of renowned and respected healers has already arrived to deliberate with us and draw conclusions as to our health this day, I will now propose a recess for the duration, and the debate will continue immediately after the serving of light refreshments . . ."

I was extremely pleased with what I had said. All the patients in the hut had followed me with smiling faces. The doctors who had come in for their daily rounds, and heard parts of the speech, were also smiling. I was in euphoria. I was cheerful. Yael was astonished at the change that had taken place this morning. She was also smiling, so it seemed, as I lectured her on the main points of my speech. The first signs of this cheerfulness had already appeared during the first days after my head operation: a kind of drunkenness accompanied by inanely "merry" speechifying. I know that this wasn't normal, and that it was a sign that a cog was loose in the machine. But I could not overcome it. While the urge was upon me, I justified it to myself by deciding that it is better to laugh than cry.

One day they brought me a wooden wheelchair. It looked as though it had seen better days, twenty or thirty years ago, or perhaps even in World War I. It was very heavy and tired. It was difficult to move even when no one was sitting in it. When somebody pushed this museum piece, its wheels turned in different directions. It behaved as though it was harnessed to four horses, one on each side and each pulling in its own direction.

They told me: "Come down from the bed, you must". I got down. Or in other words, they lifted me down. My body, which had always been heavy, was now twice or three times the weight. My head began to spin. I begged them to put me back on the bed. Should they refuse, I was certain I would slide off the chair onto the floor.

The coming days were ones of conflict between Yael and me as she served as spokesman for the doctors. She demanded that I spend more time in a sitting position on the chair. I was completely exhausted. Since the amputation my temperature was higher. Infection. Lack of sleep had also influenced my general state. Yet, when in bed I felt marvellous, occasionally.

After a few days, the situation in Hut 16 was already clear to me. This time I viewed my surroundings from a completely different viewpoint. It was still not a Garden of Eden. The leg which had been amputated also had something to say . . . But come what may, my present condition could not be compared to that of the previous month when, in the very same hut, I lay in the opposite bed.

In those days I had established no kind of rapport with any of the patients apart from Jean Claude, who lay next to me. Now a mutual awareness began to dawn. Hut 16 was divided into two wings, divided by a wall with a door over half its width. In each of the two wings there were about ten patients, most of whom were war casualties.

My acquaintance Jean Claude was still lying opposite. A dark Adonis from Dimona. He threw black looks at me: "Not long ago,"

139

he seemed to be saying, "I won a Black Belt in judo. Now, any little midget can finish me off." He was wracked with pain. His leg was no longer in a cast. But most of its flesh was gone.

One morning I was awakened by the long drawn-out polished and sweet call of a bugle. I was astonished. What was this? Morning reveille?

After a while it became clear that the sound was not issuing from a brass trumpet, but from the mouth of Abramiko, one of the casualties in Hut 16, who was nicknamed: "The Bugle". When we began to organise a daily "schedule" in the hut, he was given the job of marking the time of day: reveille, noontime and taps . . .

One day he returned from a difficult operation. Despite his drugged slumber, it was noticeable that he was in great agony. Though Hut 16 was normally inconsiderate of its patients' suffering, we imposed silence and ordered visitors to speak in whispers.

Because he was asleep we paid little attention to him. Suddenly, the hush of the hut was broken by a feeble yet drawn out poignant taps.

We turned to look at "The Bugle," who was smiling through his great pain. He whispered in an agonised voice: "That taps – was special for me. I will soon die of pain . . ."

And he immediately dropped back into sedated sleep.

My morning is always clear and good. Even if it follows upon a mad sleepless night. Towards noon my weariness increases and the amputated leg, which is swollen and infected, begins to throb. Lunch. Visitors. They again come in a steady flow. It's very nice to see them, but who can bear up to this massive onslaught? Go and tell all these emissaries of good intent, who come to fulfil the commandment of visiting the sick, how difficult it is – to repeat, time after time, day after day, the same old story in reply to the ritual question of "What's new?"

Visitors who appear between two and four in the afternoon are decidedly unwanted. These are the hours when I whisper words of love and longing in the ears of blessed sleep. But she merely touches my eyelids and then flickers away without bestowing her favours.

Evening descends. The duty nurse appears with big hypodermic syringes. Two of them. What she calls "horse injections". The one of

140

antibiotics, the second a sedative. The antibiotics perhaps help. The sedative only makes a mockery of my body. "Please turn over." Occasionally, in order to scare the nurse, I let out a shriek of pain. She recoils. It's not every nurse that knows how to plunge the needle into a body that looks like a pin-cushion because of 4 to 6 injections a day.

Parting from Yael. We'll meet again tomorrow. Darkness. Lights out. The young bastards next to me sleep like babies. Not like babies – like labourers. Their snores almost shake the walls of the hut. It's very hot. Now come the thoughts – always the thoughts . . .

Amputee. That's what you are. Amputee. No more tantrums, no more leaping, running and skipping. How many steps from the courtyard to the apartment? Sixty-nine. Better put aside any ideas of ever climbing them again. Forget them. Forget how it feels to race up them. Forget it. And also forget – you overgrown baby – hopping along the hopscotch marks left on the pavement by the neighbourhood kids when nobody is watching you. You're a cripple.

You won't swim in the sea. That's all over. In any case, you were never that great a swimmer. No climbing of ladders to prowl through the attic to discover forgotten treasures. Wheelchair. That's what you'll have. A wheelchair. Like that social worker who came to hammer it into you: You're a cripple, you've got rights. I never met an amputee. Perhaps I did, but I never gave any thought to the way he lives. How, for example, does he get into a bath on one leg? . . .

. . . I once heard that an artificial limb is a very painful thing. It is not so easy to get used to. I didn't hear – I had read: "The Legless Pilot". Was that the name of the book? God, if I have to go through everything he went through! What an ocean of suffering! What willpower! They wrote a whole book about it.

What awaits me when I reach home? How long will it be before I get home? Months? Years? What does it look like? And how will I be able to climb up to it, to such a height. What does the house look like, what does Yael look like in it, what does Tami look like in it, what will I look like in it?

What does an amputated leg look like? What's left there under the thick roll of bandages? It's swollen like a football. I understood from the doctors who came today that it's too swollen. They're not happy. Ha! They're not happy . . . This football lying on the bed is mine. The centre-forward kicks it halfway down the field, the full-back intercepts and passes it to the half-back. No! No! No! They've lost the ball, they've lost the leg. Where did the part they cut off go to? What did they do with it? It was mine. Since I was born. They could at least tell me. Tell me. Tell me . . .

"But, Yankele, you're burning the sheet again!"

The voice is that of the night-nurse. She pulls me out of my reveries. It often happens: a lighted cigarette slips from my fingers onto the sheet. "One day you'll burn the place down," the nurse holding her flashlight admonishes me. "What will happen then?"

"One less stable," I reply, "and in place of it, they'll put up something fit for patients. And now, please shine the torch on your beautiful eyes so that I'll feel better and perhaps you'll make me a cup of tea? . . ."

In the morning Cora Moskowitz, the volunteer nurse from Brazil, comes to visit. She apologises for having deserted me. She tells me about Yisrael Cohen whom she adopted in my place. Yisrael, a deputy battalion commander, was badly wounded – she doesn't quite know where – when some demolition materials that he was holding in his hands exploded. Both his hands were lost, one eye torn out and the second damaged. There was also damage to his ears. Worst of all – his chest is mutilated. And she doesn't even describe his face which was burnt and spattered with shrapnel.

The doctors, so Cora goes on to tell me, had already despaired of his life. His infected chest wounds resisted antibiotics. He was considered doomed and his wife had been told that there was no chance for him. Somehow, one of the doctors remembered a new drug from Switzerland. It was ordered urgently and his life was saved. He lives – if such can be termed life . . . He is now somewhat recovered and is already walking. Cora does not leave his bedside. She was the first witness to his awakening, when he discovered that he had no hands.

Her story shook me. I felt a burning need to see the man. I was somehow convinced that I could encourage him in some way. It was a crazy idea. How can you encourage a man in his condition? But I believed in him. Cora promised to bring him for a visit. When she left I was full of contempt for myself: How dare you still take pity on yourself? How dare you compare? But I immediately began to defend myself: O.K., he was injured very badly. But you were also injured – very badly.

4

Immediately after Cora's visit Raya Shimoni, the physiotherapist, arrived. A long pony-tail down her back, laughing eyes, upright posture. She turned to look at Jean Claude. He was making jokes but his face was pale: "Here comes my inquisitor."

Jean Claude had already been lying in bed a long time. Raya is toning up his body muscles, and especially his leg muscles, to avoid deterioration. The exercises are very painful. His paleness was no coincidence. He knew what to expect.

"I'm sorry! There's no alternative!" Raya said in an apologetic tone.

"Yes, but please, with mercy," Jean Claude begged. "Not like last time."

She began to work. The poor guy's face twisted up. Through my one eye I see how he is throwing out his hand to the metal ash-tray lying on his cupboard. I am appalled. The boy is grasping the ash-tray and it's crumpling between his fingers. Anything, rather than scream.

"Enough, criminal!" I burst out in a tone somewhere between anger and good nature. "You're murdering him."

"Forget it," Jean Claude chokes as rivulets of sweat pour down his forehead. "She simply wants to show us men how a little woman can break us. Basically, she's a good kid."

"Perhaps," I reply as my temper cools, "but she won't succeed in breaking me – that's for certain."

A shimmer of mischievousness flickers across Raya's eyes: "That we'll see in a few days time, when your turn comes."

A nurse summons me to the treatment room and helps me from the wheelchair onto the bed. The first change of dressings after the amputation. I can finally see what they did to my leg.

Dr. Parin comes into the treatment room, rubbing his hands together: "What are we anticipating today – terrible pains? Just pains? Or only twinges?"

"For your benefit, only twinges," I say and add almost in a whisper: ". . . for my benefit as well." But my heart isn't in it.

He goes to work. I daren't look at my leg. I fix my eyes on the ceiling. A sharp pain shoots through me. My hand jerks out to the handle of the window behind me, and almost tears it out of its place.

"I'm sorry," Dr. Parin says. The serious expression on his face tells me that he isn't satisfied with what he sees. He covers up the wounds, bandages them and orders the nurse to bind them tightly. The tight bandage around the sensitive wound is very painful.

I'm returned to my bed in a definitely bad mood. From time to time since the amputation a sharp, sudden pain – similar to an electric shock – passes through my body, causing me to tremble. Now, with the pressure on the leg, these electric shocks come frequently. Are they because of the tightness of the bandage?

They descended on me today: they decided to take me to the eye clinic for an examination. They remembered that I have a sick eye. They put me on the ancient wheelchair and roll me off on the trip. The clinic is at the other end of the hospital – about a kilometre. Fortunately for Yael, Menachem Talmi and Dov Goldstein of *Ma' ariv* come to visit. They save her the job of pushing the heavy chair.

How was I expected to reach the eye clinic if Yael hadn't been beside me? If my friends hadn't helped her? What sort of a hospital is this where a casualty is jolted over such great distances, on a chair that chooses its own route?

I spew out bitter thoughts as the chair bounces over the rough road, while I watch the sweat-soaked faces of my friends.

On the way we meet Dr. Kuzari. He takes one look at me and says: "You feel very bad! What's your temperature?"

"103," Yael says, "and he really does feel very bad."

"No good, no good," Dr. Kuzari sadly says and goes on his way.

We reach the eye clinic. I feel very dizzy and bilious. I'll pass out any minute. Yael summons a doctor. My state puts them in a quandary. In the queue are healthy people, with eye damage only. There's no room for a patient to lie down. Yael asks when the professor will come. Nobody knows. They find me a vacant doctor's room and place me on the examination table. I sink into delirium and pray they'll leave me here as long as possible, and that no one will disturb me.

Eventually they take me to the professor. He examines the eye on which he operated weeks ago, mumbles something that I can't catch, again covers the eye with a bandage and releases me. Yael is compelled to wheel my chair, without help, all the way back.

By evening, the pendulum has swung again and I am back in one of my lightheaded moods. I mimic some old woman who is announcing on the loud-speaker the forthcoming appearance of the "Desert Bells" troupe on the plaza between the huts. I repeat her announcements parrot fashion, in particular mimicking her Russian accent.

The actor Yossi Yadin appears. He sits by my bed and looks at me inquisitively. A few days earlier he had read my article "Thus I Was Wounded", over the Army radio service. He appears to have been impressed by it. "I had to come and see you. I just felt that way," he says. I am floating in my mad euphoria, and pay almost no attention to him. "Yankele," Yael whispers fiercely. I take no notice of her and continue to imitate the old woman whose repeated announcements of the "Desert Bells" continue to resound outside.

I sense that Yadin feels uncomfortable, but I'm still at it. I don't know what's happened to me. He pushes my chair out to the impending appearance of the "Desert Bells". After but a moment my head is in a painful whirl, and I am returned to bed. This is his chance to depart.

"You behaved very badly," Yael reprimands me. "You must pull yourself together. A man who doesn't even know you, comes all the way from Tel Aviv, and you don't even take any notice of him."

She's right. She's right. Get a move on and explain to her that it wasn't really you. It was the small devil inside who is mocking and playing with me – but oh, he makes me feel better, helps me escape!

The following morning I am worn down from lack of sleep and Dudu's screams. He is angry as usual, about somebody.

Dudu Badusa lies in the distant wing of the hut. His screams have become a part of our life. I have occasionally seen him careering by on a wheelchair, but I have never succeeded in catching a glimpse of his face.

Yael tells me that he is a unique character. Dudu's leg was amputated above the knee. His hand was also severely injured. He never allows them to change his dressings the way they did mine – without a general anaesthetic. Whenever he sees the doctors approaching, he breaks out into horrendous shrieks and warns that if they dare touch him "I will have an attack – and then it will be very bad in here." The doctors have despaired. They capitulate, and change his bandages only after anaesthetic in the operating theatre.

Dudu has arranged matters well in his wing. He has taken charge of the only wheelchair in good condition in the hut, and God help anybody who dares touch it. The same is true of the mobile public telephone. Whoever wants to ring out must do so from his bedside. From time to time his elder sister, who looks after him lovingly and devotedly, passes by and announces: "I don't know what will become of him. He was such a nice child . . ."

I take comfort: I am not the only mentally disturbed case in the hut. I have a colleague . . .

This morning, when I heard his voice, I decided to get down from the bed onto the wheelchair, to go and take a look at him at long last.

I am excited. This is the first time I have gone down without assistance. I succeed. I wheel myself to Dudu's bed, glance at him and rush back to my own. The dizziness has already begun. By my bedside, I see the smiling countenance of Shalom Rosenfeld: "What's this, Yankele, you're already rushing about?" As usual his arms are weighted with gifts. My guests never come empty-handed. They're spoiling me. After Shalom goes on his way, little Yisrael looks at me wonderingly: "What did they bring you this time?"

I pull out a packet of Kent cigarettes from my drawer and toss it over to him. He catches it, puts it into his cupboard, and exposes two bright rows of gleaming teeth: "Thanks. I don't smoke. Chocolate, if possible . . ."

In the gallery of Hut 16, Yisrael is one of the nicest and friendliest characters. But he is haunted by a great shame: most of the casualties in here were wounded in battle, while he is only a road accident injury. He served as an army dispatch rider on a motor bike, was in too great a hurry, overturned and broke his thigh.

"Yankele," he turns his merry eyes on me, "you must do something for me. You lot are all heroes. Visitors come and you tell them about

Tel Fahar. Visitors come to him – and he was wounded at Shekh Sueid. That one over there – in the Old City . . . I'm the only one with nothing to tell. Can I say that I overturned on a motor bike because I didn't drive but flew?"

It took but a few minutes to put together a totally incredible story, of which he could be proud: "Upon enlistment, Yisrael was unusually successful in the pilot's examination. His talents were already noticeable in a course which he would have finished as top of his class, if he had not left camp without permission to go to his home in Ashdod on the eve of the passing-out parade. During the war he made many sorties over Egypt, during which he destroyed 18 aircraft on the ground and in the air. In his last sortie his luck ran out, and his plane was damaged by anti-aircraft fire. Despite the heavy smoke pouring out of the plane, he hoped to save it and even succeeded in reaching Israeli territory. When the plane was close to disintegrating, his superiors ordered him to abandon it. He jumped. The jump wasn't successful. His thigh was broken. He was collected by a helicopter and brought to hospital."

Yisrael's eyes sparkled with glee. The story enthused him. Henceforward, all the men in the room made a point of telling visitors the story of Yisrael's bravery in loud voices. Some of the visitors are requested to go over to him to say a nice word: "The boy's broken up. He cannot forgive himself because the plane crashed. He blames himself for millions of pounds of damage. He must be encouraged."

Some are tempted to go over. One man in the prime of life, after gazing at him with awe came back to me today: "What boys you are! Such a youngster and already a pilot! Difficult to believe . . ."

Little Yisrael listens to the remarks and contorts. He pulls a pillow over his head, and it sounds as though stifled groans are coming out from under. Occasionally he manages to control his laughter, and while his "story" is being told, reproaches his friends with an apologetic expression on his face: "Boys, it was nothing special. I was just like everybody else . . ."

The boy is a natural wonder. At least, so the doctors believe. When he was brought to the hut, he was wrapped in a kind of plaster dressing that began at his ankles and ended at his arm-pits. Only his shoulders, arms and head were visible. Not a position to relish, but the irrepressible Yisrael made a habit of turning his body, in a

147

manner that I could never understand, over onto a wheeled stretcher-bed, and then pushed himself backwards and forward with the help of two crutches, like a sailor manoeuvring his boat against the current with the help of paddles. Whenever the doctors caught him, they would reprimand him severely, and he would put on the face of an innocent baby, and answer in a pitiful voice: "Really? And I thought I was allowed to . . ."

None – not even the most stern of doctors – could withstand his smile.

Well before the doctors expected it, Yisrael was ready to be taken out of his plaster cast, to progress to a cartoon-like contraption: an iron pipe hanging over the length of the bed with ropes and chains dropping from it. Yisrael's legs were tied high up on this frightening installation.

When they tied him to it, his face fell: "I wasn't made for this torture rack." The moment the doctors were out of the room, he released himself from the knots. "Just look at what I can do," he crowed with delight as he clambered like a monkey along the metal pipe above the bed.

"Idiot!" I yelled at him in panic, "do you want to spend the rest of your life in hospital?"

"Are you mad?" he laughingly answered from his upside down position. "I'm young and God loves me. You'll see, I'll be out of here before all of you."

He was right – the bastard.

5

Since I was moved to Hut 16, my ankle hurts a lot.

Incredible: the pains come from a part of the leg that doesn't exist at all. The part that was amputated. From time to time I unthinkingly raise the sheet to find out why the leg is so painful, and suddenly remember that it isn't there any more.

When the doctors pass by on their daily rounds, I complain about pain in the missing leg. As usual, they mumble something indecipherable and continue on to the next patient. From the whispered conversation between themselves, I catch hold of something that sounds like "phantom pain".

Their deliberate avoidance of the question irritates me no end: I'm entitled to know what's happening to my body.

I was lucky. A doctor acquaintance comes to visit me in the afternoon. I ask him whether he has ever heard of the concept "phantom pain". "Certainly," the doctor exclaims, "it means imaginary pains. I'm certain that you get them. They were right in telling you to expect them. There's no way around it. It's a part of the whole business."

Now my curiosity is satisfied. I learnt, in simple language, that the nerve ends of the stump act as though the leg was not amputated. Because they were used to reporting pain to the brain, they continue to carry out their function faithfully.

The following day, when the doctors visit, I declare: "Those imaginary pains that you told me about yesterday – how long will they continue?" I went on to explain everything that I had discovered.

They were amazed: "We told you all? We could never have done so!"

"It's a fact," I reply. "From whom else would I have found out?"

My small revenge. It became clear that in this hospital there was an iron-clad rule to ignore such pains. I, as one who was victimised by them, was convinced that this was a radical mistake, and said so. They reply in kind. Every time I pass water, the leg aches. I asked Dr. Horoshovksy, a young doctor with a sharp sense of humour, what could be done about it.

"Oh, it's easy," he answers in his pronounced French accent. "Stop passing water." A draw. One all . . .

One morning, when Raya the physiotherapist had finished administering to Jean Claude his daily ration of torture, she came over to my bed and announced in a very cheerful voice: "So that's it. Today we start on you."

With full confidence in my prowess, I advised her not to pit her strength against me. She replied: "Let's wait and see." She suggested placing one hand on the ankle of my healthy leg, and then we'll see whether I can move it.

I burst out laughing: "Alright, go ahead."

Her small feminine hand lightly gripped my leg. I was surprised by her strength. I tried to lift the leg but couldn't. I tried again, drawing on all the resources of my strength, and failed.

"So and so," I groaned at her, "you so and so."

She replied with a friendly smile: "I only wanted to put you down a peg. You couldn't succeed because you're weak after all you have gone through. We'll soon see the day when you can beat me with your little finger."

I like this girl more and more. I'm embarrassed because of my weakness. It was hard to accept that I had deteriorated to such an extent.

6

We recoil from pity and react mercilessly to those who dare bestow it upon us. The manner in which we handled one visitor, whose artificial visage particularly irritated us, is typical. He apparently considered that an apologetic mask was suited for wear when addressing the doomed.

When my comrades spotted the man, they instinctively exchanged glances which plainly indicated their resolve to take care of him. "The Bugle" watched his mournful eyes tripping up and down the rows of beds and asked politely: "Excuse me, sir, are you looking for something?"

The man replied in the affirmative and mentioned the name of his casualty.

Jean Claude, it appears, had discerned the relationship of the visitor to the casualty. He was no more than a distant acquaintance. Jean Claude heard the man's answer, gave a heart-rending sigh, and turned his back. The man remained paralysed in the centre of the hut. All very righteously looked away.

"So," the man wondered, "where can I find him?"

Silence.

"Do you think that he's left the hut?" he tried his luck again.

Somebody replied in a hushed tone: "Are you sure that you're not his father or some relative?"

"No, no," the man answered nervously. "I only worked for him once."

"Ah!" somebody answered. "That's simpler. They took him away two hours ago."

"Where to?"

"The pathological institute. They wanted to know what had happened."

The man's face literally turned black. By some kind of a miracle, the boy of whom we were speaking innocently entered at that moment. In an instant the unfortunate visitor's face turned white as the walls of the hut.

If this was the way we handled innocent visitors, it was nothing compared to the treatment meted out to a casualty who took pity on himself.

I was again taken to the operating theatre for some patching works on my amputated leg. It was still very swollen and infected.

They're still treating it at least three times a day. They put on dressings soaked with liquids that draw the accumulated muck out of it, and fasten them with a very tight elastic bandage. From time to time I again try my luck with the nurse in charge, in the hope that I will convince her to break doctors' orders, and not tighten the bandage so much – but in vain. I continue to battle with my pains. They are many-faceted: an irritating itch: cruel electric shocks, imaginary pains. As for my insomnia, I draw a memory out of the depths: the chloralhydrate that was prescribed by the psychiatrist. I ask Anka, the ward sister, to invite her. Dr. Floro, the psychiatrist, immediately reproached me for my exaggerated light-headedness.

I agree. She's right. But awareness of my lunacy doesn't help me overcome the prankster-devil. It's an irresistible urge.

I would later find out that the psychiatrist had discussed the matter with Yael the same day, and told her that I was off my tracks. In other words: it was possible that I was insane to some degree or other. She added that it was not out of the question that this behaviour resulted from the brain operation.

Yael rushed to Dr. Kuzari who calmed her down. He vigorously denied any possibility that the operation might have endangered my sanity.

In the evening, as the nurse distributed sleeping pills and injected sedatives, she told me that she had an enema, by which they would introduce a sedative into my body. In a temper I demanded that she immediately bring the liquid in a drinking vessel. The nurse gave way after a loud argument.

I took the shallow dish with the drug, and swallowed its contents in one gulp. Oh, oh! What a horror! Who concocted this devil's brew? I dived for the candy and fruit on my table, to rid myself of the terrible taste.

A short while later they were to rebroadcast, for the second time, an interview with Dan Shilon in which he relates the circumstances of our miraculous encounter on the Syrian Heights. Dan's story had greatly moved the radio public, and echoes of that reaction had reached my ears. I awaited the repeat broadcast in great excitement. I had missed the first, for at that time I wasn't capable of listening to the radio.

Meanwhile a cloud of pink fog approached and engulfed me rapidly. A cool stream flowed through my chest. I hovered above the earth, floating gently. On the distant horizon, I could make out Yael, Alexander and Ziva, my friends. From a great distance, his voice dimmed, I could hear Dan talking about me. I wanted so much to hear, but the voices were steadily weakening. A voice on the radio said that despite the distressing story, the listeners need not worry: I am fit and in good shape. Stormy bursts of applause.

. . . Stormy bursts of applause. I am well and in good shape. Well and in good shape. House of Israel, have no cares. Only one leg less. Dan, Dan my friend, you thought that I was whole. Then, when you addressed the good people you didn't yet know – and neither did I. But now, I don't care. Now I feel good floating in nowhere, rocking in a warm darkness, soft and safe and sealed as in a womb. Stormy bursts of applause. Stormy bursts of applause. Hallelujah. Hallelujah . . .

7

Morning finds me happy. The drug put me to sleep for four full consecutive hours! None of that Bacchanalian gaiety. Today I'm more normal. I contentedly shave and wash. I decided that I must dedicate this new and beautiful day with some suitably unusual act.

I drag myself into the wheelchair, and jet out into the still cool morning outside. Today, I say to myself, we will begin to exercise the weak muscles, and will also stroll around a bit in the outside world. Slowly-slowly, my arms still strong, I wheel the chair along the path between the huts. Spontaneously I burst into song, to the great astonishment of early-rising patients poised in the hut doorways. But I quickly feel my strength waning. I turn the chair around to face the hut.

When Yael arrives at her customary hour, she is surprised to find me waiting for her in a wheelchair. "I slept last night, I slept last night," I tell her as though I had experienced a miracle.

Dusk. they bring us a good-looking boy supported by two nurses. To our astonishment, a belt is placed beneath his chin and its two ends are tied to the head of the bed. His head is now stretched backwards, with no possibility of mobility.

Within a few minutes we learn his story from the nurse: the boy reached Sharm-e-Shekh on the Red Sea, and decided to bathe in the waters. But he was the victim of classical unreliability of statistics. Despite the usually very deep waters off the beach, this boy dived headlong into very shallow water. He broke his neck discs and would be operated on tomorrow.

Somebody nicknamed him "Sharm-e-Shekh" and the cheerful Hut 16 choir was already serenading him with the pop hit of that name.

"Sharm" grinned from ear to ear.

The second morning that I go out for a tour in the chair, I continued until I reached my breaking point. With the last of my strength, I decided to try for a few more yards. Each morning I set myself a target further away before I turned back to the hut.

8

One day, Raya – with whom I'm already in love (with Yael's permission) – comes with a primitive pair of crutches in her hands: "That's for you."

I panic. It is on such crutches that one sees amputee beggars in rags – broken men – hobbling around. Am I to be one of them? Is that how it is to be? Stumbling around on wooden crutches, a figure of pity?

My panic increases as the moments pass. If she brought me crutches, then she intends me to walk – I mean, to hop with their

153

help. Inconceivable. How can I do it? I'll fall! I'll break my bones! It's beyond me!

"You'll see, it'll be alright," Raya says as though she had read my thoughts. "We'll do it by stages. Everyone succeeds. You'll also succeed. No need to worry."

She bends over me and clamps an elastic bandage onto my healthy leg, to prevent a too rapid flow of blood into the veins. Then she demonstrates how you walk on crutches, supports me under the armpits and stands me up. I try to co-operate. Not without fear. She succeeds in placing one crutch under my arm-pit. I'm suddenly overcome by dizziness and my amputated leg begins strangely to vibrate and tremble as though in spasms. I drop on the bed.

"Alright, that's enough for today," Raya panics. "We'll try again tomorrow. It will work. You'll see that it will work."

A stone lifts from my heart. I have been granted a temporary reprieve.

The following day Raya returns. It seems to me that she's paler. I feared to renew the attempt, and I feared failure. Yet, I made up my mind not to break.

I stood on my healthy leg. Upright. For the first time since June 9, when we went up the Golan Heights. The world seemed completely different. The way a healthy man sees it. This was a normal vantage point. I am suddenly so tall. I see things which I had never seen from this angle. I have to lower my eyes to see my comrades lying on their beds. I no longer see them from the side. I no longer see from below.

I am astonished at the heaviness of my body. As though it had heavy weights tied to it. Tons dragging me downwards to the floor. A leaden man. A cold sweat breaks out on my naked back. The crutches are clumsy and uncomfortable. Raya stands behind me, and I feel her breath on my shoulder. I don't hear her instructions, and yet I fulfil them mechanically. God, I'm walking! I'm walking! I took a step. I moved my gawky body and took a step forward. And now the crutches. They take the place of a leg.

The bed is already a mile behind me. But I have taken no more than six, seven, eight paces. I know that if Raya demands that I continue – I will fall. I can't go on. My arms tremble from the effort. Please, back. To the bed. To the refuge.

"Every time, every time I wash this lousy floor, you have to tramp around here?" Toni Hadar, the heavily-set cleaning woman reprimands Raya. "How am I supposed to finish my work like this?"

God sent me this pleasant cleaning woman. A miracle. He heard my prayers, God did. Cleaning women are at the top of the hospital hierarchy. They must be obeyed. Raya shrugs her shoulders and says: "We'll go back to the bed."

I drop on the bed puffing and panting, as though I had climbed to the peak of a mountain. I can't even reply to Yael's compliments. I'm heavy with disappointment: if that's all I'm capable of doing, I'm an insect. Why are the others so fortunate. How does Dudu Badusa manage to jump on one leg from one end of the hut to the other?

9

"What could possibly have hurt a child like that?" little Yisrael's voice ponders in my ears, as he curiously indicates the giant ball of bandages enveloping the palm of the new casualty – who has just been wheeled into our room, deep in sedated sleep.

His question remained unanswered. We return to our own affairs. One courts his agonies, another looks for music on the radio, a third reads. The business of doing nothing. The boy was almost forgotten.

"Nurse nu-rse, n-urse!" three piercing shrieks in the vacuum of the room wrenched us out of our preoccupations.

The boy has awoken, he has been thrust out of the merciful sleep of sedation. We studied him each in our own way. One with worldly apathy, another with scholarly interest and a third dares participate in his trouble.

It was expected, but the sobs, shaking shoulders and shattering sighs were those of a baby or a small child, and who could withstand such heart-rending cries?

We waited for salvation in a white gown – and it didn't come. Somebody shouted towards the distant nurses' station: "Hey, you there, nurse! The boy has awoken, something must be done." We all knew what it was in such a case: an injection of Patidin, the wonder drug, of which so many ccs are given to the body. It was always good as an epilogue to anaesthesia. But the nurse didn't answer. She was apparently busy.

The boy calmed down a little, perhaps exhausted by the sobbing. For a moment there was silence. And then, suddenly, he opened his mouth and arose as though involuntarily in a swift movement that threatened to break the infusion tube attached to his arm. He opened his eyes wide, glanced to the right and left across the room – and then said quietly, in the voice of a hypnotised man, yet as though weighing and considering every word carefully: "Nurse, nurse, damn your father! If you don't appear immediately, but immediately – we'll see that you're turned out at night, at midnight, for a special parade in full dress, with full combat equipment with all weapons! Cleaned! At ease, you piece of s . . . t!

He dropped back to rest quietly on his bed. He smiled to himself as though with satisfaction. The speech astonished us. Such a well-organised and thought out tirade by a man who has just undergone a serious operation, and while in acute pain – is no mean feat. Somebody giggled, and another echoed it. A slight pause, and we were all swept into stormy uncontrollable laughter, until our chests ached and our breath caught.

Between the guffaws we attempted to give a graphic description of a nurse appearing on midnight parade with full combat kit and with weapons, but nobody succeeded in completing a sentence; the words drowned in laughter.

The scene required only the final touch of the painter's brush: the elderly couple, apparently visitors, who stopped in the doorway of the ward and looked at us with astonished eyes. And no sooner did we catch sight of this flabbergasted couple than we burst into fresh gales of laughter. The whole ward seemed like a ship rocking in a stormy sea. And then, at last, the nurse came running in with the duty doctor to see what was the cause of the riot.

Not one of us could explain, because no one could get out a word before laughter again rolled up leaving us helpless and choked. Only Yisrael succeeded in saying "Additional parade", and then, with difficulty: "With full kit . . . with, with f-u-l-l k-i-t."

These details did not satisfy the curiosity of the doctor and the nurse.

"But what happened? Really, what happened?" the nurse kept repeating.

But her face was already breaking into a slight smile, which slowly spread and then she too was drawn into the general contagion. Even the doctor was incapable of preserving his professional impassiveness, and his lips released a few chuckles of suppressed laughter.

And as we were already hysterical, why not elaborate upon the subject? Somebody maliciously indicated the elderly couple who was still standing in the doorway and exlaimed: "They – they are at fault."

The malicious witticism rocked the room even more. The nurse suddenly remembered her obligations. She sobered up, composed her features into a stern expression and called out to the couple: "Out! These are critical cases! What sort of irresponsibility is this? Now is no time to visit! A little bit of consideration!"

Night. The hut is asleep. The influence of my sedatives is already waning. I lay awake for a long time, chain-smoking, and begging for the moment when the night-nurse would make her rounds, in order to exchange a few words with her.

Suddenly my ears catch a stifled sound. I listen carefully. The sobbing is coming from the boy's bed. I try to see him, but a thick darkness separates us. I can only make out a blurred shape pounding on the spring-bed that creaks underneath.

The whimpers are mixed with groans and mutterings that sound like appeals for aid. "Father, mother." The agonies of a young boy. I remembered how starved I was, during the difficult hours, for somebody to share my misery with me.

At first, I decided to say nothing. I hoped he would fall asleep again, but the faint cries continued and gained intensity. Something must be done. I rose heavily from the bed, dropped into the wheelchair and rolled over to him.

"What is it, boy, why are you crying?"

He answered with difficulty: "It hurts me, God, it hurts me terribly." I decided to be tough: "Look here, friend, we all hurt here, and some very badly. But nobody's crying. You've already seen that nobody cries here. We're all men, and you must also be a man – so that you don't put the hut to shame. True, we're all soldiers and you're still a child. But you must learn from them. You too will be a soldier some day."

I almost fell off my chair when he said: "What child are you talking about? I'm also a soldier." I had thought that he was fifteen at most. He was so skinny and short.

I recovered and resorted to a mixture of teacher and commander: "If you are a soldier, then you must certainly conquer. What happened? How did you get hit?"

He slowly gained control, pulled at his nose and said: "I was stupid. I enlisted two months ago. A private. I was working with a machine-gun. I thought there was no bullet and I pulled the trigger while my other hand was over the barrel. The hand went. The hand went, it left me" – and he again burst into tears. "If you only knew what pains, mother!"

I smiled into my moustache. He has come to tell me about pains. I suggested that he go outside and breathe some clear and cool air, the best remedy for those who can't sleep. I accompanied him. On the way, Deborah the night-nurse stopped us. When she saw his face swollen from tears, she decided that he needed another pain-killing injection. She lay him down on a stretcher in the corridor and jabbed the needle into him. I exchanged some courtesies with the nurse and returned to my bed, like a Boy Scout who has done his good deed for the day.

The light of a torch dazzled me and awoke me. The nurse faced me in panic. "Dudu is gone! He's vanished! He isn't in his bed. He's not outside. Where has the little idiot gone?" She was shaken. The boy's befuddled by sedation and pain-killer. Perhaps he's gone out for a walk and can't find the way back to the hut. I dropped onto my wheelchair and went outside with the nurse. I circled around the hut until I found him: in a dark corner, under some lofty trees, stood a bed and mattress. Dudu was sleeping the sleep of the just. The injections had done their thing. The nurse and I looked at each other and burst out laughing.

In the morning I found him back in bed. When he awoke, he again began crying. Comfort and encouragement from the patients and nurses were of no avail. He went on sobbing with his face to the wall until the noon hours. I understood that something must be done. But what?

I remembered the distant days when I was a raw recruit. I remembered that I had feared a lance corporal, was in terror of a sergeant and had respect for an officer. And then I had an idea:

I consulted quietly with my comrades, Jean Claude, Little Yisrael and Eli "Hanger".

A few minutes later Jean Claude turned to Dudu, pointed to me and declared in reproachful tones: "You know, the colonel is terribly angry with you. He says that you put the army and him to shame. All sorts of visitors come – and what do they see? – a soldier weeping. The colonel will have you thrown out of the room. He doesn't stand for things like that. Be careful."

My face was hidden behind the pages of a newspaper. I sneaked a look and saw the boy rapidly change colour. He threw glances of awe and then of dread at me: "But he spoke to me yesterday. How can it be? He's really a colonel? A battalion commander? I've never spoken to anybody as important as that . . ."

Jean Claude, with a respectful and righteous expression, shrugged his shoulders and nodded his head: "Yes, that's the way he is. Sometimes like a father, sometimes tears us to bits. But he's the commander here and that's the situation."

From behind the cover of my newspaper I dispatched a threatening look at Little Yisrael. He was fighting his laughter. One outburst from him and the whole performance would be irretrievably ruined.

Dudu stared at me worriedly, as though to say: "It can't be. A battalion commander – lying opposite me? Just like that – facing a raw recruit? And he spoke to me yesterday . . ." His sobbing weakened somewhat.

At night everybody's pains got worse. Even Dudu's. He writhed in agony. I went down to Aharon Kaufman, the medical orderly, and asked him to give an injection to the boy. He refused. Drug dosages must be limited at some point and apart from that the doctor hasn't given any orders on the subject.

I went over to Dudu and again fixed him with a tough gaze, which I had rehearsed for his benefit, and asked him to calm down. "I can't, sir, I can't," he answered almost in entreaty. "I want to, but I can't."

I remembered Avramiko's strategem, the orderly who had looked after me in Hut 40. I decided to imitate it: "Listen here. The orderly here doesn't want to give you Patidin. But, as commander of the hut, I have a little bit of influence in the hospital. I'll go and get you the strongest and most soothing drug there is. But know one thing, if you let out one groan after swallowing the pill, I'll send you to military prison when you finish with the hospital."

I went back to Aharon and asked for some sort of pill. Perhaps I'll manage to calm Dudu down. He gave me a Novalgin tablet, suited for relieving light pain, and not for the severe ones with which the boy was inflicted.

I went back to him brandishing the pill in my hand, as though it was a treasure beyond value. He swallowed it joyously. A few moments passed, and he was already breathing steadily in a deep sleep.

I went back to Aharon, puffed with self-satisfaction but by now a victim to my own pains: "I quietened the hut down for you. Now give me something serious against pains."

"Novalgin," he declared with a cunning smile.

"No! Something stronger – perhaps some Vilan. Something serious that will put me to sleep for an hour or two."

"Go to the devil!" Aharon declared and went about his affairs.

I went to bed. I didn't have a battalion commander to play dirty tricks on me.

One day while he was trying to solve a crossword, I noticed Dudu looking at me hesitantly from time to time, I sensed that he wanted to ask something, but didn't dare for, after all, a raw recruit is not entitled to approach a senior officer.

Finally, when I could no longer get the better of a smile that pacified him, he found the courage and with great hesitancy, almost in a whisper, said: "Sir, excuse me, sir, can I bother you for a moment? I'm solving a crossword. Perhaps you know who wrote the poem 'To A Bird'? I can't seem to think of it."

"Bialik," I declared.

That same moment, Little Yisrael reacted with the speed of a jet pilot: "Idiot," he called over to Dudu, "aren't you ashamed to bother the commander with such nonsense?"

Dudu, who was in any case small, shrank still further.

The boy recuperated slowly, and I was already tired of play-acting. But my comrades, who were enjoying the game, begged me to continue for at least a while longer. Dudu – as they tried to convince me – would not be harmed if he didn't know the truth. He would even have something to brag about to his friends, raw re-

160

cruits like him, that he had lived and breathed day and night in the close proximity of a battalion commander.

All soap bubbles must burst. One day, when I returned from my morning tour, and Dudu wasn't in the hut, Yisrael clattered over to me on his crutches: "Listen, the kid has discovered everything. I don't know how. He told us today that you're just a sergeant, just a lousy sergeant who tricked him . . . ."

10

I hear Cora's voice: "I've brought you a visitor."

She short-circuited me out of a nightmarish reverie. The visitor stood facing me. The monster stood facing me. I had, in my time seen many a soul-chilling vision, but nothing like this.

"This is Yisrael Cohen," Cora said. "I promised and I've kept my promise."

I should have smiled at him. I know that that is the way I'm supposed to behave, but I couldn't. I just couldn't. I was too taken aback.

The man's face was a burnt and scarred mask. One eye was covered, and two hideous stumps hung in place of hands. Grotesques which they're even careful not to show in horror movies. If it was for this man that Cora had abandoned me – then she was to be forgiven. If she could spend so much time in his company – then she is a heroine. Simply a heroine.

Yisrael smiles at me: "You've been asleep, eh?"

The simple ordinary human voice coming out of the distorted body drew me back out of shock. It was unanticipated and astonishing. The simple ordinary routine question reminded me that I was faced by a human being. I could already bring myself to force a smile. And even to exchange small talk and hear something of the story of his injury.

But I could not deny my relief when Cora arose and announced that the time had come to return Yisrael to bed. You can only bear such sights in small doses.

That night, Yisrael came back in my dreams. We walked together. In a world of dark horrors. I stumbled along on crutches that threw me face down to lick the crumbled earth, then lifted me only to drop me again, while hollow gusts of laughter circled us. Yisrael held out his arms to pick up the grey shards that lay strewn about us, – and he had no hands! Then the war began, and I was given command of my tank, but I sank down to the bottom of the turret, for I had no legs on which to stand.

Today was a "minor holiday". I achieved Hut 25, which was my first home in Tel Hashomer, under my own steam. I rang the bell and the door opened. "You have a visitor," I declared in great glee. The nurses Rahel, the "Indian" Hanna, madonna Rivka, the other Hanna and Aliza looked at me with surprise. Who was this uninvited guest who trumpeted his arrival so gaily?

After a moment, Hanna raised her hands to her head: "It's Yankele; God, how you've changed."

I never expected the joyous reception which the staff of the hut accorded me. They saw me sitting for the first time. For the first time they heard me laughing.

We could not possibly exclude ourselves from celebrating the surprise party in honour of Jean Claude's ritual circumcision. I'd better place matters in their proper context: not for Jean Claude himself. He had undergone this joyful ceremony a long time ago. But for his son, just born.

Jean Claude had already been rejoicing for weeks over the boy that was to be born. A boy, not a girl. That he had decided. He had brought his wife especially from their home-town Dimona, so that she might give birth near him in Tel Hashomer. But he found no peace: he was still bedridden. He made a momentous decision. To get off his bed. He ordered a volunteer to wheel him in a chair to his wife. When he got down into the chair, his face turned pale and he bit his lips. By the time he came back, his pallor was that of a freshly bleached sheet. But behind all the agonies could be seen the sparkle of his joy: the family was about to grow. A boy would be born.

And that's how it was: a son was born. When the infant was eight days old, the gay bunch in Hut 16 decided to mark the occasion. Bottles of wine and cakes appeared – and the party began.

One of the most eager participants was "Grandfather", who was liberally dispensing blessings and compliments to the Lord and His creations, and wishing Jean Claude great-grandchildren and-great-great-grandchildren. "Grandfather" is an elderly Yemenite who joined us a few days ago. One of the few civilians hospitalised in the hut. Grandfather likes his liquor. His injury, we soon discovered, was a broken leg as the result of a drunken fall.

When he was brought to us, the evening before his operation, he was hugging a bottle of wine from which he deeply imbibed from time to time. The nurses wanted to take the bottle away, for the grapes of Bacchus are not among the medicines prescribed by the learned doctors. The old man let loose a chain of such violent and vituperative curses that the nurses recoiled and finally gave way.

The following day he was taken to the operating theatre. He awoke from anaesthesia before being transferred from the stretcher to bed. The first words to escape his lips, in a scream, were: "Wine, wine – where's my wine?" He got it. And since then had got wine regularly, for if the nurse did not fulfil his wish immediately, he would raise hell and bombard the poor patients around him with any object within reach.

Now, as our merrymaking reached its peak, a procession marched into the hut. It was headed by a stretcher bearing a young boy deep in slumber, followed by two attendants dressed in green. Tailing them, as though in a funeral procession, marched a worried family entourage, its women weeping bitterly.

When the stretcher halted at the centre of the party, we awarded the casualty a glance. Not so bad. A mere fractured leg. We can continue. But look at the horrified faces of the entourage. Their eyes open wide and their mouths agape. They take in this battered rabble of humanity singing at the top of their voices; the empty bottles strewn across the floor, the half-filled bottles clutched in hands, or appended to mouths; and the slices of cake spread everywhere.

It was obvious that they thought they had by mistake stumbled into hell at the height of an orgy. The inhabitants would soon choke over their vomit and be returned to the madhouse.

The stretcher-bearers were oblivious to events around them. They moved on with their burden. Speechless, the entourage followed the stretcher. But their eyes continued to bore into us.

When they had lain their dear one in his bed, they sat around him – these miserables – and continued weeping.

The rejoicing in our room continued. From my vantage point I could see how their sour and angry looks darted at the participants.

"Enough, enough," one of them called over.

No reaction.

A moment later: "I ask you, this boy is very sick. Dangerously ill. Don't shout."

No reaction.

Two of them got up and very deliberately strode over to the focal point of rejoicing: "What do you think this is here? A madhouse? This is a hospital. We will complain to the management. We'll call the police. They'll restore order, they'll get rid of you. What right do you have to do what you're doing? You're criminals, you!"

They ranted on and on. The veterans of the hut, all of whom were valiant warriors, listened attentively. The attentive expressions slowly gave way to amusement: Just imagine it – police! They'll throw us out of the hospital. We've got no right to be here . . .

"Sir, you're crazy," Roberto quietly answered in his South American accent, "you're mad. You've only just come and you're already giving orders? What are you doing here? Visitors aren't allowed into this hut at this hour. It interferes with the patients' rest . . . Nurse!!! The visitors are bothering us. It's already late at night, and they don't let us sleep. Nurse!!! Quickly!"

11

After Jean Claude's son's circumcision celebration, many of us arose in the morning with a hangover. Some vomited all night. We all lusted for the morning cup of coffee. We had a duty roster. Each day, one of the patients who hadn't been wounded in the legs would bring coffee for all of us from the hospital kitchen. This time it was Big Yisrael's turn (not to be confused with Little Yisrael whom we've already met).

Big Yisrael was in the habit of shirking his duties, he was prodded forth by blows from crutches and lusty reproaches. Nevertheless, he did not get up.

We had another account to settle with him, because he often tried to arouse pity for himself, although his wounds were extremely light.

That evening we revenged ourselves upon Yisrael. He, as usual, did not stay in the hut. He was off to visit one or other of his acquaintances in the distant huts.

We had to take a nurse into our confidence. Luckily, the nurse on night duty was Estie Aharonson who was blessed with a sense of humour, and usually enjoyed our pranks. Nevertheless, after joining in our merriment, she would turn serious, adopt a professional posture and say: "You lot are not behaving . . ."

We asked her to double my evening dose of chloralhydrate. This was the bitter drug. We told her that we intended to feed the drug to Yisrael to teach him that crime doesn't pay.

She was shocked: "Are you mad? It's forbidden! It will kill him. You can't take chloralhydrate orally. Only madmen like Yankele take it that way."

We begged and pleaded and entreated until she finally capitulated. The nurses also didn't love Big Yisrael. "Actually, I'm not taking any risk," she declared to assuage her own conscience. "He will in any case notice the terrible taste immediately."

The following morning after our temperature check, Eli "Hanger" went over to Big Yisrael and shook him: "Hey, get up! It's your turn to bring coffee!"

"Leave me alone," Yisrael growled in his sleep. "I don't intend to wake up for your coffee."

"Get up – we're calling you," Eli was obstinate.

"Nothing more to say about it!" Yisrael grew angry although still half asleep. He suddenly remembered: "In any case, it was my turn yesterday and not today."

"O.K.," Eli replied in a generous tone, "this time we'll let you be."

Yisrael turned over and went back to sleep.

It just goes to show that we were still prepared to give Yisrael a last chance . . .

Friendly Fariente went to fetch the coffee as usual. We poured a cup for Yisrael, sweetened it with a lot of sugar, and added the chloralhydrate to the thick mixture. We shook Yisrael who was still deep in slumber: "Yisrael, get up! Coffee." His sleep was clearly untroubled. He grunted something and slumbered on.

"Yisrael, wake up! Coffee!"

All eyes were pinned on his bed. Yisrael grunted, lifted his head slightly, mumbled something and stuck an exploratory hand out towards the coffee. He sipped with closed eyes once, gulped a second time, contorted his face, and shouted: "Pfeui! This coffee's bitter."

But he swallowed the coffee down to the dregs and went back to sleep.

At eight o'clock he was asleep. At nine, he was asleep. At ten, he was asleep. And all this despite the racket of blaring transistors and the lively morning traffic.

At eleven, when his girl – a teacher from the south of the country – arrived, she looked at him with astonishment: "Sleeping to this hour?" She sits beside him and waits. Yisrael is still in a distant world. Eventually her patience is exhausted and she shakes him. He opens one eye and declares: "No coffee", and back he goes to his sunshine world.

He awoke at three in the afternoon.

"You bastards," he growls through clenched lips when he finds out what we did to him. "The devil made bastards like you . . ."

12

Raya declares that I am king of the crutches, and she lies, of course. I hate the crutches. They take more than I can give; my armpits are sore and my hands blistered. I prefer to remain in bed. My head still spins every time I get up.

I can't see an end to my stay in hospital.

I've grown accustomed to the way of life here. Adaptation? Acceptance? Stagnation? It's a fact that even reading with my good eye doesn't attract me at all, and demands a mental effort that I'm not capable of making.

The days flit past, and are like unto each other as two drops of water. The long days. The nights that are even longer. Visitors still descend in masses. Tami, my little daughter, visits me every day. I sometimes take her for a short ride on my wheelchair and she shrieks in delight: "Lovely, my Daddy's got a wheelchair."

Doctors' rounds is the time for levity, especially with Dr. Parin and Dr. Horoshovski. Anka, the ward sister, wrings her hands in desperation when she hears my merry speeches. The psychiatrist looks in occasionally to ask what's new.

I answer her, in a cantor's chant, that there will only be an improvement when they sack all the hospital cooks, because a man can go mad eating this tasteless muck. I add that even the worst of army cooks creates better food under the most difficult conditions, and that when I see the same chicken served me day after day – I am filled with hatred for the whole poultry industry. Under such conditions, how can she expect any improvement? From the expression on the psychiatrist's face it was easy to see that she was finally convinced that I had completely gone off the tracks, with no hope of return.

From the doctors' frowns and snatches of overheard conversation, I learn that no real improvement has taken place. Though I've already been a long time in the hut, what little that is left of my leg is still very swollen, and there's certainly no point for the time being in thinking of fitting an artificial limb. The electric shocks of imaginary pain in the missing ankle continue to strike, and often they twist me up in agony.

13

Here and there the word "leave" can be heard. This refers to a short Saturday excursion from the hospital.

Most of my comrades have already been out on holiday at least once, some even a few times. Yael reports that she occasionally brings up the subject with the doctors. But they tell her the time is not yet ripe. They have their reasons: first, I still run a temperature. Secondly, sterility must be preserved, and this is impossible to guarantee at home. Thirdly, the great number of pills that I take every day – 27. They come in all sizes and colours, and Yael might confuse them at home. Fourthly, my bandages are still being changed three or four times a day, and this Yael will also not know how to do.

She is disappointed.

As for me, I have mixed feelings about anything connected with going home. On the one hand I am longing to see it after such a long time. How many months have passed since I enlisted? Four? For me – an eternity. I would like to lie in my own bed. To play with Tami in her room, to smell the odours of the kitchen. To be at home in a house which I only entered a few short months before the war.

On the other hand, I'm afraid of being cut off from the hospital. I don't believe that I can bear the jogging along the road. I haven't yet forgotten the ambulance that brought me from Rambam Hospital to Tel Hashomer. At home, I'll also be cut off from now familiar surroundings. From my wounded comrades. What will happen if I suffer heavy pain at home? Who will save me? Who will comfort me with drugs? The hospital is my home now, the home of Yaacov Haelyon, the casualty. Will my house in Tel Aviv know how to give me the same degree of security?

The longing to return home, and the fear of returning alternate. But a Thursday inevitably arrives when Dr. Parin announces to Yael that I can go out on holiday. I receive the message while still of two minds.

The following day Yael reports to ward sister Anka to be taught the great mysteries of my case. She comes back loaded down with packages, escorted by Anka who smiles good-naturedly at me. She carries pills and bottles with a liquid for dampening the bandages. In place of changing the bandages, it has been decided to inject the liquid medicaments into the dressings, by means of a big syringe that we have received.

Dr. Eli Antebi appears to give last instructions. The ceremony troubles me. I feel as though I am about to be severed from my safe refuge. I have a frightening thought: I will certainly be in agony at home.

They have recently considerably reduced the dose of analgesics that I am given. Rightly so. My body may become addicted. I could become a morphine addict. But now, in my present situation while my body is in agony, it's difficult to be rational about it. The temptation inherent in a drug and its ability to lessen pain, is too attractive to permit clear-headed judgement and long-term thinking. The drug drives away the pains – and that is what is most important to me for the moment.

I asked the doctor to supply me, against any possible eventuality, with a Vilan pill. The doctor grimaced unhappily. Vilan is a strong drug. I gave my word of honour not to use it, unless I really suffer pains that cannot be borne. It's already known in the ward that I keep my promises. Dr. Antebi nods at Anka. The pill is added to the big collection in Yael's hands.

I am convinced that I have disappointed Yael. She expected me to be excited about my first trip home. I, on the other hand, crept into my shell. I was deep in depression. The car sped through familiar streets near home. Boys and girls in school uniform came out of the Herzliya Gymnasium, the flower stall stood in its usual place by Café Exodus. The sun poured down with the blaze of end of summer. Nothing had changed.

. . . Nothing had changed. An ordinary Friday. Like the one when I left in the evening carrying a small haversack, off to war. I departed at dusk and now I was returning in daylight. A flower stall – just like then. School kids – just like then. Soon we would pass the sun-flower-seed vendor.

I'm going home. Cars are parked, bumper to bumper, on both sides of the street. Just touching, as always. The street cleaner tries to collect the scattered garbage. In another hour, another will re-place her. As usual. The milkman, wearing high waders even in summer, with difficulty pushes his motor cart. He's already old, poor man. I don't see the postman – he must have already finished his round. Is there any mail in the box? A few days ago Yael brought to the hospital a reminder from the income tax. I haven't yet made an annual declaration. Really, I must report the "income" I received.

Things are as usual. As though the war had never been. As though the murderous volcano on the road to Tel Fahar had never exploded. As though there had never been a shell which hit my head, and one to follow that shot splinters into my legs. Everything as usual. A boy hugs his girl's waist and she returns a smile. The skies are blue and smiling. Everything as usual. There is love in the world and flowers and sunflower seeds. Only I am not as usual. I went out at night on two legs, and am returning by day on one.

Life is back to normal and the war is over. Their war, and mine? How will I climb 69 steps on one leg? For ever, on one leg.

And here's the hopscotch drawn on the pavement. Hallo, hop-scotch. The girls of the neighbourhood are now eating lunch. They've abandoned the game. The pattern remains. Ha, the pattern remains. But not for you. You can no longer skip down it surreptitiously. Not for you. The milkman hasn't yet finished his rounds. He goes up and down, up and down steps. His shirt sticky from sweat, and his sour smell, as always, broadcasts his presence from a distance.

First, we take out the wheelchair. Then the crutches, the other packages and the expensive drugs. The problem – in other words me – remains inside. How will I get from the padded car seat up to the flat? Third floor over the pillars.

I say: "I'll walk on crutches."

They say: "Certainly not. You barely manage on level ground, how are you going to go up stairs?"

I say: "I'll make it whatever happens."

They: "Not to be considered."

I: "What will be will be. Either this way, or I go straight back to the hospital."

They: "You will not go back to the hospital. But if you intend to climb on crutches, you will make the return journey in an ambulance. You'll roll down the stairs and break bones, for certain."

I give in and am beaten. As always.

I'm carried up on crossed hands, a "Sabbath chair" as the children call it. My disgrace. When we reached the doorway, I was tired and wrung out as though after a long march. I dropped helplessly into an armchair. My good old armchair. The sweat poured from my body. I closed my eyes.

I didn't imagine my return home this way. Tired, exhausted, frightened and keeping up appearances. Where's the surge of joy? The uplift? The good feeling of belonging?

A cold drink restores my spirits. My eyes pass around the room. What hadn't Yael done to make my return a happy one! The house is alight with splashes of colour – bunches of fragrant flowers. The table is laden down with cakes and my favourite nibbles. The apartment is clean and sparkling.

My friends who brought me, and the good neighbours who heard us ascend the stairs, close in on me with festive expressions, as though saying: "How do you like to be home?"

I try to answer in the language that they expect, and return their smiles.

Tami erupts over me: "Daddy!"

She breaks my heart, this little one. After the first hug, she backs off and examines me with an inquisitive and thorough gaze. Her father is very strange. One leg touches the floor, and the other? "What's that, Daddy? . ."

"Oh, nothing, we gave the leg in for repair."

Then the family on its own. After a little while I escape to my bed. A new one. Yael bought it especially, as a surprise, for my arrival. Lower, so that it will be easy to get onto. What that woman doesn't think of!

170

I couldn't relax. Every few minutes, Tami burst in despite Yael's warning and the closed door. This was no simple affair – they'd returned her father!

The telephone didn't stop ringing. God, how many people worry about my health! How many people are happy that I've returned home! Everyone wanted to visit. Yael forbade it.

At night Yael touched my hand. It betrayed my fever. "You're burning," she said. She turned out the light. My eyes wouldn't close. A few times during the night Yael asked: "Why don't you sleep?" She also couldn't drop off. I tried to lie without moving, so that she shouldn't worry.

The following day, Saturday, Yael said she would return me to hospital. I refused. I wanted to stay. I refused to succumb. Visitors, visitors, visitors. Bandage changing ceremonies. Tami is astounded at the quantity of medicines that I swallow. The delicacy with which my visitors – my best friends talk to me depresses me. They're trying to act "naturally". I'm not the only one playing "things as usual". They as well. It's funny . . .

On Sunday morning, when the hour came to get ready for the return to hospital, I announce in the most vigorous voice that I could muster, that under no circumstances would I go down on somebody's hands. I did not want to leave the house the way they brought met into it. There were arguments, and this time I was victorious.

Yigal Simon descended in front of me. If I fall, he will stop me with his body. Yael walked beside me. I hopped down holding a crutch in my right hand, and the bannister in my left. I did it. Alone. Without help. I won!

I raced over to my bed in the hospital. I had returned home!

Nevertheless, that visit was worthwhile. It relieved me from my attacks of light-headedness.

Henceforward I went home almost every weekend. If the first holiday was a frightened, cautious glimpse at the outside world, those that followed became a refreshment, an open window.

171

BOOK 4

THE WAY BACK

1

"Down to the dining hall!"

"What?"

"Down to the dining hall. This isn't a hospital. No room service here. Forget what it was like in hospital."

"It hurts? We're sorry. Here there are no little tablets against pain. Forget what you had in hospital."

"Have you showered yet?"

"No."

"Then go down to the bathroom and take a shower. This isn't a hospital. There's no washing in bed here. All that is over. Please go and shower."

"Chloralhydrate? What's that? We're sorry. There isn't any here."

"But without it I can't sleep."

"There is none! Perhaps we'll give you a sleeping pill."

"But chloralhydrate is the only thing that puts me to sleep. Tablets don't have any effect on me."

"No!"

"What do you mean, no? I must. The psychiatrist ordered . . ."

"Yes? But here we have none."

I send a questioning glance into the new darkness, across an unfamiliar bed. Where have they brought me today? What is this place? I'm in the hands of the Inquisition.

Something whispered this morning, some hidden sense, that I mustn't agree to go where they want to take me. It's very bad. They took me against my will and threw me in here. What a regime! What hard-heartedness.

What's this. Don't they know who I am? What happened to me? Don't they know I can't go to the dining-room? That if they don't drug me against pain, I won't be able to bear the suffering? That only – only chloralhydrate puts me to sleep! "Here there is none," "Forget it. We are not a hospital." Gentlemen, gentlemen, I'm wounded. I've lost a leg. What are you? A sports club? Some spartan camp for developing toughness? It won't work that way. Not with me.

Today you exploited my weakness and disorientation. If you are a "rehabilitation centre", then please rehabilitate, but without torture...

This morning, during doctors' rounds, it was decided: Jean Claude and Yankele are moving today to the rehabilitation centre. In other words, they're leaving Hut 16.

Yael packed my belongings and also helped Jean Claude. We started out along the road that leads to the rehabilitation centre, facing the hospital.

Nobody bothered to talk to us, involve us in the decision, or even explain to us what goes on there in the centre. The only thing we heard about the centre was: "They make artificial limbs."

I rolled into a strange world of which I knew nothing. A good world? A bad world? That I would find out in the course of time. Meanwhile, hostile. All these noes – each was like a slap in the face. With one sharp blow, the routine and treatment to which I had become accustomed in Hut 16 were wiped out.

When I awoke the following day – wonder of wonders, I had fallen asleep without drugs – a cool morning breeze was wafting through the room, perfumed with early fall, a message from the open spaces.

I examined the new room with curiosity. Five beds in my row, and four facing. Some of them empty. I glanced at my watch and noticed that my neighbours were sleeping soundly despite the late hour. It seems that they don't waken you here to take temperatures.

After a while, the hut began to come to life. Transistors boomed out. Figures hobbling around on crutches, or rolling in wheelchairs, passed down the corridor facing my bed. Most are dressed in civilian clothes, not in hospital pyjamas. Conversations between rooms are carried out in the loudest possible tones. Somebody was holding a dirty dialogue with one of the medical orderlies. A voice called out through the hut "Food, food", and the inmates moved towards the dining-room. I didn't get down. I wasn't hungry.

Later I became aware of friends and acquaintances. To my right lies Ron, my neighbour from Hut 25. His two legs are in casts and his eye is covered. My eye has already been stripped of its patches. They told me that Dudu is in my room, but has gone away on holiday and isn't back yet. Ezra, my platoon commander during the war, lies in a neighbouring room. He was injured a short while after me. His leg remained beside the tank.

The first morning flits by. Doctors' rounds are over. Dr. Weigel serves as ward doctor. He is furious at Dudu and somebody called Avi for extending their leave: "I'll throw them out of the hospital. What do they think this is here?"

Somebody rolls into the room on a wheelchair. He introduces himself as Lazar Eckstein. I'd heard his name in hospital. He's from Mea Sha'arim in Jerusalem. He got caught up in the company of some young warriors, most of whom weren't even half his age. A fifty year old with a thick beard. Silver hairs running through it added years to his age. His booming voice rang out from one end of the hut to the other.

"I'm the father of everybody here," he declared to me in a musical Jewish accent. "What's with you? Healthy already? Yes? Healthy already? It'll be alright, you don't need to worry. We'll all be alright. You're healthy. There's not long to go. Just a little longer. The Name, blessed be He, will help and we'll all come out of here in one piece and strong. The important thing is your state of mind. That's the important thing. Laugh a lot. Forget the pains. It's not good, not good to think about them. Here everybody's a member of the gang. They're all hundred percent. Look at me, here. Everything will be alright."

A smile radiates from my face at the man in the blue pyjamas.

"Lazar," I hear a young voice from the nearby room, "Lazar, you jumping on people again? Enough of the noise, Lazar. Enough, my head aches!"

"Shuki," Lazar responds in friendly tones, "somebody new has arrived. We must get to know him, he must get to know us. We must explain to him, so that he knows what goes on here. A new boy has arrived, Shuki. I'll be over to you in a minute."

Lazar Eckstein – good, innocent and vociferous. How did he roll into our world? I would hear his story in the course of time. During the War of Independence he fought gallantly on one of the strongpoints near Jerusalem. In the Six Day War he was already the father of ten offspring. He asked to enlist and was refused. Lazar did not despair. He abandoned all his plumbing tools, and volunteered for the Army Rabbinate Burial Squad.

During the battle for Jerusalem, a plane fell and its pilot was

177

killed. Unluckily, he lay in the heart of a minefield. Lazar, with his deep faith, did not flinch. He went into the midst of the mines to extricate the body. One of the mines waylaid him as he returned. His leg was amputated.

In the afternoon I have a very pleasant visit from Little Yisrael. "I missed you, my adopted brother," he said, exposing his shining teeth as usual, and winking towards the girl who had pushed his wheelchair from the hospital as though to say: "And what do you think of her?"

The girl, a physiotherapist, had come as a volunteer from Canada immediately after the war. She only knows five or six words in Hebrew. Yisrael, on the other hand, only knows five or six English words. Yet, his charms had captivated her heart. While I was still in Hut 16, he asked me to enrich his English. I taught him to say "I love you . . ." They don't talk much, but her hand almost never leaves his.

I decided to break my "hunger strike". In the evening I went down to the dining hall. The thought of sitting at a table had until now deterred me. Nevertheless, I decided to try it. How many months was it since I last sat at a table? A lively conversation was in full swing. Stinging remarks about the quality of the food, and the smallness of portions, liberally sprinkled with the fervent wish that the cook who prepared this meal will always have only this to eat. The insults were so flowery and obscene that I wouldn't have wanted to be in that cook's shoes at that moment.

While eating, I feel a warm wave of emotion spread through me. So, the devil isn't so terrible. I can eat at a table, like healthy people. The taste of life as it was before I was injured.

I feel at ease. I think about the hut. Whereas Hut 16 was made up of two large halls, our hut is divided into many rooms. Two are big, housing nine beds, and the others have three or four beds. The centre of the hut is occupied by treatment rooms and the nurses' station. I have been put in one of the big rooms.

2

Take it or not? Drink, swallow and sleep like a human being.

Yael had smuggled the drug from the hospital, and prepared a plate of fruit to disguise the taste before she left. Well, why hesitate. It's not a dangerous drug. A few moments of foul taste in the mouth, and then – into the bosom of sleep. Why not? After all, the psychiatrist said so. Why disdain her orders?

No, leave the chloralhydrate alone. Take control of yourself. One day you'll have to be broken of all these drugs. The longer you delay, the harder it will be. If you're a man, decide that today's the day. They don't give drugs to anybody here. You don't need to be different. At least try it. Put your willpower to the test. Test yourself. Test whether your character's strong, or weak and despicable. Fight yourself. What's wrong? You've faced tougher things than this, so stand up to temptation. When you went off on leave for the first time, they gave you Vilan to take home. You were in agony at home, and the Vilan winked at you. But you didn't take it. Say no this time. Don't take.

I can always try the old childish trick – counting sheep crossing the bridge. One sheep, two, three, a brown one. A black one. I'm a black sheep myself if I don't overcome the temptation. Six sheep. Seven sheep . . . What sort of a strange world this rehabilitation is . . . Ten sheep. Eleven. Twenty. The boy shepherd. The boy shepherd with a pack on his back. Twenty-seven sheep. Twenty-eight. I first heard of the rehabilitation centre from Yigal, an Army officer. He asked us to accompany him on a visit to a comrade who was lying here. On the main road he stopped and asked us to get out. "You'll be better off not coming in there with me. Too much shock. Paralysed, maimed, amputees." We got out and waited on the roadside. How many sheep have already crossed the bridge? I got mixed up. Start again from the beginning . . .

No, no. The view isn't pleasant. But now it's us. So what? We'll manage somehow. We'll get out of this, with God's help, as Lazar says. It's a fact that people do leave here. Take for instance that boy who used to come to my friend Amiram Chen's house. Did I ever notice that he had only one flesh and blood leg? I didn't sense anything apart from a shadow of a limp. It was only after my leg was amputated that Amiram told me that this boy had had his leg cut above the knee. Not so terrible. It can't be seen through pants. And that old man who came to see me the day after the operation. He even said that it's possible to swim in the sea.

The important thing – let's get it over and done with. So that

179

they'll send me home. I want to work, to go to the theatre, to friends. Let them do what they've got to do and let me go. And let them find a way to finish off the pains. And especially the imaginary pains. The doctors don't talk about them, as though they're nursing a secret. I'll have to do something about it. If I decided to get down and go to eat at a table, I can also break with sleeping drugs. If they are imaginary pains, it means they don't exist except in my imagination. After all, I don't have a sole to my foot, I don't have an ankle and I don't have a shin. I must fight this strange phenomenon. If I succeed in convincing myself that what seems to hurt can't really hurt, perhaps I'll succeed in ridding myself of these illusions. It's possible to try. And if I must try, then let's begin now . . .

A movie will be shown on the big lawn. It's worth trying. Until the movie comes on, Lazar dances about on one leg. He's in a good mood today: he was visited this afternoon by a multitude who poured out of a loaded pick-up. All of them – his sons . . .

After a few moments of waiting for the movie, my eyes blur and close.

Yael turns the wheelchair back towards the hut. In a dark corner of the lawn a group of rehabilitation veterans sits. They're talking about "rights". While listening to the conversation, I remembered the social worker who came the day after my amputation, and said that I had entered the family of disabled, and could expect some benefits. The subject hadn't bothered me until today. The conversation here, on the lawn, was lively and awakened my curiosity.

"It's possible," somebody said, "to get a gasoline station. That's a good business."

"A pox on 'it's possible'," his colleague responded. "Only those with pull in the Ministry of Defence Rehabilitation Department get a gasoline station!"

"Or somebody who smashes the tables there," a third added. "If you don't create some kind of a fuss there, you won't get anything."

"And what about the car? Is it true that they let you buy a big American car without taxes?" somebody asks. Apparently a new recruit to rehabilitation, just like me.

"Yes, of course," the expert answers cynically. "When you break your spinal cord. Only paralysis cases get them. For us, there are restrictions. Anyone who lost his leg above the knee – gets a car up to 20 horsepower. Anybody below the knee – up to 17 horsepower."

"Not so bad, not so bad," the raw recruit mumbles. "I didn't have a car at all before the war. Now I'll have a Peugeot or a Cortina or a Taunus. Fantastic."

"You made a good deal," the cynic replies. "You gave a leg, you receive a car."

The raw recruit hesitantly asks whether help is given to change apartments. He lives on the fourth floor and will have difficulty climbing steps.

"Of course you'll get a flat. You deserve it. The state looks after you, my son," the cynic continued to conduct the conversation. "The state says: You were injured, ah-ah, not so good. I compensate the heroes of the homeland. You will get a loan which will perhaps, with difficulty, allow you to move into some lousy neighbourhood, and you'll have to pay it off for the rest of your life. You didn't make a good deal. Instead of fighting, you should have been a new immigrant. They get much better and much bigger loans."

"Do you think so? Can't be," the raw recruit says and changes the subject. "I don't know whether I'll be able to find work as a welder without a leg. Where will I get the money to pay off loans?"

"And where will you get the money to pay for the tax-free car?"

The content of this conversation isn't to my liking. I wonder whether the cynic is right. I was in a hurry to get back to my room. Rehabilitation or no rehabilitation, my leg is already crying hallelujah.

On their return from the movie, Dudu Badusa and Avi Lavi, my neighbours in the room, wage a peculiar battle. One beats the other on his amputated limb, while issueing war cries such as "I'll show you! Amputated mug", and "Shut up, disabled lump".

The macabre humour of rehabilitation: the one who is maimed jokes at the limp of the amputee, and they both laugh. The amputee mocks the strange hooks that replace the other's hand, and explains how to use them to pinch a girl, and they both revel in it. The artificial legs sometimes serve as improvised flower vases, and the visitors shudder. The shock on visitors' faces causes pleasure and laughter. Shuki Kaufman announces to all who enter: "Shalom, sir, cripples lie here."

There are those who make use of every opportunity to visit home. The king is Yitzhak Ganis. Already at two in the afternoon, he hovers around the doctor's room. No sooner does the doctor depart, then he rushes to his bed, pulls on pants and a shirt, combs his hair and escapes in a waiting friend's car. He's back early in the morning: "Anybody ask about me? Has the doctor arrived yet?"

"Don't ask, don't ask," Ron tells him. "The doctor came last night, heard you'd bolted and turned as red as a beetroot. He said he'd throw you out of the hospital."

Ganis blanches for a moment, but catches on to the deceit and grunts: "Pigs." Since we're still in our beds, and his day began a long time ago, he as usual volunteers to pour out the good coffee that he brought from home.

The space around the nurses' station and the entrance to the hut serve as our community social centre. The patients sit and talk from morning to the late hours of the night. Lazar says that he can't go back to his work as a plumber. Haim, a building carpenter, wonders what trade he will find now. Ezra Brosh, a driving teacher, is convinced that he will still be able to carry on. I am happy that I can continue my work as a journalist, if only things work out alright.

The conversation usually turns to the subject of cars. Most of the candidates for rehabilitation have never owned an automobile. They are bemused at the possibility of acquiring a model of which they could never have dreamt on their previous salaries. The youngsters, the "conscripts", are especially enthusiastic. A daily car fair takes place here. Automobile agencies rush to the rehabilitation centre as though to an international fair. Where else can they find such a concentration of potential buyers? Every agent brings a long convoy of all the models that he sells. None have any faults. All are roadworthy. All were as if built specially for the needs of the disabled. The boys are impressed and convinced – and change their minds the following day, when another agent comes to denigrate his predecessor's collection. These shows arouse nausea in me: the agents look like vultures hovering over the carcasses.

The subject passes from automobiles to gossip about the doctors, the nurses, the physiotherapists and everybody else. They good-naturedly touch on all the women on the staff. "Oh, oh! – they're hungry!" – the women say of them, not without some enjoyment. The participants in these conversations have a lot to say about medical treatment, but surprisingly they almost never mention the war.

The conversations don't take place on an empty stomach. We may be sinned against as far as food is concerned, but there's always plenty of coffee. Not hospital coffee, with its taste of ashes and chlorine mixed in water, but the best coffee. A quarter of an hour hasn't passed since the last round, and one of our experts has already been sent to the kitchen. Usually Ganis goes. He has acquired the title of coffee chef.

The composition of the group taking part in these sit-ins constantly changes. One gets up and goes to the workshop to try on a leg or hand. Another remembers his turn to exercise in physiotherapy. Others go to the work therapy rooms, to kill a few spare hours in handicrafts.

The gay bunch attracts some of the rehabilitation centre staff who are popular with the casualties. One of the participants in these discussions is the secretary of the centre, Simoha Goldberg. He comes with laden hands, transistors, watches, razor blades and a variety of other gadgetry. He's always ready to hear out any request, and to do everything to fulfil it, and we repay him with coffee.

Another great subscriber to our coffee is Yoske Arbiv from the workshop, a man of unusual dimensions. His pot-belly trumpets his arrival long before the rest of his body appears. He is sometimes joined by his partner in leg manufacture, Haim Potakovski. He is less valuable than Yoske, but just as devoted. Shlomo Freund, who prepares artificial hands, also appears. He never misses anything that's going on in the theatre world. When he comes to chat with us, he's prepared to analyse every literary creation; he repeatedly declares that the true heroes of the war are not those who lie here, but their good wives. "And in passing, have a little cognac. . ."

3

And the good coffee spilling over finally drew me to the workshop. I wait and watch. Poised fearfully on a high bed and ready for anything. Yoske and Haim are busy with my damaged leg. They tell me they'll fashion me a temporary leg. I was surprised, and curious to learn the peculiar qualities and qualifications of a "temporary leg".

Its purpose, Yoske and Haim patiently explain, is to prepare me for that great day when I will be granted the leg on which I will go

183

out to meet life. Firstly, so that I don't forget to walk. "You'd be surprised how quickly the brain centres forget the tasks they were given by the Creator."

After a day or two they again invite me to the workshop. They display a wondrously ugly object. At one end hangs my shoe, filled with wood stuffing, and with an iron pipe projecting out of it. At the end of the pipe are some wooden cubes. Between these are various bolts and screws and a strange unrecognisable installation.

"Here. It's yours. The leg," they say.

I quake.

"Just a moment, we'll attach it to your cast." They ignore the incredulous expression on my face, and get on with their work.

I left the workshop on two legs. One natural, formed in my mother's womb. The second, a most weighty creation which the most satanic imagination couldn't call a leg.

I stopped on the wide lawn. A few casualties were strolling with their visitors and children. A little boy, about five years old, passed by me half running and half skipping. He suddenly pulled up, came back and stood facing me, while he very thoroughly examined the "thing" that was hanging from me.

"What a funny leg," he said, perhaps to himself and perhaps to me, "it should be taken out."

Why he wanted to remove it, I couldn't understand. But he meant what he said and began to tug at the leg with all his strength. I was so astonished that I didn't stop him. His mother came at a run and pulled him away, blushing furiously and mumbling apologies.

After they left, I burst out laughing.

"What are you laughing at, Yankele? Are you happy? Oh, I see they've already given you a temporary leg. That's progress, that's progress."

I knew the voice. I raised my eyes. It required a small effort to recognise the man: Yisrael Cohen. That monster that Cora had brought to Hut 16 two months ago. What wondrous changes had taken place! His face was much improved. The scars remained, but were blurred. His skin was no longer so pale. And the main thing, two arms hung in the sleeves on both sides of his body. Was this a trick? No. Not a trick. Artificial arms. In place of palms and fingers, two hooks extended from each sleeve.

One day they began to film us. We became actors in a movie. The movie, apparently intended for medical education, showed us – the disabled – in various activities.

We sat around a table in the dining-hall and were asked to eat. We were all actors, but Yisrael Cohen was the star. The lens focussed on him, while he tried to raise food to his mouth. It took great effort. But he was obstinate and would not despair.

He had already been trying to feed himself for some time. But the hooks that served in place of palms deceived him. A spoonful of soup overturned and its contents poured over his trousers.

A piece of meat slipped between the tines of a fork, time and again, until it was trapped. He had especial difficulty in raising a cup of water to his mouth.

"Patience, boys," he said to the cameramen, "it may not work the hundredth time, but I'll succeed on the hundred and first."

Of course, he succeeded. As always.

Only yesterday he came and displayed a written sheet before us proudly. "I wrote the lot," he said. "With these hooks."

It took him a whole week, day by day, until he mastered the pen well enough to write the page.

After the filming, he slipped behind the back of one of the crew. He showed us the wallet that he had "pickpocketed" from the cameraman, with a skill that would provide tough competition for somebody with flesh and blood hands. He returned the wallet to its owner, and declared: "Not much more left. Only to learn how to button my trousers and soap myself in the bath. But we'll overcome that as well."

I went over to shake his hand. The effort he had made in eating with a knife and fork was deserving of a compliment. He gave me a "hand". I suddenly trembled: God, I'd shaken his hand as though it was that of any other man. I didn't even notice the chill of the hooks. And how naturally he extended them . . .

What's preferable? Or better: what's worse? To be maimed or amptutated? Or in the jargon of the inhabitants of the hut: "A Trumpeldor" (one armed Jewish hero of the Czarist wars) or "a Douglas Bader" (legless RAF pilot)?

Opinions were divided. Each was convinced that the limb he had lost was the most essential. The "pilots" said that it was possible to manage even without a hand. Without a leg, a man could not move. An artificial hand hanging from the shoulder doesn't hurt. But if you put all your body-weight on an artificial leg, "it hurts, oh boy how it hurts".

"Yes," a young "Trumpeldor" shouted. "Have you tried to caress a girl with one hand? Have you considered what she thinks when she feels the second hand, the one made of plastic? Have you tried to drive with one hand? And have you, for example, tried to fight somebody?"

"Ah, you amputees," somebody reproached. "A leg, a hand. What would happen if you'd lost your prick? Be grateful that it's only a hand or a leg."

A hand or a leg. Must consult Shuki Kaufman. He lost both a hand and a leg. On the face of it there's no greater expert for deciding this weighty problem. But he's shut himself away with his tape recorder, which is blaring out "I Had a Boy that I Loved". Is Shuki in love with somebody? I wouldn't know. But a lot of girls chase him.

On my way to the hut the sun was behind my back and threw my shadow forwards. I looked at the shadow. Two legs. Not like a week ago. Not like two weeks ago, when the left one was shorter. I felt an unexpected pleasant sensation: again on two legs!

"Ah, you've already got your temporary? Good luck. Really, best of luck," says Yitzhak Ganis, my neighbour, as I sprawl on my bed. I was still excited at what I had seen reflected in my shadow.

Good and smiling Ganis still has to undergo a lot of operations and pour us many cups of coffee. A short while after leaving rehabilitation – he would be killed in a traffic accident.

My temporary leg, attached to my body by the cast, doesn't leave me even at night. It can't be removed. Ron, lying next to me, jokes: "Tell me. Do you go to bed at home with your shoes on? . . ."

"Ha," I reply dryly, "ha, ha, ha."

I try to walk on the "temporary" as though it was a real leg. It doesn't work. The moment my body-weight transfers to it, I feel a sharp pain which forces me to lift it straight away.

I don't despair, but the intervals between attempts get ever longer. If it hurts so much, how will I progress?

I escape to the wheelchair. The tempting and comfortable refuge.

A hunger strike is declared in the hut. We are demanding distribution of hot tea. The food is the subject of incessant bitterness. The quantities are small, portions are handed out stingily and the taste is insipid.

The rehabilitation nurses, Leah Bornstein and Tova Tal, shake their heads sadly: "What do you want? The food is brought from the hospital, we don't prepare it and we don't decide the quantity."

We have no other address for our grievances, and it's growing day by day. "What's this? Are they starving us? What do we care about caloric content? We want food."

The duty medical orderly is panicked by the strike. This was all he needed. The hungry bunch soon break the strike. The following day, the fact of the strike was publicised, and now we get hot tea, and – wonder of wonders – a bottle of oil to add taste to the bland and insipid salad.

4

A few days after they "assembled" my temporary leg, I was summoned to the physiotherapy hall to learn how to walk.

I wheeled my chair into the hall which resembled a large gymnasium. Swedish ladders hung from one wall, a hoop for basket-ball in another corner, bundles of weights for lifting, and springs for stretching were strewn here and there.

So this is the place where people are taught, among other things, a lesson that they had forgotten: how to walk.

A large group is bunched around the basket-ball hoop, trying to get the ball in. Its members seem completely healthy. Another group is exercising on mattresses. At the end of the hall I spot somebody in a wheelchair and a physiotherapist, dressed in green, leaning over him raising and lowering his arms. Not far from them, another physiotherapist and a boy equipped like me with a temporary leg. They were kicking a ball, about the size of a tennis ball, backwards and forwards.

In an inside room, deep in the hut, men are lying on mattresses while physiotherapists move their limbs. In another room, somebody is walking on a "final" limb – not on a "temporary" like mine. His limp is pronounced.

"You, what are you looking for here?" – That is Major Ruth Sheinfeld, the commandant of physiotherapy.

"I was invited."

"Ah, you are. Dina! Come here."

Dina, a young dark-haired girl whose belt proclaims that she is not yet a qualified physiotherapist but only a student, takes me under her wing: "Come on, let's play football."

I look at her in astonishment. Football? Me? With this young girl? Where? I parted company with football a long time ago, and this young girl seems more suited to love-play than any other kind. I smile to show that I understood her joke.

"Come on then," she says.

She places herself facing me and explains: "I'll kick the ball to you, and you kick it back."

I didn't quite understand what the game was about, and why we were doing it, but I accepted the ruling. She kicked to me, and I . . . What do I do? I can't kick with my healthy leg because then I'll be putting all my weight on the amputated leg. And it's certainly not possible with the temporary leg.

"Well," the girl says, "why don't you return it?"

I shrug my shoulders: "How?"

"Once with your healthy leg and once with the other," she explains patiently. "Try it, O.K.?"

When the ball comes to me, I raise my whole body, lean on the crutches and kick with the healthy leg.

"That's no trick," she says. "Without leaning on the crutches! Put them on the floor, please." When the ball comes the second time, I transfer my body-weight onto the temporary leg and kick with the healthy one. A terrific pain rushed through my body. A groan escapes my lips.

"Hurts a little, eh?" the girl says sympathetically. "But there's no alternative, you must try."

We go on. It's a torture that cannot be described in words. After a few passes, when my body is already soaked in sweat, she releases me: "We've done enough for today. We'll go on tomorrow."

I roll, aching all over, back to the hut. If the beginning is so bad, what will the continuation be like? Football isn't my sport.

Therefore, handball. In the afternoon hours of the same day, a ball bursts into our room. It is followed by the stormy entrance of a good-looking girl: "Come on, boys. Let's have a game."

"That's Dahlia, Professor Shapira's wife. She dabbles in sport therapy," Ganis tells me. "Come on let's play a bit. There'll be no problem for you."

I roll with my comrades over to the physiotherapy hall. A volley-ball net is now stretched across its width. I settle down to be a spectator, but the girl doesn't let me alone. She called me over with a big smile: "Come on, join in."

My comrades organise themselves sitting along both sides of the net. Dahlia lowers it towards the floor. Now I understand how I can participate in the game. The players play sitting down. I am happy for the opportunity to stretch my bones. Not only that: It's been a long road to this volley-ball net . . .

The game progresses with great enthusiasm. Shouts of joy and anger whenever the ball is lost. I don't play as well as I used to. For some reason, my hands miss their mark by a few inches.

In the evening, after turning off the lights, my neighbour Ron turns to me: "Tell me, is something wrong with you? I noticed your misses today, and remembered that they happen often. For example, when you tap the ash off your cigarette, or pour water from the jug into a cup. Perhaps it's because of your eye?"

I really don't know. Ron is right. My misses are strange. I hadn't thought about them. My attention was centred on my leg. The eye is no more than an appendix, treated every few weeks in the eye clinic.

The following day, I am again Dina's guest.

"Today, no football," she announces to me. "We'll learn to walk between the parallel bars."

Dina explains what I must do. Lay the crutches down, and lean with both arms on the parallel bars. "Simply try to walk. Once on the healthy leg, and once on the other. Don't rush. Slowly – slowly, so that it won't hurt too much. You'll see that within a few days you'll be making nice progress."

She takes up a position next to me. I try to walk. The healthy leg moves forward. Nicely. Now, I must transfer my body-weight onto the temporary leg. A step. The sharp and recognisable pain rocks me in an instant back onto the healthy leg. On it, I can rest with no problems. No, there's no difference between football and the parallel bars. Both are versions of hell.

As time passes, somebody calls Dina from the depths of the hall. "Go on trying," she says, "I'll be back straight away."

Failure. That's what you are. A coward. You don't dare. You

don't know how to bear pain. Without it, it's impossible to progress.
You're not the only one who's in pain. Others here are just like you.
They've tried and succeeded. You afraid? Of what? You're despicable, son, miserable. If you don't fight your weakness, you'll remain
here. On a wheelchair. Begin to walk, for Christ's sake!

I take my hands off the parallel bar, place my body firmly on both
legs, and without holding anything, stride forwards. A step, two,
three, four . . .

"Stop! What are you doing?" Dina, who was on her way over
screamed. "You mustn't without hands, you mustn't! You don't
know."

That same moment, I came to myself – grasped what I had done.
In a powerful pressing stream, as though from a fireman's hose,
pains flooded through all my limbs. I almost passed out. Again, without knowing what I was doing, I grasped Dina's face between my
two hands, and kissed her on the cheek: "I walked! Do you understand
that! I walked . . ."

She blushed: "Yes, that was very nice. But don't dare repeat it.
I'm responsible for you and had they caught you, I would get it on
the head. It's too early for you, too early and dangerous. That's
the reason why we stopped playing football . . ."

My pride was but equal to my torment. I knew that what I had
done on the spur of the moment would be very difficult to repeat with
a cool head. I had walked! On both my legs! Four paces!

5

I wait with unbearable impatience for Saturday leave. I already want
to climb the wooden steps placed in the centre of the hall. The pro-
gressive brethren amongst us practise climbing up and down stairs to
ready themselves for what waits at home.

I went over to them. I laid my crutches down beside them, and
grasped the rails on both sides. Major Ruti dashed over. "What are
you doing? You mustn't. First of all learn to walk, and then climb
steps. I don't like people doing things without permission. When we
say that you're ready – then climb. Not now. What's this? You want
to break your leg? Haven't you gone through enough?"

"But, Ruti," I told her, "I've already climbed steps in my own home, even before I had this temporary leg. I only want to learn to climb without crutches, with the help of the rail alone."

"Certainly not," she replies decisively.

"In that case, certainly yes," I retort boldly.

She gives way. She has a heart of gold. To be on the safe side, she stands next to me. The climb and descent are very tiring and take a lot of energy. I practise, and practise again. I don't fall.

"What you won't do for your leave!" Ruti shakes her head in wonder. "Enough, enough. You already know how to handle steps..."

That same Saturday I climbed the steps of my home, supported by a rail in one hand and a crutch in the other. On Saturday night, before darkness fell, as we stood by the car in which Yael was to return me to hospital, I saw the horror with which people were staring at me, people who were not familiar with the sights which are so natural in rehabilitation.

I was wearing short pants, with the temporary leg sticking out below. Two old people came towards me, stopped for a moment and threw me a long, puzzled and shocked look. It was some time before they realised that their curiosity was neither polite nor pleasant, and they quickly passed me, careful to move in a wide arc, while continuing to look back.

They began to take us to theatre and entertainment programmes.

After the evening meal, a convoy of private cars or military vehicles would cluster at the entrance to the hut. We would climb into them, or were lifted in by others. The conglomeration of unfortunates would be spewed out close to the entrance to the hall, under the shocked eyes of the audience.

It is easy to imagine the reactions of those who came to pass a pleasant evening at the theatre and suddenly found themselves joined by a large public of variegated limbless, a motley of passengers on wheelchairs, the more fortunate hopping on crutches, maimed, scarred and bandaged.

There were those that turned their eyes aside. In my heart, I blessed them. The others – the majority – looked at us with curiosity, pity, evaluating and calculating. I didn't find their gaze pleasant.

"What is it? What have we got to be ashamed of," Dudu replied one day when I reproached him for attending a performance in the

Soldiers' Club in pyjamas. Dudu astonished the audience there by hopping at terrifying speed on one leg up the stairs without the aid of crutches.

He is injured, he is an amputee, everything goes – so he said.

Displays of this kind (imagine long-bearded Lazar, dressed in pyjamas, humming Hassidic tunes, gambolling in the foyer of a theatre) are perhaps a subject for psychological research. I think they were a form of defiance: We are heroes! For us, these social conventions are nil! It won't hurt you, the healthy ones, to be a little shocked. Some of us, for the same reason allowed ourselves to chew steaks through the performance, and smoke cigarettes. No usher was summoned. "Our wounded" can do whatever they want . . .

"A rat, a rat!" a woman's scream pierced the silence in the hut. I rushed on my wheelchair towards the dining-hall from where the voice came. I saw Hagit Yaron, the cute little volunteer, standing as white as a sheet and pointing at a rat racing along the window-frame. Uri Rosenman stood next to her, roaring with laughter. I joined in his laughter.

"What are you laughing at?" she was insulted. "She, it, passed right next to me."

The rat appeared while the two were sitting with books and notebooks, studying. All Uri's memories, and all the knowledge that he had acquired during his twenty-one years, had as though poured out through the hole made by the bullet in his brain. Uri forgot the alphabet, didn't know how to read, and forgot the simplest arithmetic. He decided to quickly make up what he had lost. When he mentioned the period of time that he had allocated to this, people shook their heads: the boy's crazy.

The day was too short for him: early in the morning, he would limp over to the speech therapist, to improve the diction of his cut and twisted mouth.

From the speech therapist he passed on to the physiotherapist to exercise his paralysed arm, which he hoped to restore to usefulness, though he was told that the chances were extremely slight. He ignored the prognosis.

As soon as he finished exercises, he turned to school books. Here, Hagit stood by him. The beautiful twelfth grade schoolgirl, who herself faced the pressures of matriculation examinations, was his private teacher. Every day they would sit to a late hour at night. Hagit taught, and Uri silently absorbed her words. Her clear tones and his rasping voice mingled together, and it was difficult to decide whose happiness was the greatest when Uri took yet another step forwards.

"Laughter over a rat will cost you dearly," Hagit said as her panic died down. "Just wait till you see the homework I'm going to assign you! Three times more than usual!" Uri smiled.

6

"Get up, Yaacov, get up!" Who's shaking me with such a heavy hand? I unwillingly force my gummed eyelids apart. Yoske, Yoske Arbiv from the workshop.

"Get up, Yaacov, I've brought you the limb. Try it on, try it on, boy."

An unexpected gift. In his hand he holds an artificial leg, almost finished. This will be the leg on which I go out into the world. I wake up with a warm feeling: I can't believe it, I've got my leg!

I don't know how you get into a leg like this. Yoske helps me: first you must pull on a nylon sock, and then a wool sock, and then force the stump into it. As though in passing, he says: "I wanted you to get up on the right side this morning. Today's going to be a happy day. Now – are you happy?"

"Very happy, Yoske, really happy. But you're mad. You didn't have to get up this early for me."

"See here, I could guess how you've been waiting for this leg . . ."

With great difficulty I got into the new leg, and with great caution tried to transfer my weight onto it. It hurt.

"Don't panic," Yoske soothes me. "When they put in a false tooth, the body doesn't like it so well at first. Some time passes and you get used to it. Don't forget that your stump is still very sensitive. Anything touches it and you go through the ceiling. Don't give up if it doesn't work at first. You'll come to the workshop, and we'll fix it a number of times before you feel secure in it. What's important now is to get used to it."

I decided to try. I started out leaning on my crutch. A very short distance. The space from my bed to the one at the far end of the room. Yoske stopped me and said: "Enough! Now take it off. At least in the first stages, you eat it a spoon at a time. If you don't – you'll damage the stump, and it will swell up – you'll have to wait a long time before you can try it again."

He went out, taking the limb with him. They don't trust us. They're afraid that, despite their instructions and prohibitions, we won't overcome our desires.

At lunch time, I was called to the workshop. I rolled over in a wheelchair with little Ruti Shai, my regular physiotherapist. We took the limb to exercise with it. The first lesson was very short. They were careful not to damage or tire the stump. After the lesson, Ruti ordered me to return the artificial leg to the workshop. I picked it up and took it with me to my room. After all, when they finally give a man a leg in place of the natural one taken away from him, why can't he keep it with him – caress it with his eyes and secretly put it on? Put it on? Is that the right word? A leg: do you put on a leg? That sounds a bit thick. Discordant. But there's no other way. You can't dress up in a leg, or even pull it on like a sock. And certainly not instal it. "I put it on, like a shoe," the old man who came to console me, told me the day after they amputated my leg. And so, put it on . . .

The days pass. From time to time I try to walk with the new leg, with a little help from the crutches. But, it's a vain illusion. First step – okay. Second step – not bad. If so, then everything's alright. But no! The leg starts issuing a long series of audible shrieks of protest. I must hop on my good leg to my bed, and take it off quickly.

I believe that the more exercise, the more I walk on my new leg, the less pain there will be. All you need is to get used to it, learn to control yourself. Pain? No matter!! You've got no alternative. Otherwise you'll never get out of here.

When no one's looking, I pull some sharp tricks of my own. I go behind the rehabilitation centre, and fling my crutches as far as I can. Now, there's no alternative. I can't walk with them. I won't be able to go anywhere, unless I walk. With the first steps, I am in high spirits and proud of the idea. Immediately afterwards, the leg begins to broadcast pain messages which grow with each additional step. One more step and the pains turn into an inferno of agony. Halfway, I curse myself for a stupid idea. I must sit on the ground and rest. The moment I arise and start walking, the pains will be stronger than they were. The stretch that still remains to reach the crutches is a nightmare. The crutches seem at the end of the world. When will I reach them?

Covered in cold sweat, I pounce on them and with the last of my strength reach the bed. There, I remove the artificial limb to find that the stump has swollen up considerably and the bandages are soaked in blood. That's it! Now I won't be able to get into it all day. Perhaps not even tomorrow.

Yoske and Haim, artificial leg experts, come from the workshop to visit me. They persuade me to behave calmly, to be patient. "This isn't a simple matter," they say. "When they cut a leg, it means that they've cut muscles, bones, nerves, ligaments, blood vessels. Whatever remains is very sensitive. You must be careful. If you're not careful we'll have no alternative but to take the limb away from you."

Each body responds differently to the artificial leg. It to a great extent depends on the success of the surgeon who amputated; on the success of the technicians in adapting the artificial limb in a manner which won't press, and won't damage the sensitive points that remain on the stump; on the different number of sensitive points that each one has. And finally, on the character of the leg bearer himself – in other words, the amputee.

Meanwhile, I don't sense any progress, and am downcast.

Now I cannot but be angry with myself, because of what I thought of Peewee, the first leg amputee that I met. I first saw him the day after I arrived in Tel Hashomer. He was moving around on a wheelchair. One pyjama leg was empty. His leg had been amputated during the war. Because he was injured only in the leg, he was among the first to arrive in the rehabilitation centre, and was among the first war-wounded to be fitted with an artificial limb. When I came to the rehabilitation centre, he was already leaning on crutches, carrying the limb and complaining about the pain that it gave him.

Every time I went to the workshop, I would see him consulting with Haim and Yoske as to changes so that the leg would fit more comfortably.

I was contemptuous of his complaints. It had already come to my notice that the staff classified the casualties into two types: those who battle to overcome their pains, and the weak who surrender to the adversary. I pigeon-holed him into the last group. Why does he complain so much? When you get down to it he's wearing nothing but a shoe – somewhat higher, but still a mere shoe. Why does he buzz around everyone with his whining?

And in my smug ignorance I behaved improperly towards him, at least in my thoughts. An artificial limb isn't a shoe. A stump is not the sole of a foot. And the road to be traversed by the untutored traveller is long and strait.

"You're a thief, Dudu," Ron accuses Dudu Badusa.

"Shame on you," says Ganis. "A girl comes to visit her cousin, what do you do? Take her away from her poor relative. In a flash! She's already yours. You're short of girls? They stick to you, don't they?! It should only happen to me. I'm married, I . . . And the cousin? Remains alone. He has no visitor, he's left with nothing. He only has the bastard Dudu in the next bed, who pinches his visitors. Ah Dudu, that's not the way. Shame on you!"

Dudu is angry. Or at least, he impersonates someone who's angry, but you don't know whether or not he's really smiling to himself: "Oop! I'm fed up with the lot of you. You've got nothing to do except pick on me. You, Ganis, who asked you to shove your nose into everything? Go and make coffee. That suits you better."

After a moment he softens: "She's nice, isn't she?"

"Cousin!" Ron turned to reproach the girl, a sixteen year old high school student. "Pay attention to your cousin. Address him only, please. Don't talk to strangers. You're a minor. Mommy and Daddy won't approve. Dudu is a dangerous man for little girls to know!"

Dudu breaks into deep laughter, but the "cousin" blushes to her ear-lobes, mumbles an apology in a weak voice, and hastens to turn her face to her injured relative, so that he shouldn't feel neglected.

"Ah, leave those pigs alone," her cousin calms her. "They've got nothing better to do, so they jump on people."

Though he isn't particularly attractive right now, with all his wrappings and trappings, the girls stick to Dudu. He was always a Don Juan. And now, even as a casualty, his bed is a focal point for the girls, while we try to figure out how they all got there. But the "cousin" had really captured his heart. The wild Dudu vanished. In his place, a new creature – friendly, gentle and well-mannered to his fellow-men. And in later days he would marry Ruti, the "cousin".

7

The days dribble by slowly. There's no great change. There is no untouched spot left on the artificial limb. It is a motley of patches on patches, the result of attempts to repair and adjust it. Haim and Yoske weary of it and shrug their shoulders helplessly: they cannot find the root of its evil. As opposed to others, I have no external marks that indicated where the limb is damaging flesh. They can't succeed in finding the source of pain. The doctors also offer no solution. One whispered in my ear that, in his opinion, a mistake had been made. They should have waited a few more months before the burden of the artificial leg was loaded on my amputated stump.

Recently, it's been deceiving me. It allows me to walk a few paces without any pain, and then it suddenly attacks. Each time anew I delude myself that at long last I have adapted to the new limb, that the long episode of agony is over – and each time I am cruelly awoken from the illusion.

One day, while Professor Shapira is present on his weekly visit, the leg shows off its tricks. I pass down the corridor and shout to the professor: "Look, look, it doesn't hurt. I can walk."

He turns a happy smile on me, puts me at the end of the corridor so that I should demonstrate. I walk upright, without any hint of a limp. After a few steps, the illusion passes. My leg is as though caught in a vice. I try to hide my pain, not to destroy the performance. Unwittingly, my teeth bite deep into my lips. The professor comes nearer and says quietly: "Enough, I can see you're suffering. It's not worth the effort."

The group outings to places of entertainment have an advantage. You don't stand alone facing the gaze of the masses. One day, Yael and my good friends, Bubi and Odeda, decide to take me out to see the film "The Six Days" at Mograbi Cinema. They say it's well done and I'll certainly want to see the reconstruction of the battle of Tel Fahar, in which I participated.

The first time out without the protection of my hospital "family".

I agree readily. We arrive at the cinema. The fresh scars on my face, the crutches which support me, attract attention and I feel considerable discomfort. Climbing so many stairs to the balcony is difficult. As I finally sit down in a seat next to the aisle, I have to stick my leg out, because I can't bend it. Because it's hanging in thin air with no support, the pain is great. In addition, it's an obstacle for those trying to find their seats in the dark. They run into it one after the other. Some fume in silence. Others swear and one storms at me: "Perhaps you'll stick your lousy leg in its right place. What is this here, are you at home?"

I apologise and would like to be buried in a deep hole. I can't explain why I'm sitting like this. After the showing I pour out my bitterness on Yael and my friends. They absorb it with their usual patience. It will be a long time before I again acquiesce to Yael's stratagems to accustom me to normal life outside.

On my own initiative I visited the eye clinic and asked for a status report. Dr. Nissan told me that its condition has been defined. The lens has parted from the retina, and before long the eye's light will turn out for ever.

"And so, Moshe Dayan?!" I say to the eye doctor. He sadly nods his head. He was right. After a few months I completely lost the sight in my left eye.

On my visit home last Saturday, Tami touched my heart. The little one was excited about the new leg that Daddy had brought home. Questions poured out unceasingly: If I have a new leg, why don't I "wear" it? Why do I take it off like that in the middle of the day? And if I have a leg, why do I also need the "crubtches"?

I try to explain. The leg that I had was very broken. They wanted to repair it, but didn't succeed. Perhaps they will succeed yet. Meanwhile, I'm using another leg. Not as good. But it'll be alright.You mustn't worry.

She hugs me tightly and lays her head on my chest. But she immediately jumps off and walks - keeping a considerable distance – around the leg, that strange creation which had won a permanent place next to Daddy's bed. On one of her exploratory trips, she pushes it inadvertently, and it falls on the floor. She looks with horrified eyes at the leg lying on the floor, her mouth silently twists up, and then she suddenly bursts into bitter tears, close to hysteria.

I hasten to hold her tight: "But why, Tami, why, my Tami – why are you crying?"

She refuses to be comforted. Only after a long time do I succeed in getting anything out of her: "Your leg . . . your new leg . . . it fell over . . . it hurt you terribly . . ."

198

In an hour-long intimate tête-à-tête with Yael, who is sitting by her bedside before she falls asleep, she confesses her fears: "I don't want what happened to Daddy to happen to me. I will never, never, be a soldier . . ."

A lot of people come and ask to see me. Apparently people who have read my articles in *Ma'ariv*. I yawn to myself: they look at me like some animal in a cage. Nevertheless I take a liking to those who bother to come to the hospital to participate in some way in our suffering. Among others, editors of school newspapers come here to write articles. They send their papers to me, so that I can read their interviews with me (Headline: "The Wounded – Their Spirits Are Good!"). I receive many letters. One, Semadar Ben Shoshan from Beersheba religiously writes at least once a week. A second, Yael Gelman, a young officer in Armoured Corps Headquarters, also writes regularly. I feel obliged to treat the many letters very seriously, including those I receive from children in the lower classes of schools. It isn't an unpleasant obligation.

One of the most moving letters came from Haifa. It read:

"I was the man who received you on a stretcher, when you were taken off the helicopter that brought you from the Syrian Heights. You were wounded over your whole body, drenched in blood from head to foot. You were one of many. By chance, my eye spotted the tag attached to your body. I saw your name. I was shaken. I was among your loyal readers. I'd never seen you before. And now – to meet in this way . . .

"I must admit, that because of your unconscious and so badly injured condition I rolled the stretcher without believing that you had any chance of awaking, of living. Now, reading your article again, I find that I was wrong and I am happy, very happy."

Time plods slowly by and nothing changes. Dr. Parin, who is relieving Professor Shapira during his holiday, looks at me with his usual mocking expression, but turns serious and after a moment orders the artificial limb to be thrown away. It's no longer suitable. Small comfort. Perhaps I'll manage better with the new one.

Externally, I try to keep up a tranquil, gay, and even mischievous appearance. I'm the only one who knows that I am lying, keeping up appearances in order not to expose weakness. People are being released from the hospital one after the other. Among them, some who were wounded, mostly by mines, long after the war ended. And me – the veteran – I remain.

I find an escape valve! I become a traffic offender. I got a new car not long ago. It's standing by the entrance to the hut. Every morning, after treatment in the workshop or in physiotherapy, I get into the car and start out on my way. I race it at full speed, pump the accelerator till it touches the floor. Luckily, I'm not caught by a traffic policeman. But even if I should be, I wouldn't be sorry. It may even be that I wanted it to happen. That they lock me up, that the car overturns, that I'll get in a fight. Frustration seeking a release – and this is its mask.

Upon my return from the mad excursions, I am calm. At least for a time, until the pressure builds up again. Nobody follows me, or guesses the reason for my mysterious absences.

Friends give me contradictory advice. Doctors who are not doctors confuse me: "Don't leave them alone – in other words, the doctors of the rehabilitation centre. Needle them and continue needling them until they find out what's causing the trouble. In my opinion, you must simply leave the hospital. Go home, rest for a few months, and come back fresh. Here they won't help you. Pick yourself up and go to a country where the doctors are specialists in dealing with cases like yours. They don't have enough experience here. Before they find out the reason for the failure, your hair will turn white."

In conversations among the veterans of the group, whose longevity is a sign of their bad luck, poison diffuse. They levy accusations at the doctors – and I don't know whether founded or unfounded – and question their capability. Activities of this sort only make things worse.

Stagnation is stupefying. You don't know whose advice to take, whom to believe. Finally, I ignore one and all, and expect affairs to arrange themselves without any initiative or intervention on my part. It's the easiest way, the most convenient way. I continue to go to the workshop, but without hope or anticipation. I similarly keep up my visits to the physiotherapy hall. There's not much point in it. My muscles are already strong, and no physiotherapist is capable of holding me down like Raya did in Hut 16. I go almost every day to the hospital, where my leg is given special medical baths. The jets of hot water pumped over my leg are apparently supposed to reduce the sensitivity. It doesn't work. The scars of the amputation haven't yet healed over.

8

One hot afternoon I sat in a wheelchair by the nurses' station. I was deep in my own thoughts. I hated the weakness that kept me sitting idly. I couldn't doze because of the great uproar. And I knew that even should I fall asleep, some visitor would appear to tear me out of my slumber.

I couldn't read. I lacked the necessary patience and concentration to transfer myself into another world.

I also didn't have anything to say to my comrades revelling alongside me. I was immersed in a disturbing nothingness, listening to time whose slow passive rhythm was addling my senses. I was contemptuous of myself: why do events which climax so quickly for others slow down for me? As time passes by, my complaints over the pains weaken. There were no external symptoms. Wouldn't it be natural – so I thought – that the doctors would begin to believe that my agonies were not physical pain, but lack of willpower? I almost began to believe it myself: here is a man who cannot bear a pain to which many others stand up. Weak character, me, miserable . . .

My thoughts were suddenly broken off. My name was called: "You have a visitor." I twisted up my face in distaste. Visitors were a nuisance. I'm too weary for idle conversation. Sooner or later they'll revert to the state of my health, and this is the last thing I want to talk about right now.

I turned my head with deliberate and contemptuous slowness towards the door. A strange unknown girl stood there. I hoped it was a mistake. She hadn't come to me. Perhaps one of the boys' usual tricks. She asked for somebody else, and they pointed to me and said: There he is, over there.

Well, it can't be helped. It seems that she really is looking for me.

I wheel my chair towards the girl and invite her to sit down. "Are you sure it's me that you want?" She was silent. She tilted her head to one side. After a moment, she nodded affirmatively. She had come to me.

She had something, this girl. Not the usual. A sad face. A somewhat obstinate line across her tight mouth. Downcast, so it seemed to me. The expression on her face sent a flood of self-hatred through me. The contempt that I had displayed for her earlier now seemed despicable.

Silence. Discomfort of the kind between two people who both expect to answer, and therefore don't initiate the conversation. I come to the girl's aid, and smile at her. "Have you got a cigarette? Mine are over there in the room – and I'm too lazy." And then: "I'm all yours, can I help you with something?"

Her mouth opens as though to say something. She hesitates. Returns to her silence. How long is this silence thick between us? Seconds? Minutes?

"Nevertheless?"

She found the courage and blurted out quickly: "My name's Tamar. You fought at Tel Fahar, didn't you? I have a few questions that are bothering me. If you don't mind?"

I nod my head encouragingly. This visit, the visitor, aroused my curiosity. Her eyes sparkle in her face. As our glances meet, I hasten to look away so she shouldn't be embarrassed.

"I wanted you to tell me about Moshe Segal," her words scatter my thoughts. In one breath she blurted out, as though the words had burst out of their own accord.

Moshe Segal?.. Moshe Segal?.. Who's she talking about? Who does she mean. I don't remember anybody of that name . . . He wasn't in our company. I'm not sure that I can satisfy her curiosity.

"I'm sorry, I don't know . . . I don't think I've ever met a man by that name," I say. A cloud of despair crosses her face. I have disappointed her. She came, so she said, especially from Jerusalem. I can't help her. Why is she interested in this man?

"Really, I'm trying to remember. It seems to me that I didn't meet him," I repeat what I had already said: "Are you sure there's a connection between us?"

"Yes, certainly! He, like you, fought on Tel Fahar."

"Let's see, Moshe Segal, to what unit did he belong? Was he . . . was he wounded?"

No. Not wounded. That I understand from the shake of her brown-haired head. No. Not wounded. Her eyes tell me what happened to him. There's no need for her to say anything else. I already know! What a slow grasp I have!

Her voice is choking as she reveals: "He fell there. He was my fiancé. He was killed and I want to know everything about it. Everything I can find out. He was in the Golani Brigade, and they told me that he was attached for a while to a tank company – in other words, to you. And so I came . . . But I understand if you didn't meet him . . .

We lift our eyes, which until now had been avoiding each other. She, because of her embarrassment. Me, because of mine. We both feel the need to break the depression hanging over our heads. We smiled.

From here on the conversation needed no prodding. The most difficult of all had already been said ("My fiancé fell"). And all I have to do is tell her everything that I heard of the battle on Tel Fahar. To my surprise, she knows much more than I do, and fills in many details that I lacked. It appears that she had already interrogated many.

When we part, evening is already falling. She goes on her way, and I follow her somewhat stooped walk, until she vanishes from sight.

9

Night. I couldn't sleep. It was hot.

The snoring of the sleepers fills the air of the hut. I dropped onto the wheelchair, and rolled myself out onto the grass plaza.

I sat relaxed and smoked. After a short while the silence was split by the screech of wheels that hadn't been oiled for a long time. By the light of the moon, I noticed the "boy". He too came in a wheelchair.

The "boy" had recently been transferred from another hospital.

A war injury, about twenty years old and very innocent. Skinny body, pale face and hair growing wild, his leg in a thick cast from the sole of his foot up to the upper thigh. The doctors hoped to save it. But he had to wait a few weeks till he would be again invited to the operating theatre.

His nickname, the "boy", was given him the moment he arrived. At first he was a little insulted: "What's this? I'm not a boy!" But after a few days, he took to the nickname, and would use it himself: "Nurse! The 'boy' wants to know what we're getting for lunch today!"

And a while longer and the terror reflected in his eyes died away and he adapted himself to the coarse language of the hut, the macabre jokes and the contemptuous stares.

He now recognised me and waved his hand.

"Hey, boy," I call. "You're not asleep? Your mother will come tomorrow and hear that her little one didn't sleep at night, she'll be very angry. Would you like a cigarette?"

"I don't smoke, don't you know? But I've got some chocolate, that the good aunts brought today. Apart from that, the lousy jokes about my mother are wearing a little thin."

I smoked, and he chewed chocolate. We suddenly noticed a movement on the far side of the lawn. Two figures rose out of the shrubs. A man and a woman. He in blue hospital pyjamas, and she in a short skirt and light blouse. The girl straightened her clothes. They grasped each other around the waist and moved away towards the clinic hut. Those shrubs, on the corner of the lawn, were already known as the "den of vice".

"Ah!" the "boy" grunted. "I'd be prepared to break my other leg to do to a girl what that bastard just did. Tell me, is it true what they say that the students of the nurses' school give?"

"Boy," I waved a remonstrative finger at him, "your mother is coming tomorrow . . ."

"Stop it," he reproached me, "How many times must I tell you that I'm fed up to the teeth with those jokes?"

Women were our first and most important subject of discussion. Especially at night, after lights out, when slumber was in no hurry to come and lusts awaken. There was not a single girl – nurse, volunteer or even visitor – who wasn't examined closely, and undressed by hungry stares. In the nightly symposiums we would dissect in great detail their physical assets, and debate them with great enthusiasm. One remembered brown eyes, while his colleague contended that they were blue. One said that her legs were exceptional, and the other that "They were not that good".

Not everybody participated in these conversations. But there was not one who didn't show an interest in them. Whoever remained silent did so because of his delicacy or shyness, and because he didn't want to display his yearnings in public.

"Look here," the "boy" said. He spoke in a low voice as though apologising. "Don't think that I'm just a lecher. Don't see me as I am now. When I was in uniform, I did fantastically well with girls. Now, after four months – no, it's actually almost five – I've done nothing. Perhaps it's because I was stupid and kept changing them like mad. If I had found myself a regular girl, perhaps I wouldn't have had to talk about it now. Why don't they make some kind of an arrangement in the hospital to solve the problem?"

He pondered for a moment, rolled the silver paper of the chocolate into a ball, and gave a short laugh: "Do you hear what happened to that bastard, Dani? He screwed a girl in the physiotherapy room. No more and no less. He told me yesterday. He simply arranged to be the last for treatment on that day, and volunteered to lock the windows, but 'forgot' to close one.

"Towards evening, he took that volunteer that visited him, you know, the one with black hair and a mini and maddening breasts, and they both went in through the window. He told me that she found it difficult to climb, and he had to help her. He, without one leg, helped her! Fantastic."

Again he sank for a moment into his thoughts, and said: "Yes, explain to me – there's one thing I don't understand. Those girls aren't disgusted when they lie with one of us? After all, when I look in a mirror, I'm disgusted by my own appearance. That reminds me: in the hospital that I came from, there was one – an orderly or a a doctor or a psychologist, the devil knows – that used to invite a few of the bunch for a conversation. You know, preparatory talks about the world that awaits us. He warned us that our future sex life will be full of crises, or something similar. And that we shouldn't be surprised if the girls don't want to be with us. His remarks were very encouraging, you know. Somebody doesn't even manage to grasp that he hasn't got a leg, or eye, or a hand – and he's already got to worry about another part of him that does remain, and still functions up to par . . .

"Well, to get back to Dani. They got in, so he told me, to the physiotherapy room, arranged a few mattresses, and went to work! As they got near the end, they heard the voices of two physiotherapists. God knows what brought them there at that hour. Dani realised that they were on the way to the room where he was. The girl almost had a heart attack, but he didn't lose his cool or desire: Come on, let's finish, he told her. It will take three or four minutes till they get to the room."

The "boy" leaned forward, groaned, with difficulty raised his leg – the one in a cast – and laid it very carefully on the bench. "It's bothering me a little, the leg," he said apologetically. "Do you think the worms have already started to eat it?"

"We must go to sleep," he said, "but I've still got to tell you about an annoying thing that happened to me in the hospital where I was. You know, soldier girls used to come to help the nurses, just like they do here. In place of their leave, or because they had nothing else to do, I don't know exactly. And so, two beauties – Atara and Tova – once came to our ward. Really they were something special. Very cute. We immediately explained to the nurses that they could forget about them. We had much more important jobs for them than washing pots and pans, or changing sheets. They must sit with us. The nurses were already well trained and didn't argue too much.

"After only a day or two, we became attached to the girls, and they to us. The atmosphere in the ward had become really pleasant. The feminine touch, if you understand. One of them devoted most of her time to the boy paralysed up to his shoulders. Believe it or not, the first time he smiled it was for her.

"After a few days, one of them came to us. Red eyes. Weeping. She said that the supervisor of girl soldiers in the hospital had decided to transfer them to another hut. No explanations were given. I was furious. I decided to go to their commanding officer and make a scandal. I knocked politely on the door, went in and explained why I had come. She said that she was very sorry, but she had no time for me. If I want to talk to her, then please would I walk along with her. She got up and went out of the room. She strode quickly, and I was compelled to hobble after her with the plastered leg. I don't know whether she behaved this way deliberately. It was very painful. I bit my lips and tried not to lose her. I again asked why she'd taken the girls away from us. She replied that she doesn't owe me any explanation. I told her about the attachment that had developed between them and the casualties, and then she looked at me coldly. Do you know what she said? That it was just because of that attachment that she was transferring them. 'I don't want one of them to fall in love with a cripple . . .' "

The "boy's" voice was choked: "The newspapers write that we are heroes, that we are brave, that we are really fighting the toughest war. All that is blah-blah. The journalists will get fed up of writing. All the people who respect us will forget. We get up one morning without a hand, or without a leg, and hear remarks like those of that woman, who is so careful of her soldier girls in case they fall in love with a casualty. Go and tell her what the soldier girl succeeded in doing with the paralysed boy who lay on his bed and didn't smile until she came."

10

My continued investigations among those doctors who are prepared to share their knowledge with me, give rise to some suppositions about my pain. It could be caused by the continued growth of a nerve which was amputated with the leg. There is often a wild growth of nerve at the cut-off point. Having no way out, it winds around like a worm on the spot where it's growing. Some are lucky, and their wild nerve finds a pocket deep into the flesh – and then has no contact with the artificial limb. "It's possibly your bad luck that it grew right under the skin. Any touch on the artificial leg, when you place your body-weight on it, stimulates it and hurts."

In desperation, I go on interrogating. Other doctors are also not satisfied with the nerve end, which is not covered by more than a thin layer of skin – in other words, there isn't enough buffer between it and the limb. They're also not pleased with bone which is hanging right under the skin, and with edema that has taken up most of the lower area of the stump.

I don't understand why my doctors don't treat these problems. Possibly they're hoping that time and habit will do their own work. No explanations are offered.

One particular doctor who is in my confidence, agrees with me that the cause of the pain is the growth of a wild nerve, and that there is need for an operation. But he doesn't have the authority to argue with the seniors. I beg him to give me an injection of Novocaine. I had heard that it was possible to know whether the wild nerve was the pain centre, from the leg's reaction after the injection. He hesitates. There is an infected sore on my leg. The injection is forbidden, because the needle-prick in flesh may transfer the infection. Finally, he gives way. He is himself curious to know the results.

Two hours of pleasure, the like of which I have not had since coming to the rehabilitation centre. A few minutes after the Novocaine entered my flesh, I felt no more pain. For the first time I threw the crutches away and walked hundreds of yards without their help. Distances of which I had not dreamt in my wildest dreams. I revelled in it like a boy. Here I am walking on two legs without any pain. As in that long ago time, before the war. I walked and walked and walked, distributing broad smiles among my comrades, who look at me with astonished eyes.

Two hours of happiness. But all rejoicing must have its end. The influence of the drug began to wear off. Luckily I'm not far away from the hut. I foresee the outcome, and rush towards it. On the way to my room the influence of the drug comes to an end, and the pains return in full force.

Now I know what is before me. There's nothing left but to convince the doctors to accept my opinion: they must operate to remove the wild nerve. It will be a difficult battle.

Though I am recorded as hospitalised in the rehabilitation centre, my sorties out increase. I don't sleep there any longer, but in my own home. Every morning I report back to the centre.

And as time passes, I even take two trips far, far away from Tel Aviv. The one southwards, and the other north.

11

I leaned against its steel. It was still warm, though dusk and a chill had already descended over the drifting sands of Sinai. I stretched out a loving hand and caressed its big body. Its gun-barrel stretched over my head like the trunk of an elephant, and its muscles were not tensed, it was no longer threatening, as I had once believed it to be, certain that it would defend me.

What an encounter.

I left it burning and scarred, and now found it again ready for battle with its barrel blackened from test firing. My tank.

I went down to Sinai. Somebody decided it would be good for me to see our large areas of conquest. Just an ordinary tour. But somebody higher up decided to give me a present: driving down the road, our way suddenly blocked by a rapidly crossing convoy of armour.

And here, among hundreds of racing tons, like an immense herd of gigantic elephants, white masks stared out at me. Under the helmets, I discovered the dusty faces of my comrades from the company, who had fought with me at Tel Fahar. They saw me. Excited hand waving. There was no time. The convoy was racing on. A drill. One, Nachum

Shuki, jumped off the tank as it was moving, ran over to me, hugged me tight and returned to his heavy vehicle, whose driver had slowed down.

Hours later we came up on their resting place. There I met my colleagues, veteran war horses. They were embarrassed and didn't know how to behave towards me. They were whole, and I hobbled on crutches. It was a conversation read between the lines. The trivial and not the important was spoken. Suddenly one of my comrades, Gideon Shapira, approached, and said: "Don't you want to see your tank?"

I looked at him with astonished eyes. He must be kidding me. How is it possible? My tank was finished. Hit, burnt, its steel buckled. "No, seriously!" my friend said. "Come, I'll show you."

I walked behind him with the rest of my somewhat entertained colleagues trailing behind. I saw it: it was no different from any of the other tanks. I looked at it lovingly and hastened to caress its steel. Men grow attached to their inanimate helpmates as well.

Its body was decorated with scars. To the front gaped a hole, made by a shell that penetrated into the turret ("We are wounded, we are wounded," Eli Albert and Shimon, my turret crew, shouted . .)The hole is there. The turret roof, from outside, is scratched and dented. This was another shell that burst on the armour and threw splinters at my head ("God! I can't see! I'm also wounded" . . .).

Everything remains as it was. Almost. The bloodstains have been washed off. The clods of soil and soot have been scrubbed. Again a warrior of the line. My battle-experienced dinosaur.

"Shalom, tank," I whispered to it. It didn't answer. They tend to forget those who leave them. I threw a last look at it. It stood facing me unmoved and silent, squat on the hot sands. Ready to go again when summoned. But it won't be me that calls it. New lords and masters.

After a while, exactly one year to the day after I was injured, I climbed it.

I've come back to you, Tel Fahar. On crutches, I've returned. My shoes crash your soil. And I am your lord.

Now you look like a nature reserve. But we know, both of us, that you're nothing but a horrible memento of the nature of man's cruelty.

Poppies grow among the trenches. Alex Krinski's blood enriched the spot where the poppy blooms. Rusted over cartridge cases tell the story of his death.

A geranium climbed up the wall of a house. The house is destroyed, but the geranium lives. How many bodies sprawled on the ground from which you blossom, beautiful flower?

Magnificent lily of the valley, who are you trying to deceive? We have eyes in our heads, and they see other eyes returning our gaze, the loopholes of a bunker from which two Gorianov machine-gun barrels spewed death.

Nature has dealt kindly with you, Tel Fahar, smoothed away the blood with an expert hand and powdered your flowers. An innocent young girl, in short pants, is plucking the flowers of blood.

A commercial van stops. It unloads a tray full of cakes, and then another and a third. What is the celebration today? Who is the man bearing them so reverently?

No, there's no special reason. The man, just an ordinary man, is a baker from Ramat Gan. One of those who adopted us. Somebody whispers in my ear: "His son fell in the war. As a paratrooper."

We are again sitting on the plaza in front of the hut. The conversation turns round to the question of whether a man who is paralysed can make love to his wife. And the corollary, can he father children? The answer is in the affirmative. There are those who have investigated. It turns out that his partner must be the active one in bed. "That's good, that's good," some is heard to mumble. Even we whose sensitivities have been blunted, feel for the even less fortunate and suffered because of their distress.

Once the subject is exhausted, the bunch turns to discuss its own affairs, while gorging on the cakes.

I decided to ride a bicycle. Why a bicycle? Because there it is. The kashrut supervisor rode it over, leaned it against the hut wall, and vanished into the kitchen.

I quickly rolled to my room, locked on the limb and in leaps and bounds aided by my crutches, reached the bicycle.

"What are you doing?" Eli Blau, my neighbour in the room, shouts. "Are you mad?"

I didn't bother to answer. I sit on the bicycle, press down on the pedals and depart. Riding a bicycle isn't an easy matter, and that's exactly why it tempts me. The bicycle carries me along the path leading to the office of the rehabilitation centre, and draws astounded stares: How come? A cripple, with one amputated leg, riding a bicycle? I reply with jokes accompanied by merry smiles. After a while I sense that the time had come to go back.

From a distance I could see the kashrut supervisor looking about desperately, wondering where his vehicle had vanished to. The good angels of the hut hadn't bothered to tell him which way the bicycle had gone. On the contrary. They told him that it had certainly been stolen. They told him that a suspicious character in a crash helmet had been looking right and left, jumping on the bicycle and rushing off quickly. No, no, they weren't able to stop him. How could they? In their condition? . .

The victim didn't spot me. I circled around and brought the bicycle to the hidden side of the hut. I hobbled to the entrance on my crutches. "Your bicycle," I asked the supervisor, "what is it doing behind the hut?"

That evening I went home as usual to sleep. Yael washed Tami in the bath, while I sprawled in the armchair and read a paper. Apparently Yael asked her to lift her leg, so that she could soap it. The clear voice of my daughter rang out from the bath: "Who do you think I am – Daddy, that I can stand on one leg? . ."

12

One sunlit January day, I strode quite fast, leaning on one crutch, towards the workshop. Sprinklers spread clouds of silvery drops into the air. The spray wet my clothes, and its cold touch was pleasant.

It was a nice day. A festive day. Yael's birthday.

My friends, the artificial limb sculpturers, stood in the workshop, and with them Professor Shapira. All of them looked at me with laughing eyes. The golden day had touched them too. My body was presented for final inspection. It passed.

"And so," the professor said, "I don't see any reason why you shouldn't be released today. You've been here long enough."

My heart missed a beat. A warmth flowed through me. Is he serious, this man? Can I really go home?

Fat Yoske is standing closest to me. I grab his face in my two hands and kiss him. Hearty hand-shakes and a bottle of cognac appears from somewhere. "To life", "Thank you", "To health", "You were a tough nut", "In time, I think, the situation will improve", "Only don't forget us . . ."

Joyous return to the hut. Emptying the cupboard by my bed. Toothbrush, soap, candies, books, a packet of sleeping pills that had rolled into a corner, a bundle of letters sent by unknowns, a plastic box with the splinters taken from my body.

The nurses' wet eyes. Leah Bernstein and Toya Tal who have helped and supported me through the difficult times. My eyes are also damp. Prolonged kisses. An emotional parting from the orderlies, Yitzhak Sinai, Shimon Walnerman, Eliezer Carmi, Reuven Druker. Parting from the physiotherapists, who lately have had their muscles strengthened by me. Again kisses. Parting from the house of agonies, which is also a reservoir of love and a repository of gratitude. The house of great hopes.

Hand-shakes with those remaining. Those who look on with jealousy. That same jealousy with which I regarded those who preceded me in departing. Some roll their wheelchairs after me. Their gaze glued to my back. Wake up, wake up. Is this a sweet illusion? Not a night's dream, from which you will be awoken by the cry: "Breakfast, breakfast, get up for breakfast!?"

No, no dream. No, not an illusion. The truth. Reality. You're leaving. You're walking. You're really walking. How much time has gone by? How much time!! Eight full months, which are 240 days, which again are 5 760 hours! Three hundred and fifty thousand minutes! Eight months, God! An eternity! And now you turn your back on them. You get in a car. Not to come back. And perhaps yes. To visit. All those magnificent souls who comforted you. In Hut 25 and in Hut 16 and in Hut 40 and in Hut 42 and in the operating theatre, in the rehabilitation centre, in the physiotherapy halls and in the workshop . . . All the good souls who bothered over you, and whom you bothered. Those who received you as a broken man, sprayed with metal, torn, mashed, scarred – and now return you to life. True, not whole. A little worn here and there, scarred here and there. But who could ask for more?

Go, go and say goodbye to all. Don't forget anyone.

Shalom to the pathways twisting between the huts (whose potholes made me feel so bad) and shalom to the world-shaking speeches I made on subjects irrelevant to the world; shalom to the plastic bed-pan and the chrome bed-pan. Farewell to the psychiatrist who feared for my sanity and to the green-clothed stretcher bearers who brought me in and carried me out so many times from the operating theatres (and especially to the one who stared at me in shocked surprise: "For fifteen years I've been taking people to the operating theatre, and I've never yet met one like you who bellows out songs before they cut him"). Shalom to the wheelchairs that took me to and fro here to there, and to all the medicines with which I wasn't stuffed and which still remain. Farewell to blue pyjamas that I didn't wear, and to the nappies they gave us instead of towels. Shalom to the cleaning women who went to the bother of collecting the cigarette stubs and the ashes that I threw on the floor, during the endless sleepless nights (and a special shalom to Toni Hadad from 16, the cleaning woman I loved most of all).

Shalom to the volunteers, and a wink to the beautiful girls who kept the secret of their attractive femininity, and caused some of us to smile in our sleep. (And a special shalom to Hagit Yaron whose dimples and smile drove all of us crazy.)

Shalom to all the nurses, and especially to Tami Lipschitz, of the round face, with only her beautiful eyes showing behind the operating theatre mask, who didn't know that we knew how apprehensive she was for us. Farewell to the nurses whose eyes peered at me at nights, and whose anxious voices I heard: "Why don't you sleep? It'll soon be morning." Shalom to all the doctors who helped to bring me to my present condition. Farewell to the X-ray technicians and anaesthetists ("Now to sleep. Good night.").

Shalom to my good colleagues who remain here, and for whom my heart aches. Farewell to the white beds that don't succeed in cooling down before a new patient arrives on them. Shalom to the whiteness, to the smell of the hospital that sticks to me. Farewell to everything and everybody that I have forgotten. Farewell to all those I didn't remember. Shalom, shalom, shalom.

I've come home. It's already night. Many shining faces and pyramids of pastry awaited me. Bouquets of flowers in all the colours of the rainbow, and a warm hug from Yael. I mustn't be surprised, it's her birthday today. But, no. She's forgotten hers. I am the one who has been born into a new world.

213

After a month I return to the hospital. An operation. Again to Hut 16.

"Lie quietly and don't dare get up from the bed," Dr. Parin says to me after the operation. "I'm tired of opening zip-fasteners in your leg. You lie in that bed for a month, and God help you if you get up from it."

He extends a hand, the fingers of which are half-closed as though holding a fistful of sand grains: "You should see what grew on your leg! I took out a full fistful of that nerve!"

I smile and gloat over my victory. The victory of an illiterate over all the wise men of Hippocrates. I was the one who made the diagnosis. They couldn't believe that my pains were neither exaggerated nor the fruits of my imagination. And now – have I reached the end?

No. Not yet.

Another half-dozen months will pass while I still drag my crutches with me. There's no way around it. I must consult more doctors. New York. Six months. Friendly looking Dr. Lipman and Dr. Jer, speaking English, escort me in to more operating theatres. The zip-fastener again. American experts fit me with a new and comfortable artificial leg. I must rush home. Yael is about to give me a son.

About two weeks after my return to Israel, my son Uri is born. That same Uri to whom I committed myself ceremonially in the ears of the recovery room nurse, after my brain operation. Uri was born in Tel Hashomer. The hospital that returned me to life gave life to my small son.

Have I reached the end?

No. The debt must be paid off in instalments. My whole life. Sometimes the instalments are large, and then I again am a guest of the hospital.

13

October 1970. I'm in Paris. A guide is leading a group of tourists and lecturing them: "The Eiffel Tower was built in the year 18 . . . It was erected in honour of . . . It was assembled of so many iron girders . . . They weigh so many tons . . . So many suicides jump from its heights every year . . . Elevators take the passengers up and down. I wouldn't suggest that you use the steps, ha, ha . . ."

An idea flashed across my brain: the steps! Now settle accounts with your body: show me its strength. Go down the steps! From the beginning to the very end. And without stopping, if you please. If you don't succeed . . .

Standing at the bottom, between the spreadeagled legs of the tower, shaking as though from malaria and pouring with sweat, I knew I was victorious: over the tower, over my leg, over the first Syrian shell, and the second Syrian mortar bomb.

EPILOGUE

The war isn't over.

One Friday, in September 1969, with the War of Attrition at its peak, the telephone rang in my home. Yael answered. At the other end of the line, the voice of my doctor and friend Henry Horoshvisky.

"Yael," he said, "when Yaacov gets in, tell him to get in touch with me immediately. It's urgent."

I phoned him when I got home, and after a few moments was in my car racing to Tel Hashomer.

"A tough case," the doctor told me, "perhaps you can help."

On one of the beds in Hut 17 lay a beautiful, dark-haired girl with a face the colour of the sheet.

"She has to be encouraged," the doctor said. "I'm afraid that she will do something desperate."

Two days earlier, Lieutenant Iris Zaharoni stood at the opening of a bunker on the Suez Canal. A shell suddenly dropped. One leg was torn off, and the other so badly injured that it could expect the same fate.

"Iris," I called to her, "Iris."

She opened a pair of large green eyes. Struggled to turn them to me. I sensed that a drugged fog stood like a curtain between me and her vacant gaze.

"Iris," I whispered, "you'll see, everything will be alright." I didn't believe what I was saying. I knew I was talking to deaf ears. She was already deep in delirium. I left the room.

The following day, I came again, and the next and the next. I felt weighted by a heavy responsibility – a responsibility that no one had given me: she mustn't kill herself, she mustn't kill herself . . .

One day, she smiled at me and I knew: the danger was over.

Iris's struggle was more bitter than mine. First of all, she was a woman. Secondly, I was only injured in one leg. She in both. To this day, she is still in hospital much of the time.

And yet, amid all the treatment and operations, she finished her first year of study in the university with high marks. Shuki Kaufman finished the Technion with honours. Without a hand and without a leg. Yisrael Cohen, without both his hands, graduated in economics and holds a senior position in a co-operative. Eli Margoliot is manager of a successful plant in Haifa. Gadi Refen, who should have received mention in dispatches for his bravery in hospital, won – if I forgot to tell it before – a medal for valour in battle. He returned to the army. Ruti gave Dudu Badusi, a taxi driver and one of the nicest people I ever met, two children. Uri Rosenman, whose chances of recovery were doubted by many, proved that willpower can surpass the wisdom and prognosis of medicine.

The war isn't over. Simcha Holtzberg – the "father of the wounded" still has his hands full of work.

But the tin soldiers, standing on their one leg, are as steady as their comrades on two. Not only in fairy tales.

POSTSCRIPT OCTOBER 1973: THE DEBT

"When they lay me blind and hurting beside the tank – I suddenly remembered something else that you wrote. The words of the book crossed my brain in a sudden flash: you related that they lay you beside the tank.

You said that the Syrians fired on the tank. It was a tempting target. To you, the bullets sounded like hail. And then the shell aimed at the tank, and you were wounded a second time.

I thought: God, it can happen to me. I can also hear the patter of hail on my tank. I asked the men who pulled me out to move me away from the tank. They began to carry me. We were not very far away when I heard a tremendous noise. The shell that I had feared had reached the tank. But we were no longer within the effective range of its shrapnel."

I am now sitting beside Aran's bed in Hadassah Hospital, Jerusalem. He is talking faintly and slowly – slowly. Those moments of mine return without me having to close my eyes. Apparently so similar to those that I now witness.

Strange, I think to myself, I thought I had become inured. I had seen far worse sights than those before me now. I had seen my own face in a mirror. Casualties lay beside me who were far worse injured than him. But my heart is beating like a tribal drum, and I fear that my eyes are wet.

Is it because Aran, lying with closed eyes, is gripping my hand so fiercely? Is it because I don't know what to answer? Is it because I fear that any word said in answer – which he so obviously expects – will be crude or trite or out of place?

Strange, strange . . .

Does this emotion which I find so hard to hold back derive from the fact that my friend so many years younger than me grew up alongside me from the age of eight? Is it because I see myself, my own painful experiences, in him? Is he not – me?

"We have some happy news for you" – they said to Yael, my wife – "Yankele is wounded."

Wounded – meaning alive. Therefore, happy.

Those were Aran's parents. It was them whom I asked to be informed about my injury, as the evacuation half-track took me down the slopes of the Golan Heights to the field hospital.

Yael remembers it well. She received this news at ten at night on June 9, 1967.

"I have some news for you. Aran is wounded," I told his parents. My heart would not let me add the word – happy. Even though I knew that his injury was much lighter than mine. I just could not do it. On the way to them I thought to myself whether to use the word. I dreaded their reaction.

I felt a tremor as the brave mother lay her head on my shoulder, and muttered: "You're repaying a debt. You're redeeming a promissory note."

The obligation to repay promissory notes of this kind is a miserable one.

To try and stop my stream of thought, and because I didn't really know what to do with myself, I glanced at my watch. The time – ten at night. A few days later I would check and remember: also the 9th of the month.

The first blow as I commanded the tank, with half my body outside – and without fearing any danger in the inferno on the slopes of Tel Fahar – was a terrible blow. When I awoke after an immeasurable period of time, I found that I was blind. Days to come would clarify that only one eye was injured beyond repair. The second returned to me after some time.

Aran was sent to the Canal on the day of the invasion. He rushed in his vehicle through the inferno of fire and tried to do the best he could. Without hesitation in the middle of battle, he raised half his body outside the tank to operate the machine-gun fixed on the turret. He also had no sense of impending danger.

Aran: "I suddenly took a terrible blow. Time passed – I know not how long – until I awoke and found that I was blind."

Only a few days would pass, thank God, before to everyone's joy it would become clear that only one eye was damaged beyond repair. There was a considerable improvement in the second and it would continue to do its work faithfully. If we can judge by his morale, and the way in which he behaves, he will certainly recover quickly.

But this was not the end of the bond between our stories: while his mind was functioning faintly through the mists of his injury and terrible bruising, he remembered another chapter of my book and decided to recapitulate its text:

While I lay in his condition, I wrote that after the first shock and while still in the tank, I thought that I must find the radio and call for help for my wounded crewmen. I desperately looked for the switch on the radio box. It seemed to me that my efforts had failed, and there was no answer to my cry – and I faded into the fog of lost consciousness.

Aran: "I remembered the story, and decided that I must do the same as you. I groped for the switch to call for help."

Aran remembers nothing of what happened after that. Did he also sink into the same fog?

I awoke from my coma to sense that somebody was interfering with my rest. The unknown was trying to tow me, spread as I was over the tank turret, in order to get me down.

Through my daze I managed to establish that the soothing voice I heard was that of my tank driver.

Aran: "Somebody began to drag me down from the tank. Of course, I couldn't see him. After a moment, when I heard his voice, I knew that it was my tank driver . . ."

When they put him in a bed in the intensive treatment ward of Hadassah Hospital, he remembered his parents and wanted to inform them. He could not talk. He asked for a pen and paper, and wrote without seeing what he wrote: "Phone number . . ."

His strength failed him.

A little while later, when he again recouped energy, they asked for the phone number of his parents. They thought that it was their number that Aran was trying to write on the paper.

Aran told them that it was not his parents' home: "There is someone who owes them the news. When he was wounded in the Six Day War, he asked them to phone my parents, and I received the notice. If you don't believe, read his book. Now, he must repay the debt."

The "he" was me . . .

October 19, 1973.